Scandinavian
Studies in
Criminology

SCANDINAVIA UNIVERSITY BOOKS
Universitetsforlaget, Oslo – Bergen – Tromsø
Munksgaard, Copenhagen
Esselte Studium, Stockholm – Gothenburg – Lund

Scandinavian
Studies in
Criminology

VOLUME 7

*Policing
Scandinavia*

UNIVERSITETSFORLAGET

Distribution offices:
NORWAY
Universitetsforlaget
Box 2977, Tøyen
Oslo 6

UNITED KINGDOM
Global Book Resources Ltd.
109 Great Russell Street
London WC1B 3NA

UNITED STATES and CANADA
Columbia University Press
135 South Broadway
Irvington-on-Hudson, N.Y. 10533

PRINTED IN NORWAY BY
DREYER AKSJESELSKAP
STAVANGER

CONTENTS

Introduction – By Ragnar Hauge 1

Criminal Policy and Repression in Capitalist Societies – The Scandinavian Case
– By Leif Lenke 5

Reinforcing the Police – Actors, Interests and Strategies – by Håkon Lorentzen   31

The Proactive Police – By Henning Koch 51

The 1976 Police Strike in Finland – By Tuija Mäkinen and Hannu Takala ..   87

Police Investigations and the Personal Integrity of the Suspect in Scandinavia
– By Anders Bratholm 107

Violent Criminality and Social Control during Stockholm's Urbanization – By
Sven Sperlings 125

Finnish Gypsies and the Police – By Martti Grønfors 147

Work Adjustment of Swedish Policemen – By Jan Forslin 157

Policing Labour Conflicts – By Jørgen Jepsen 177

The Police and Social Conflicts – The Menstad Conflict of 1931 – By Per Ole
Johansen 207

The Authors 245

INTRODUCTION

BY *Ragnar Hauge*

Criminological research in Scandinavia – as in most other countries – has traditionally concentrated on the study of the law-breaker. The purpose of this research has been to differentiate between law-breakers and law-abiding individuals in order to be able to say something about the causes of criminality.

During the last 10–20 years, however, this traditional focus has gradually changed. To an increasing extent interests have moved away from those committing offences to those defining what constitutes a breach of the law and determines who is the law-breaker – those who through their political influence decide the content of the law and also the agencies and authorities empowered to enforce the regulations.

This move has generated a radical change in the presentation of problems. Traditionally, the fact that young people to a much higher degree than adults are registered as criminals has led to the question why the young are much more involved in criminality than adults. But the problem can also be posed as a question why acts that are most common among youths are to a larger degree criminalized than acts commonly engaged in by adults – or why the law-enforcement apparatus is mostly geared towards catching young law-breakers. Furthermore, while customarily changes in the size of the prison population have been viewed as a consequence of changes in the crime rate, the question has been raised whether the former could be due to changes in societal conditions creating a need to keep more or fewer individuals imprisoned.

In many ways this trend in research interests indicates that the borderlines between criminology and disciplines such as sociology of law and political science are partially disappearing. At the same time, historical and economic methods of analysis have entered the field. Thus criminology is now less clearly defined – but at the same time more diverse, and richer in nuances.

In this volume we present some work within one of the many newly opened criminological research areas during the last decade, police research.

In the first article, *Leif Lenke* uses as a starting point the large differences in the size of the prison population in Finland, on the one hand, and the other Scandinavian countries, on the other. On the basis of an analysis of the development of criminal policy in the countries concerned, he maintains that the high Finnish prison figures result from a much more repressive control system in Finland than in the other countries – a difference which, according to him, may be derived from differences in the political climate.

The article by *Håkon Lorentzen* is also based on a comparison between the different Scandinavian countries. He describes the strong reinforcement and reorganization of the police that we have witnessed during the last 10–15 years, and asks which conditions have been decisive in this development and which arguments it rests on.

One approach towards increasing the effectivity of the police is to increase the amount of time spent on patrolling and thus intensify the surveillance. *Henning Koch* concentrates on the conditions in Århus – the second largest city in Denmark – where in 1974 the amount of time spent on patrol duty was increased, with the aim of making the police more effective. In his article he tries to elucidate subsequent effects – did the change lead to higher efficiency as measured in numbers of recorded offences and did it influence the individual policeman's handling of encountered cases?

Tuija Mäkinen and *Hannu Takala* pursue the same issue. What happens when the police are out of action – as in a strike? The data in their article are collected from a strike occurring among the uniformed police in Finland in February 1976, a strike lasting almost a month. On the basis of interviews with the public, investigation of police journals, hospital journals and other sources, they report on the population's attitude towards the strike and its effects with regard to crimes and violations against public peace and order.

The effectivity of the police, however, is largely dependent on the means they utilize. And within the criminal justice system, the police often tread a fine line between legality and efficiency. The law stipulates what the policeman can and cannot do in the course of investigation. At the same time it is demanded that he shall be as effective as possible with respect to solving crimes. But to act in accordance with the law can in many cases mean that the police have to disregard the most effective measures in the investigative work. In his article, *Anders Bratholm* describes the legal framework adopted in Scandinavia concerning the protection of the personal integrity of the suspect – and to what extent the police act within these borderlines.

What is the relationship between crime development, societal conditions, and social control as mirrored in the activity of the police? In an attempt to illustrate this relationship, *Sven Sperlings* looks at the development of violent crimes in Stockholm during the latter part of the nineteenth century. Despite increased industrialization and a strong population increase, particularly in the working class, the registered violent criminality sharply decreased. Was the reason an actual decrease in violent crimes, a lessened recording of such criminality on the part of the police, people's tendency to solve the conflicts among themselves without involving the police – or do other explanations exist?

Martti Grönfors deals with the conflict that exists between gypsies and the police, in data gathered from Finland. Through material based on interviews with policemen in two large cities, he tries to portray the attitudes of the police towards gypsies – in relation to the gypsies' attitudes towards the police.

In his article, *Jan Forslin* raises the question of the adaptation of the police to their professional role. His contribution is a study of the views on the police profession expressed by a group of Swedish policemen in 1968 – when they all were recruits – and in 1974, after six years of experience. The results show that they had great expectations concerning work conditions and career when they began in their profession. Six years later they were much less enthusiastic – in most areas their expectations had been far from fulfilled, and their optimism with respect to future work conditions had diminished. But at the same time they viewed as good the possibilities of changing to other and better paid professions. Nonetheless, a large majority wanted to remain in the police force – in a working situation that was regarded as rather unattractive in many aspects.

Although the task of the police most often consists of intervening in conflicts between individual citizens or between single citizens and the state, on certain occasions the police are brought into conflicts where groups of citizens or social classes clash. This may happen, for example, in demonstrations, riots or labour conflicts. In these instances, the police must either take the part of mediator or choose sides between the conflicting parties.

Two of the articles examine the role of the police in labour conflicts. *Jørgen Jepsen* offers a presentation of a series of such conflicts in Danish industrial life during the last couple of years, and poses the question which factors determine the voluntary or coerced choice made by the police and the rest of the criminal justice apparatus in selecting what he labels 'absorption' or 'confrontation'. *Per Ole Johansen's* topic is the most well-known and dramatic labour conflict in Norway during the period between the two world wars, and he describes how the role of the police progressively changed as the conflict intensified.

The articles included in this volume do not aim at covering all the police research in Scandinavia. Rather, the choice is determined by a wish to present the broad scope of this research – while at the same time wanting to shed light on the problems of policing Scandinavia.

Criminal Policy and Repression in Capitalist Societies – the Scandinavian Case

BY *Leif Lenke*

1. INTRODUCTION

In traditional criminology there is a strong tendency to perceive criminal policy as something rather unrelated to the class and political structure of society. Reform 'waves' and changes in the level of criminal repression are looked upon as effects of 'industrialization' or 'international streams of thought' or as determined by 'scientific development', etc. In the same manner, varieties in police behaviour (discrimination, etc.) are often described as dependent upon factors such as 'education', 'tradition', 'relations to the mass media', or as a 'response to behaviour of the public', etc.

In this article I will try to construct an alternative model for variations in crime control strategies and police behaviour. In my opinion these variations are better explained by a model built upon the concepts of political structure and conflict. My thesis is that the *level of repression in criminal policy in capitalistic countries is determined by the level of manifest political conflict and by the balance of power between the different classes in these societies.*

In an attempt to show these relationships, I will use the method of cross-national comparisons in combination with a longitudinal analysis. The study proceeds in different stages, and I will begin by comparing the four Nordic countries[1] with respect to criminal policy and the level of criminal repression. Then, I will compare the social structures of the countries and construct a theoretical model to explain the relationship between these social structures and the levels of crime repression. The next stage will be to test this model in two different ways. First, through a longitudinal study within the four countries and, in the next step, with a correlational analysis of international data concerning the level of political conflict and crime repression.

2.1 CRIMINAL POLICY IN THE NORDIC COUNTRIES

The point of departure for this study is Nils Christie's important work on the different rates of prison populations in the Nordic countries (Christie, 1968).[2] In that study Christie showed the prison population of Finland to be approximately double that of each of the other three countries. (See diagram on page 7.) The prison population rate of Finland was about 150 prisoners per 100,000 inhabitants in the 1960s, placing Finland in a high position in an international comparison among Western industrialized societies. Only the United States ranked higher, with a rate of 200–250, i.e. several times higher than that of the other Nordic countries (von Hofer, 1975).

An expected assumption would be that such differences in rates reflect the levels of criminality in the different societies. For the Nordic countries, however, this is not the case.[3] In comparison to Sweden and Denmark, the Finnish crime rate was about one-third as high at the time this comparison was made – during the 1960s (Anttila, 1973, p. 89).

The explanation for the difference in prison population rates must be looked for elsewhere. The best explanation, I think, is that the penalties in Finland are much harsher[4] than in the other Scandinavian countries. This applies to theft (Anttila, 1973 p. 83), with thieves comprising the bulk of the prisoners,[5] but also to other offences such as 'drunken driving'.

Christie also made this assumption and tried to explain the deviance of the Finnish control system as a consequence of applying a different yardstick with regard to suffering. Christie writes (1968):

> Let us now concern ourselves entirely with the diverging country, Finland. As one can see from the diagram, the curve for Finland resembles, at any rate to some degree, the curves from the other countries right up to 1918. At that date, however, the Finnish figures increase from 100 to 250 prisoners per 100 000 inhabitants, and later fluctuate around 200, while the prison populations in the other Nordic countries are stabilised at a quite modest level compared with Finland.
>
> It is difficult to come to any other conclusion than that these Finnish figures reflect *another frame of reference as regards suffering* than is found in the other Nordic countries. Had the Finnish figures lain at the same high level all the time, they could perhaps have been regarded as an expression of a firmly implanted different attitude towards the use of detention. But the resemblances to the other Nordic countries up to 1918 make it altogether more natural to regard the increased level of imprisonment as a result of the break with Russia in December 1917, a bloody civil war, causing wounds that are not yet completely healed, and furthermore two wars against an overwhelming foe. It is quite reasonable to suppose that this has created a scale of suffering peculiar to Finland. Three years' imprisonment in Finland is the counterpart of one year in Norway.

From this quotation and also from Christie's further writings on the same topic (Christie, 1974 p. 123), it is obvious that his model is not a conflict model, i.e. that the political structure and an *ongoing* political conflict are of no significant importance in his explanation.

To me, however, such a model of consensus is hardly convincing. Many countries have participated in wars without showing as similarly high a prison

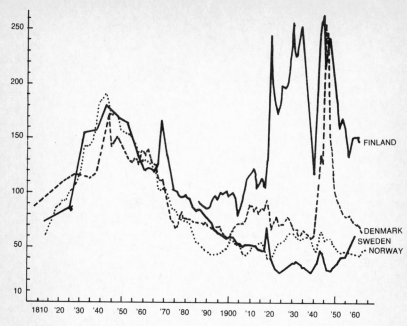

Number of persons imprisoned per 100,000 of the population in Denmark, Finland, Norway, and Sweden. (Source: Christie 1968).

population rate as that of Finland. Furthermore, it is possible to show that the large prison population is not an isolated repressive phenomenon in the Finnish control system, but rather a single part of a control policy system that differs in almost every respect from the control policies in the other Scandinavian countries.

Besides the more *punitive legislation* and *application of law* in the courts, it is also reported that the Finnish *police* have extensive power in comparison with their colleagues in the other Nordic countries, as regards retaining persons in custody before formal charging, i.e. before they have the right to be brought before a judge or be freed. According to Anttila (1973, p. 77) the time limit in Finland is 17 days, as compared with 3 days in Sweden and 24 hours in Denmark and Norway (Andenaes, 1969 p. 202).[6]

The Finnish police also have extensive power to take people into custody for identification (SOU 1979:6 p. 304) and when public drunkenness was still criminalized in Scandinavia, they also arrested people for 'drunkenness' 5–10 times more often than was the case in the other countries. This occurred in spite of a lower consumption of alcohol per head (in the 1960s) and also a lower degree of urbanization in Finland, factors of importance to the level of drunkenness.[7]

Another example of deviance in the Finnish control system is that the police – as well as the courts – are thought to use class discrimination to a higher degree than is the case in the other countries. This is shown in a comparative interview study made by the Finnish sociologist Allardt (1975, p. 133). Representative samples from the four countries were asked to answer the question: 'Do you think persons from different social classes are treated differently or alike in the courts and by the police?'

Courts	Finland	Denmark	Sweden	Norway
Treat people:				
Equal	30	42	53	50
Unequal	58	37	37	36
Don't know	12	21	10	14
	100 %	100 %	100 %	100 %
Police				
Treat people:				
Equal	36	49	51	45
Unequal	54	33	41	41
Don't know	11	18	8	14
	100 %	100 %	100 %	100 %

The table shows a significant difference between the countries. A majority of the Finns believe their control system is discriminatory. The relevance of this public opinion could ultimately be questioned, as it is just an attitude and does not reflect actual discrimination.

Another study carried out in the 1960s (with a similar methodology) indicates, however, that this attitude is grounded upon reality. Extensive surveys of 'self-reported criminality' were made on representative samples of conscripts in the four countries. These studies did not, however, show a large extent of social discrimination. This result had, however, one exception – Finland. The results were interpreted by Anttila (1973, p. 121) as follows: 'In Finland, Jaakkola showed that in the study of "hidden delinquency" the risk of police contact was higher for working-class juveniles, even though their crime rates were not higher.' Such a finding was not made by authors in the other countries (Christie 1965, Werner 1971).[8]

Besides these differences concerning police, legislation and court practices, it is beyond doubt that the Finnish prison system also differs from those in the other countries. Their 'hard labour' institutions, which were abolished in 1975, had a reputation that reached far outside the borders of the country, and I think it is significant to note that principles of the so-called 'treatment ideology' have never been accepted within the Finnish prison system (Anttila, 1971). This 'ideology' – with all its shortcomings – is seen by many people as an important humanizing factor underlying the 'criminal welfare' systems of Scandinavia today. Having described the differences in criminal policy between Finland and the other Nordic countries, I will now turn to the factors that could be of importance in explaining these differences.

2.2 The political structure of the Nordic countries

Christie's diagram and analysis show that 'historical tradition' is hardly an interesting factor. The reason for this conclusion is that the significant differences between the four countries did not appear until the 1920s. It was then that Finland 'took off' and beat out its own path in criminal policy. Nor do factors like 'level of industrialization' or 'degree of urbanization' seem likely explanations, as even today Finland has a larger prison population than the other countries have had for one hundred years.

For this reason I have focussed instead upon the political factors, to determine whether they could help to explain the pattern we find in the sphere of criminal policy in the Nordic countries. I define these political factors as the level of conflict between different classes of society and also the balance of power between these classes. Even if industrialization, urbanization, religion, the parliamentary and administrative systems, etc. are very similar within the Nordic countries, it is obvious that the political structures differ significantly.

Finland's divergence in this respect is described clearly by the Finnish political scientist Nousiainen (p. 37):

> In western societies on the march towards industrialisation it has been possible to observe a successive shift to the left in politics. In different ways, implied revision of views are due to the changing circumstances and success for political parties with a clear leftist program. This has been the case in Scandinavia, where the labour parties reached leading positions, even as political majority parties. From this point of view the political situation in Finland is designed by the relative weakness of the labour movement. The Finnish policy has during the decades been described as 'conservative', due to the fact that the parliamentary, as also the extraparliamentary, power has been in the hands of the right wing.
>
> The suffrage reform (as early as 1906) made the future look very promising to the Social Democrats. Their representatives increased rapidly from 80 to 90 (out of 200) and by 1916, owing to special circumstances, they received an absolute majority in the parliament (lantdagen), Thus the party became one of the strongest socialist parties in Europe.
>
> For different reasons, such as the civil war (1918), the split of the labour movement, the isolation of the left, the land reform,[9] and the agrarian party's strong increase, the development took another track; following the Second World War, the conservatives kept a small majority in the parliament. In the years 1958–62 the leftist parties had the smallest possible majority (101 representatives) but due to profound differences in political views they were unable to use it to their own advantage.

Although there are differences in social structure and political tradition, it would be reasonable to expect that socialism should have the same possibilities in Finland as in the other Scandinavian countries. However, the agrarian party is supported by the lowest income groups in the rural areas and competes successfully with the leftist parties. /. . ./

Finally, the *split of the labour movement* has given special significance to the Finnish party system in comparison to the other Scandinavian countries. There have been several attempts to explain the strength of the Communist Party in Finland. Some have looked back in history to find an explanation for the radicalism among Finnish workers; others have put stress on the geographical proximity to Russia. Attention has also been paid to economic and institutional circumstances. Some sociologists interpret the so-called 'wasteland communism' as a kind of protest against the limited possibilities to take part in the political and social life. /. . ./

A further peculiarity in the Finnish party system is the relative stability in political strength of the parties, the sharp boundaries between the parties and the *high level of political conflict*. The main parties have for some time been static, independent organisations, suspicious of each other, counting no one as a reliable partner, not even within a short-term coalition. /. . ./

The struggle against foreign oppression, a civil war, a semi-fascist effort to conduct a coup d'état, two wars, and interior political crises, all in a relatively short time span, have split the Finnish society, have conserved a certain violent mentality and have locked individuals and parties in basic questions of social importance. The conflict between social classes and parties is thus very deep and the parliamentary system has not reached the same stability as in many other western democracies.

Nousiainens' description can be summarized in the following way:

1. The typical feature of the political structure of the Scandinavian countries is the comparatively strong influence of the working class. Through their political branches – the social democratic parties – unified labour movements have dominated the political (if not the economic) scene since the 1920s.

   The one exception is Finland. The labour movement was crushed[10] and divided into communist and social democratic branches of about the same strength, and the rivalry between these groups made it impossible to form a parliamentary working class majority until the 1960s and then only for a couple of years.

2. The second factor – and probably linked to the former – is the high level of manifest political conflict in Finland. An indicator of this was of course the civil war, but it is also possible to show that social and cultural life is much more politicized than in the other Nordic countries. In addition, Finland ranks much higher with regard to the frequency of strikes (ILO).

3.1 THE 'POLITICAL STRUCTURE' MODEL

What relevance do these factors possibly have in explaining variations in the degree of repression in criminal policy and in police behaviour, etc? My interpretation proceeds as follows: I believe that unfulfilled political demands in a society tend to lead to a high level of conflict (in the form of protests, strikes, etc.) and that this will trigger different repressive measures, including in the formation of criminal policy. The degree of repression will be determined by the degree of influence from each class of society over legislation, over the courts, and over the control apparatus, for example, the police and the prison authorities, etc. This influence can function in different ways and through different channels, from ordinary legislation and staff appointments, to more subtle opinion- and ideology-creating measures emanating from the bureaucracy and the mass media.

If this model is applied to the Nordic countries, the interpretation would be that the labour movements in Sweden, Norway, and Denmark have been more successful in achieving the fulfilment of their demands than has Finland's labour movement. This leads not only to a lower level of conflict, but also to a stronger influence over legislation and the control apparatus in the first three countries.

In Finland, however, the domination of the bourgeoisie was complete from the 1920s onward until the middle of the 1960s. Thus, they were able to reject almost all workers' demands and forced the workers to strike for every small advancement in the struggle for influence. Furthermore, in Finland the bourgeois domination over mass media is even greater than it is in the other Nordic countries, in all of which labour-owned newspaper syndicates exist. Even the state-owned radio and television corporation in Finland is less independent than in the other countries and is dominated by the parliamentary majority.

The consequences of this domination have been an almost continuous 'law-and-order' atmosphere in the society and an unchallenged 'deterrence' ideology in the control system, with stiff penalties and extensive police power.

3.2 A test – the evolution of criminal policy in the Nordic countries

To be able to test the 'political structure' model as an explanation for variations in the degree of repression in criminal policy, I will now try to show that it is possible to relate changes in repression to changes in the political structure (i.e. political conflict and the balance of power) in Scandinavia over the last century.

Since it is difficult for various reasons to find measurable factors which indicate strengths of 'political conflict' in one country over time,[12] and since political conflict obviously is connected to the balance of power,[13] I will in the following illustrate that criminal policy is strongly influenced by changes in the balance of power. My hypothesis is that stronger influence from the lower strata in society results in a lower level of repression.

Norway was the first country in Scandinavia to introduce a criminal policy based on the principles of 'individual prevention'. (This ideology is characterized by an emphasis on the rehabilitation of the offender instead of his punishment for purposes of deterrence.) 'Prosecution waivers' and 'conditional discharges' were introduced at the end of the 19th century. In addition, capital punishment was abolished by the new penal law in 1902.

This rather frenetic reform activity was not a coincidence either in point of time or geographically. The political situation in Norway was very exceptional. Norway in the 19th century had one of the most democratic constitutions in Europe,[14] as a rather independent nation under the Swedish crown. At the end of the century a struggle for total independence accelerated and was successfully carried through in 1905.

The political party behind this movement for independence was also the party behind the suffrage reform and the criminal policy reform, which gave Norway the 'most modern penal law of its time', to quote Lahti (1979). The party was referred to as the Leftist Party, *Venstre* (Kuhnle, pp. 14–15)[15] and periodically held a parliamentary majority over the conservatives during the decades around 1900. Thus the most democratic country of its time also had the most modern penal law and, also with reference to Christie's diagram, probably the lowest level of repression.

I think it is possible to see behind this rather exceptional situation the conflict between Norway and Sweden, which functioned as a sort of lid upon the social conflict *within* the country of Norway. It was important for the upper classes to accede to the demands of the lower classes in order to obtain their support and to legitimize the take-over of power from the Swedes.

Later, when the working class had entered the political arena in the years around World War I and threatened the bourgeois hegemony, the national 'honeymoon' was over and the level of conflict rose. This was also reflected in the criminal policy sphere, and a strong campaign for 'preventive detention' resulted in the 1920s in a dramatic extension of the law of 'preventive detention', giving Norway legislation for 'indeterminate sentences' that by far exceeded the corresponding legislation in Sweden and even in Finland (Glöerson, p. 41).

This rather short period of manifest political conflict ebbed in the 1930s, when the Social Democrats came to power, and to an even more marked degree during the Second World War and the German occupation. After the war criminal policy reform continued without any dramatic changes. According to the prison population rate (and other indications) Norway still has one of the lowest levels of repression in the world. These policies were challenged by a conservative 'law and order' campaign in the beginning of the 1970s (Lorentzen, 1979) but with only limited success.

In *Denmark* a similiar development was somewhat slower than in Norway. The first non-conservative Danish government introduced 'conditional discharges' in 1905.[16] A general penal reform, however, did not appear until 1930, when the new penal code was introduced by a social democratic government. Like the Norwegian penal law, the Danish code was built upon the principle of 'individual prevention'. 'Capital punishment' and 'hard labour' were abolished and 'conditional release' and extended possibilities to waive prosecution were introduced, especially for young offenders. During the decades thereafter the trend closely resembled the Norwegian one, perhaps with the exception that the 'treatment ideology' seems to have affected the Danish system even more fundamentally than the Norwegian system. (The notorious Herstedvester Institution for 'psychopaths' is an example of this.)

The development in *Sweden* was very much the same as in Denmark. The breakthrough of democracy also meant an acceleration of criminal reforms. The first non-conservative government introduced 'conditional discharge' as well as 'parole' in the same year (1906).[17] (This party also had suffrage reform in its political program.) Capital punishment was abolished in 1921, and in 1925 the Social Democrats passed a law to regulate the power of the police (Sjöholm, p. 43).

The real breakthrough for criminal policy reforms, however, did not take place until the 1930s, when the Social Democrats began their 40-year hegemony as the dominating political power. Their Minister of Justice, Karl Schlyter, started a campaign to 'empty the prisons' and thus gained an international reputation in the following decades. Several committees were formed, and the reform program covered every aspect of criminal policy and significantly extended the possibilities for usage of 'conditional discharges' and 'prosecution waivers' for juveniles. The prisons were reformed in the 1940s with the abolition of 'solitary confinement' and the introduction of 'open prisons' and a 'home leave' system. The 'loss of civil rights' for ex-convicts was also abolished, as was imprisonment for unpaid fines. The latter step meant a subsequent reduction of the intake into the prisons by more than 10,000 persons.[18] Schlyter even suggested the total abolition of the concept of 'punishment' in the new penal code, a proposal that had to be modified because of strong objections from the law committee (Beckman, p. 37).

In the 1950s and 1960s the pace within the reform movement slowed down significantly. This is hardly surprising, as the reformation in the 1930s and 1940s had been rather radical. An interesting interpretation, however, is that the slowdown indicates that prison reforms are not determined by economic factors, as the economic boom in Sweden appeared after World War II, after the reformation had already been carried out.[19] Recent decades in Sweden can be characterized very much as in Denmark and Norway. The reformation is continuing at a rather slow pace without radical changes in any direction.

While Sweden gained its reputation for a humane criminal policy, *Finland* regressed. In the beginning of the century it had been a rather progressive country, with universal suffrage as early as 1906.[20] The prison population was not at an exceptional level, although the country was under the reign of the Russian tsar until 1917, and capital punishment had not been used since the 1830s (Anttila 1966, p. 239). That no reforms were carried through during the first decades of this century was probably due to the fact that *all* legislation in Finland ceased because of the 'campaign of russification' (Wrede, p. 124).

The movement for independence ended in a class war in 1918 and the total defeat of the labour movement. The new nation was born with approximately 80,000 persons (i.e. workers taking part in the war) in concentration camps. In trying to legitimize the new state after the war, the 'white' victors did not free the 'red' vanquished as 'prisoners' of war', but criminalized them instead, charging them with treasonous rebellion, etc. In this situation – for obvious reasons – 'conditional discharges' were introduced to reduce the number of prisoners (Lahti 1977, p. 130).

After the civil war there was a short period of reconciliation. In this period the 'day-fine' system (fines meted out in proportion to daily income level) was introduced (1921). Even a new penal law, based on the principle of 'individual prevention', was presented (Granfelt, p. 116), but the political situation had already begun to shift and the penal law reform was shelved.

In the beginning of the 1920s the agitation from the now divided and weak left appeared again. The backlash this time was enormous. The communist MPs were imprisoned and their party criminalized; and in the decades to come many hundreds of their members were incarcerated for 'high treason', etc. In the field of criminal policy too this period is characterized as a time of 'hard climate' (Anttila, 1973, p. 87, Kalela, p. 105). As an indication of this 'climate' the legislation of 1930, the year of the fascist 'Lappo-movement', is very illustrative. In this year the Minister of Justice reintroduced the penalty of 'imprisonment on water-and-bread' (i.e. a form of corporal punishment) abolished in all of Scandinavia at least half of a century before.[21] The penalty was, however, again abolished when the left was able to form a government in the aftermath of the Second World War. The famous 'labour colonies' (open prisons with liberal conditions)[22] for short-term prisoners were also introduced.[23] A model was taken from the Soviet penal system (Conrad, p. 121).

After the 1948 communist take-over in Czechoslovakia, the bourgeois parties in Finland again succeeded in breaking the influence of the left and maintained their position until the 1960s, when the left recovered the power to enforce their interests. A law to regulate the power of the police was passed in 1966 for the first time (Virtanen, p. 123), by the new government, which also incurred responsibility for a penal system almost identical with the 19th-century system, a system that was with few exceptions based on the principles of deterrence.

Thus during the 1960s, a 'people's front' succeeded in breaking the right-wing domination in Finnish politics. This also meant a dramatic change in the control policy and ideology. In the following decade the government reformed the penal laws and the penal system, and almost brought Finland level with the other Nordic countries.[24]

A backlash in the 1970s has, however, retarded the democratization process in the Finnish control system. The labour movement is still split, and the prison population has again shown an upward trend since the lowest level (approx. 100) reached in the beginning of the 1970s. Christie's (1974, p. 131) comment on this is that Finland 'again is fading away from her Scandinavian neighbours'. This prophecy will perhaps prove false, but signs such as the revival of the 'classical school'[25] could very easily be interpreted in this way.

3.3 Concluding remarks

To sum up, in all the Scandinavian countries, it has been possible to show that penal reforms are a function of political influence from the lower strata of these societies. When this influence has increased,[26] measures have been taken to reduce the level of repression in criminal policy.

Some general remarks could, however, perhaps shed light over certain incongruencies in my description. It is obviously the case that the political factors play a much more visible role in the case of Finland than for the other countries. In Norway in the 1890s the 'leftist' government had a conservative expert (Getz),[27] and in Denmark (in the 1920s) the social democratic government passed a penal code based on the proposals of a commission from the former liberal period.[28]

In Sweden the break in the continuity is easier to document, while in the Finnish case almost every change in the political structure is reflected in changes in the criminal policy and vice versa.

At first this inconsistency could be seen as contradictory to the theoretical model. I think, however, that it should instead be interpreted in another way. The inconsistency could be explained by the other factor in the model, the notion of 'political conflict'. Finland, thus, is not only characterized as the country with the weakest influence from the left, but also as the country with the highest level of political conflict in both a short and a long perspective.

The interpretations of the inconsistency could be that political life in Finland is much more politicized (or polarized), and that every political act has a stronger 'ideological' significance. In Sweden and perhaps even more in Norway and Denmark, there has been more room for compromises and 'technocratic solutions' in the field of criminal policy.[29] This interpretation could also help to explain the very strong influence from forensic psychiatry and social workers (i.e., the 'treatment ideology') in these three countries, a development without parallel in Finland (Anttila, 1971).

A significant feature in the case of Finland, however, is that many 'treatment-oriented' measures were introduced, but at the same time distorted to fit the interests of the authorities. For example, 'indeterminate sentences' (preventive detention) were introduced, but without the accompanying concept of 'psychopath' and mental disturbances as mitigating factors. 'Prosecution waivers' for juveniles were introduced (1940), but were so legally restricted as to be meaningless (Lahti 1979, p. 6). Probation and parole were introduced, but the supervisors were police officers rather than social workers.

My interpretation of these distortions is that the Finnish system was thus developed in an attempt to match the modern and progressive systems in the Nordic countries but in actuality extracted only the repressive components of the 'treatment ideology'. In contrast, Swedish 'treatment ideology' in fact had almost exclusively humanizing effects on criminal policy. Thus, a 'preventive detention' sentence in the 'treatment-oriented' Swedish penal system was very much shorter than in the 'repression-oriented' Finnish system.[30]

Such an interpretation could also help to explain the particularly strong 'anti-treatment' attitude among prison activists in Finland in the 1960s (Eriksson), while in Sweden the corresponding movement (KRUM) took the opposite stand (in the beginning) and demanded that the 'treatment ideology' be put into practice.

4.1 THE POSSIBILITY OF GENERALIZING

The next step in the analysis is to determine whether it is possible to generalize the findings from the Nordic countries to other countries. To achieve this we must look for acceptable indicators of leftist influence and 'level of manifest political conflict' and correlate them with some indicators of repressive criminal policy.

To find such indicators is hardly an easy task, and all suggestions could probably be subjected to criticism. I decided to use 'prison population' rates as indicators of 'repressive criminal policy', since variation in these rates was the starting point for this study. The other indicators are even more difficult to find, especially those for 'influence from the political left'.

On the assumption, however, that a weak labour movement is forced to strike more often than a strong one – an assumption with both theoretical and empirical support (Olsson 1977, Korpi & Shalev 1979) – we could perhaps use the indicator 'strike rates'. This indicator would then take into account the 'strength of the left', but would also be a measure of 'political conflict'.

This method of analysis is supported by the Scandinavian data, which show Finland on one end of a continuum with high rates of strikes and a large prison population, followed at a distance by Denmark and the other two countries with low rates of both.

With these indicators – the 'prison population rate' and the 'strike rate' – for 19 countries with official data (i.e. western industrialized countries)[31] we get a correlation of $r_s = + 0.39$. A high 'strike rate' thus indicates a large prison population and vice versa. (See diagram on p. 18).

The correlation is significant (5 % level) but would probably be even stronger if the indicators had been more precise in measuring the actual phenomena. This can be illustrated by discussing the countries that deviate from the general pattern. Italy and Ireland (I) for instance, show very high strike

	Prison rate*	Strike rate**	Rank order strikes***
1. USA	189	1 088	6
2. Austria	104	1	18
3. Finland	101	1 412	5
4. Canada	95	1 862	1
5. New Zealand	85	400	10
6. West Germany	81	112	14
7. United Kingdom	75	1 546	4
8. Australia	70	1 560	3
9. France	61	342†	11
10. Belgium	58	422	9
11. Denmark	54	1 066	7
12. Italy	51	1 730	2
13. Switzerland	44	–	19
14. Japan	43	330	12
15. Sweden	43	14	17
16. Spain	40	215	13
17. Norway	39	104	15
18. Ireland	35	718	8
19. Netherlands	21	90	16

$r_s = + 0.39$

* Number of persons in prisons per 100,000 inhabitants, 1 January 1974 (Vetere, E. & Newman, G 1977).
** Working days lost per 1000 workers 1960–1974. (Yearbook of Labour Statistics, ILO 1970 and 1976).
*** r_s as a measurement is commented on in note 38.
† The political strike of 1968 is not included in the ILO compilation.

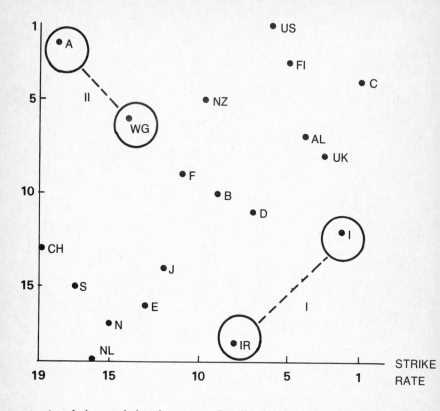

rates in relation to their prison rates. Possible interpretations of these facts are either that the strike rates are too high to indicate the 'real' level of political conflict, or that the prison rates are too low to indicate the 'real' level of repressive criminal policy.

At least for Italy the choice is easy. The level of political conflict is undoubtedly very high. It is also reasonable to assume that the political influence from the left so far has been very limited, since no labour-dominated government has ever been formed and the major communist party has not taken part in any of the almost thirty governments since the war. Thus, the high strike rate is obviously a good indicator of the level of manifest political conflict in the country.

It is more probable that the 'prison rate' is not a valid indicator of repressive criminal policy. The actual penal law is known to be far from 'permissive'[33] and was in fact introduced by the fascist government in 1930. The relatively low prison rate is therefore perhaps better explained by the extremely low rate of criminality reported in this country.[34] Even if the rate of criminality *per se* has only a very limited importance for prison rates (the correlation is $r_S = + 0.06$),[35] perhaps *extreme* crime rates would influence the prison rate in any case. (It is difficult to produce a high prison rate without access to at least some criminals.) If so, the case of Ireland could be similarly 'explained', since it reports an extremely low rate of criminality as well[36] (probably due to the influence of the Roman Catholic Church).[37]

A second deviating group of countries (II) consists of Austria and West Germany. These countries report large prison populations and low strike rates. In these cases, I think, the 'strike rate' is a reasonable indicator of a low level of manifest political conflict. According to the explanatory model we should then also expect a low incarceration rate. To find a reason why this is not the case, I think we have to return to the original formulation of the model. It then turns out that the model includes *two* specific conditions for a low level of repression in the criminal policy. One was a low level of political conflict and the other was a strong political influence from the lower classes. The latter is a practical necessity for facilitating changes in the legal rules, which remain from earlier periods of conflict, and for altering ideologies, for example from the 'deterrence ideology' to the 'treatment ideology'.

The explanatory model could be used to predict that when the lower classes in these societies form a government and thus obtain influence over the control apparatus, a reformation will take place which will change the criminal policy and, in a somewhat longer perspective, reduce the level of repression in the criminal policy.

This, in fact, is what is occurring in both West Germany and Austria, since the labour parties have come to power in the 1970s. Austria introduced a new penal code in 1975, and West Germany has also adopted 'individual prevention' measures aimed at, among other things, reducing the use of short-term imprisonment. These policies are obviously intended to lower the prison populations in these countries, where the control systems were never cleansed from the former fascist influence.

If these explanations of the two types of deviating countries are acceptable and the correlations are computed for the remaining countries, we get the following results. If only Austria is excluded from the computation, the correlation is raised from +.39 to +.58 for the remaining 18 countries. If West Germany is also excluded, we get a correlation of +.65 and, finally, if also Italy and Ireland are excluded, the correlation is .80 for the remaining 15 countries.

Another country of special interest is the United States. This country reports an extreme prison population rate of 189 per 100,000 inhabitants, which I think is probably an underestimate. The extreme prison rate has, however, no counterpart in an equally extreme strike rate (even if this rate is among the highest in the sample). The special circumstances in this case, however, are traceable, as it turns out that half of the prison population in the USA is black (Cahalan p. 39).

To understand this, it is necessary to look at the political structure of the USA, especially in the South. This region reports the most extreme prison rates, and we find a very good illustration of the 'political structure' model. Exploiting the traditional race prejudices and threatening the white workers to replace them with blacks, factory owners have succeeded in preventing almost all labour organization (Vann Woodward p. 36) and in creating a situation of 'political frustration' probably unique in the world.

To enact this policy, the authorities have been forced to resort to extremely repressive actions in all fields. Thus emerged 'cooperation between factory owners, the police, and politicians fighting the unions', to quote an expert on labour organization (Olsson p. 32).

The conclusion must be that the white ruling class oppresses the black *and* the white workers. The white workers – as they cannot direct it against the factory owners in the form of strikes or other protests – vent their frustration on the blacks and other subordinated groups. This, I think, is the primary explanation for the rather moderate strike rate of the USA in relation to the extreme prison rate.[38] Even if the pattern is most pronounced in the South, I think that it also has relevance in the rest of the country, to some degree. The labour situation in the USA has always been characterized by a divided labour market. This was earlier due to foreign immigration and during the most recent decades to inner migration when the South exported the outcasts of its semi-fascist political system to the rest of the country. This factor has probably strongly contributed to the chronic weakness and very low degree of organization of the American workers, judged on an international scale.[39] The working class is fragmented and it has not even been able to create a political party. The influence of the lower strata in the USA, especially of the groups outside the labour unions, is even weaker than that of these strata in Finland. This relationship is reflected in the correspondingly higher prison population rates found in the USA.[40]

The relationship is further illustrated if the prison population in the USA is calculated separately for whites and blacks. The prison rate is 100–150 for whites (i.e. comparable to Finland's). For Blacks, however, the prison rate is about 900[41] and thus exceeds even the South African rate of approx. 400.[42]

If the astronomic rate of imprisonment for black Americans were applied in the Swedish society, the number of prisoners on a given day would increase from approximately 3,000 to almost 75,000, and 175 new prisons of the largest model (Kumla) would be required.

4.2 Eastern Europe

The title of this study is 'Criminal Policy and Repression in Capitalist Societies'. This limitation is logical, since the theoretical model was deduced from an analysis of four capitalistic societies (the Scandinavian countries). The limited scope, however, does not necessarily mean that the model – at least to some extent – must be without relevance for other political systems too. The problem is, however, that to test the model in other types of political systems would require a new set of concepts and measurements to analyse the distribution of power and the level of manifest political conflict.

One example could be the political systems of Eastern Europe. Given the fact that these countries obviously have a markedly high level of repression in their criminal policies (including capital punishment and large prison populations), and, further, the fact that the theoretical model presented includes 'political influence from the lower strata of society' as an explanatory factor, a special commentary is perhaps appropriate. Thus, the question to be answered is: 'Why didn't the level of repression in criminal policy decrease in the Soviet Union when the working class exerted more, and even monopolized, political influence as a result of the revolution?'

The answer to this, is, in fact, that the level of repression in criminal policy *did* decrease, and that the USSR in the 1920s probably had one of the most humane criminal policies of that period. The party program of 1919 included the following principles:

- The administration of criminal justice should rely on the principle of the conditional discharge of the offender.
- Courts should express the attitude of society towards crime and the criminal through the exercise of social reprimand.
- Punishment should be without deprivation of liberty, as for example corrective labour on special public projects.
- Prisons should be transformed into educational institutions in which offenders are educated rather than isolated.
- Correctional institutions should rely on the support of the neighbouring communities to strengthen the educative aspects of their programs.[43]

That these principles were also obviously put into practice is supported by the following statement by contemporary observers:

Soviet criminology seems to assume that the 'criminal' is not a criminal. He is not to be treated as an outcast, nor to be punished for revenge or retaliation. He is an 'unfortunate', sick, weak, maladjusted, and must be trained to become a social being, a functioning member of the community. Sentences are short, and once the sentence has been served the miscreant is readmitted into everyday life, with no sting or scar of shame, no brand of having been a 'convict'. The maximum sentence for a non-political offence – murder – is ten years (before 1922 it was five years); most prison sentences run two to three years. Any sentence of less than a year's imprisonment is not carried out; the offender is left at liberty and perhaps fined. But there are other sentences ranging from severe public reprimands to fines (usually deducted from the pay) that seem to affect the delinquent as deeply as a prison sentence.

The humanitarian principles of the Communists seem actually to have been carried into effect in the prison regime for non-political criminals in the USSR. The buildings are, in most cases, those inherited from the tsarist regime, and often still inadequately improved in sanitation and amenities. But the administration is well spoken of, and is apparently as free from physical cruelty as any prisons are ever likely to be. In addition to these government prisons, however, the GPU itself maintains at Bolshevo, in the Moscow oblast, a remarkable reformatory settlement, which seems to go further in the direction of humanitarian treatment of offenders against society than anything else in the world. Nor does the Bolshevo stand alone. There are in the USSR ten other reformatory colonies on the same plan.[44]

Thus, so far, the theoretical model could obviously also have relevance for the USSR. However, this conclusion must be restricted in at least two important respects. The first is that the humane criminal policy of the 1920s was only applicable to 'ordinary criminals' and not to 'political enemies to the regime' (Ranulf, p. 188). Towards this group the regime used measures of terror and not seldom in a rather indiscriminate way (cf. the handling of 'terrorist cases' in West Germany and elsewhere today).

The second restriction is that the humane policy obviously was altered in the 1930s, at the time of large scale purges and the revival of the Gulag policy. Thus, the humane 'socialist' criminal policy of the 1920s had already faded away when USSR extended its political system to the rest of Eastern Europe at the end of World War II.

Perhaps it would be possible to meet the first objection if Ranulf's division between 'interested' and 'disinterested' tendencies to inflict punishment is introduced into the interpretation. The 'interested tendency to inflict punishment' is, according to Ranulf (p. 188), only directed at 'the political enemies of the regime', as a political necessity, and should theoretically not be confused with the 'disinterested' tendency. The latter category of punishment is directed only at 'ordinary' criminals, where motives for variation in the punishment are not obvious.[45]

To respond to the second objection, i.e. why repression in criminal policy increased in the 1930s, it is necessary to have access to indicators showing variation in the distribution of political influence and the level of political conflict. Only if it were possible to show that the distribution of power in the USSR was altered towards political centralization, with reduced influence from the lower strata of society and an increased level of political conflict as a consequence, would the 'political structure' model be supported. Such an interpretation is hardly unrealistic.

5 GENERAL DISCUSSION
5.1 Motives and Attitudes

The 'political structure' model is intentionally presented as a 'theoretical model' and not as a 'theory'. To present it as a theory, I think it would be necessary to explain 'why' the empirical findings and relationships obviously exist, and what *motives* different political groups could have in advocating different levels of repression in criminal policies. In other words, why should right-wing political groups strive to increase this form of repression, or the opposite, why should the left-wing try to decrease it? Clearly, so far almost no one has stated that criminal policy or penal law plays a significant role in class struggles.

Not being able to give a good answer to these questions, I will attempt a tentative explanation. In my view, neither the right- nor the left-wing *per se* have an 'objective interest' in a certain level of repressive criminal policy. For the right-wing, however, repression in criminal policy can function in a *political strategy aimed at exploiting middle-class fears and anxiety of lower class political activity.*[46]

The Nixon-style 'law and order' campaigns experienced in almost every western industrialized country have been aimed at reversing the swing to the left in the politics of the 1960s. A corresponding technique was used by the Nazis in Germany to overthrow the Weimar Republic in the 1930s.[47]

Polls and studies show that concern about crime in various countries is at least as widespread in the middle (and even working) class as in the upper class. Thus, it is not difficult to see the potential of this stategy, especially when the technique includes a conscious confusion between political and criminal activity. Black protest is aligned with black criminality, war demonstrations with drug trafficking, and striking workers' attacks on strike breakers with attacks on 'public safety'. In this way it is possible for the right-wing to 'criminalize' (or de-legitimize) political protest in the eyes of members of the middle class and even of politically immobilized workers.

A second question is whether we must expect *individuals and groups to act and show the attitudes* expected from the model. In other words, must a leftist government always act to reduce repression and must all reductions in repression be instigated by leftist political forces in order not to reject the model? The answer must be, No.

An illustration is the suffrage reform in Sweden at the beginning of this century, when the conservatives passed the law that extended the right to vote. No serious person would suggest that this was a result of the party's actual desires. On the contrary, the party had worked against this reform for decades and took the step out of necessity, forced by the growing power of organized labour.

In the same vein, a 'left-wing' government, of course, can be forced to act in a similar manner, for instance to enact repressive legislation to repel a 'law and order' campaign by the right-wing. Again, it is the *level of conflict* and the *balance of power* that determines the level of repression according to the macrosociological 'political structure' model, and not the wishes and attitudes of the individual actors.

This argument also has relevance to so-called 'public opinion' on these matters. A probable common belief is that members of the working class are more 'punitive' than members of other classes. This is not, however, the case, At least according to findings reported from Denmark (Kutchinsky, p. 144) not as a general statement.[48]

It could, however, very well be the case that 'public opinion' in more repressive societies reflects more punitive attitudes. Again, we must ask whether this attitude is a coincidence and a *cause* of the repression in the society or the opposite, i.e. that political conflict and oppression create punitive individuals, especially among the most oppressed classes.

If public attitudes in fact are more punitive in more repressive societies, I think this fact would be in support of the interpretation, rather than the opposite. Such conditions would promote the political exploitation of these punitive attitudes, and simultaneously increase the general political significance of criminal policy in the repressive countries.

SUMMARY

The point of departure for this study is the fact that since the 1920s Finland has reported a very high prison population rate in comparison to the other Scandinavian countries. In trying to explain this phenomenon, the criminal policy systems in Scandinavia were analysed, and it was possible to show that the high prison rate was just *one* aspect of a total repressive control system. Thus, also the police in Finland have extensive powers and act more discriminatorily than their colleagues in the other countries, the legislation and the application of the law in the courts are harsher and, finally, the prisoners are more severely treated.

From this background it was concluded that a high prison rate could be viewed as an indication of a generally high level of repression in criminal policy in Finnish society. The next step in the analysis therefore was to try to find an explanation for this repressive tendency within the Finnish control system. To achieve this, a comparative analysis of the four Scandinavian countries was made. From the process of elimination it was decided that the *political factors* were most interesting, since the four countries show strong similarities in other respects.

From this comparative analysis *a theoretical model* was constructed, stating that the reason for the more repressive criminal policy in Finland, was probably the high level of manifest political conflict and the weak political influence from the lower strata (i.e. the political left) of this society.

To test this model two different methods were used. First, a longitudinal analysis of the political circumstances under which criminal policy reforms had been introduced in the Scandinavian countries was done. With this form of analysis it was possible to show that reforms to reduce the level of repression in the criminal policy systems tended to be introduced in periods when the political influence from the lower strata was higher. The second test was made with a cross-national comparative method. An indicator of *repression in criminal policy* (prison population rates) was correlated to an indicator of *manifest political conflict* (and a weak polical influence from the lower strata) (strike rates). In support of the model a significant, positive correlation was found for the 19 industrialized western countries included in the test.

ACKNOWLEDGEMENT

I should hereby like to extend my gratitude to the following persons for their helpful critical comments on various versions of this study: Hanns von Hofer, Hans Enroth, Karsten Åström, Per-Olof Wikström, Stina Holmberg and Karen Leander at the Institute of Criminology in Stockholm.

NOTES:

[1] Only Finland, Denmark, Norway and Sweden are included. Iceland is excluded for demographical reasons (200,000 inhabitants).

[2] Christie's analysis of prison populations was referred to in a Finnish pamphlet on prison reform in 1967, *Varning för vård* (Beware of treatment). Anttila's comment on this was that Christie's figures received quite a lot of attention in Finland, and they contributed to those legal reforms (especially the abolition of drunkenness fines, often resulting in imprisonment if not paid) which have now brought Finland somewhat closer to its neighbours as far as the number of prisoners is concerned (Anttila 1971, p. 3).

[3] As shown below on page 19, the conclusion is also relevant for the other countries included in this study.

[4] Punishments in Finland are harsher in terms of length of sentences as well as the greater risk of being sentenced to imprisonment (Sveri).

[5] According to Aromaa (p. 13), 41 % of the prisoners in Finnish penal institutions were convicted of theft and burglary etc, 25 % of 'crimes of violence' (incl. robberies), and 20 % of 'drunken driving'. The corresponding figures for Sweden were 60 %, 13 %, and 14 % respectively (SOU 1971 p. 290).

[6] The Chief Public Prosecutor's report (Stockholm 1974, p. 40) states that 'there is an internationally accepted norm that temporary deprivation of liberty shall be examined by a judge within 24 hours'. This norm is obviously not accepted in either Finland or Sweden.

[7] Differences in drinking habits and behaviour could perhaps also partly account for the Finnish rate of 'public drunkenness' before this behaviour was decriminalized in 1969.

[8] Findings indicating a low degree of social discrimination in the Swedish criminal justice system are also reported by Carlsson (1972), Janson (1976), and Tham (1979).

[9] The 'land reform' was a fundamental political reform, 'aimed at creating a wall of ideological defence against the Bolsjevik revolution'. In the states bordering the new Soviet state, millions of crofters were given land or allowed to buy land at sharply reduced prices. In Finland no fewer than 115,000 became landowners during the years following the civil war in 1918. (Hataja, p. 8).

[10] Of a population of about 3 millions, 80,000 persons were sent to concentration camps after defeat in the Finnish civil war. Of these 10,000 were executed or died in epidemics in the camps (Puntila p. 121).

[11] Leftist governments in Finland ruled during 1944–48 and 1966–71 as coalition governments with communists, social democrats and agrarians. Also between 1958–62 the left had a majority in parliament, but was not able to form a government.

[12] One indicator of 'political conflict' is 'strikes'. In a longitudinal perspective, however, the phenomenon of 'strikes' is strongly dependent on international, economic terms of trade. Also the nature of strikes has changed from 'many, small but long' to 'few, large but short'. For these reasons 'strikes' are difficult to use as indicators of 'political conflict' over time in one country. These problems, however, are diminished if 'strikes' are used as an indicator in a cross-national comparison during a specific period of time, and such a comparison is made below in this study.

[13] The relationship between 'distribution of power' and 'political conflict' is discussed below in § 5.3.

[14] This judgement was made by Engels (Lorenz p. 25).

[15] A valuable study on the emergence of the 'Nordic welfare state', using a comparative, longitudinal approach, is presented by Kuhnle.

[16] The legislation of this government was rather contradictory. The Minister of Justice in Denmark, Mr. Alberti, succeeded in getting a law passed re-introducing flogging for serious sexual crimes. (The legislation was motivated by a 'wave of hooliganism' including sexual assaults etc., but met with protests from all sectors in parliament and even from the King.) The special law lasted only a few years, and the Minister himself was forced to resign and was later convicted of, and sentenced to 8 years imprisonment (hard labour) for, embezzlement of the enormous sum of 15,000,000 million DCr (Danstrup p. 467).

[17] Karl Staaf, the liberal and first non-conservative Prime Minister of Sweden personally participated in the drafting and passage of the penal reform (Carlsson p. 600).

[18] As the average time spent in prison was very short for this group of prisoners, the 'prison rate' (number of persons in penal institutions on a certain day) per 100,000 inhabitants was reduced by only 10–20 %.

[19] The 'prison rate' rose, however, very rapidly during the 1950s, in spite of the reforms. Although 'crime rate' certainly is not a good indicator of 'prison rates' (Christie 1974), in general, I think that the 'crime boom' of the 1950s was an important factor behind this. When the crime rates continued to increase in the 1960s, however, the 'prison rate' did not follow suit. The interpretation is then, that *extreme* changes in the 'crime rates' *can* influence the prison rates under special circumstances, and that the prison rate of the 1950s probably would have increased even more without the reforms of the 1940s.

[20] The Finnish situation at that time was obviously a parallel to the Norwegian situation at the same time period, mentioned above. To keep the nation together against foreign supremacy the internal ruling class had to meet demands from the other classes and, thus, reduce the level of conflict within the country (Wrede p. 128).

[21] The Minister succeeded in passing three laws in the same year and their contents are very illustrative. The first law criminalized 'public statements of a defamatory character about the legal order of society'. The next law was aimed at 'protecting the peace of the labour market', and the third was the re-introduction of the 'water-and-bread'-penalty *(Svensk Juristtidning* 1930, p. 480).

[22] The function of these 'labour colonies' or 'work camps' is described and evaluated by Uusitalo.

[23] Besides reducing the repression, this government, however, also sharpened the penalties for theft. This fact is potentially damaging to the theoretical model suggested in this study. A closer look will show that the political situation in this period was extreme. The post-war years in Finland produced a nearly chaotic situation with a demobilized army, 10 % of the population displaced, and a 'boom' in registered criminality *(Svensk Juristtidning* 1951, p. 231). See further discussion on this topic in § 5.2 below.

[24] The Police Act of 1966. Furthermore, the prison system was reformed by a new law to regulate the conditions in the prisons. The principle of rehabilitation was stressed (BRÅ-report), and a home-leave system was introduced. Of special importance to the prison rate was the decriminalization of public drunkenness and later the abolition of 'preventive detention' for non-violent offenders. Finally, the loss of civil rights for ex-convicts was ended, capital punishment (not inflicted in peace-time) was abolished, and the principle of absolute prosecution was reduced (Lahti 1977, p. 142).

[25] The so-called 'new classical school' is the name of a movement in penal 'reform' which seeks the solution for future criminal policy in the past (i.e. the 19th century). Rationality, calculation, foreseeability, proportionality, and deterrence are basic concepts of this school's policy in place of social determination, rehabilitation, treatment and care. The school proclaims that its goals are progressive and non-repressive, but apparently accepts the conservative perception of man and carries the burden of a very enthusiastic support from the right-wing politicians in Scandinavia and in the USA.

[26] An increasing influence from the lower strata could also be called 'increased democracy'.

[27] See Røstad, p. 399.

[28] See *Svensk Juristtidning* 1925, p. 139, and 1930, p. 435.

[29] This interpretation is in line with Dahl's (p. 89). She states that Getz – the conservative expert of the 'left' (liberal) government – 'imported' his ideas and techniques from abroad, and that his reform proposals were seldom aimed at solving acute social problems in the Norwegian society.

[30] A 'preventive detention' sentence in Sweden in the 1940s seldom exceeded 1 year (Strahl p. 137), which was in fact also the 'minimum time'. This practice was in line with Schlyter's statement at the Criminal Policy meeting in Finland in 1949, that he was opposed to the American form of 'indeterminate sentences'. He would rather see a development in the other direction *towards a radical decrease in the use of incarceration for criminal offenders.* (Aulie p. 108). In Finland the 'preventive detention' practice was 2–3 years 'in addition to the term of imprisonment' (Anttila 1966, p. 241).

[31] Only countries with officially registered rates are included. Excluded are, thus, East European countries, Greece (after the coup d'état in 1967), and also extremely small nations like Iceland, Luxembourg, Lichtenstein, etc.

[32] The ideal case would, of course, be to have perfect indicators of the two correlated phenomena 'criminal policy repressiveness' and 'political conflict'. Thus, the 'prison population rate' must, at least to some extent, also be influenced by, for example, crime rates, and 'strike rates' to some extent influenced by forms of labour organization, access to funds, legislation etc. These other influences therefore must be expected to vary between countries in dissimilar directions, and thus conceal the relationship between the phenomena to be studied, and decrease the correlation between them.

[33] See Lenke (1974) on the sentencing practices in Italy and other European countries.

[34] See Interpol – International Crime Statistics. In 1968 Italy together with Spain ranked among the lowest of all industrialized countries.

[35] The correlation is computed for crimes against property for the 13 countries in the sample for which statistical information was available in the Interpol statistics.

[36] *Statistical Yearbook of Ireland 1974*, Table 225.

[37] Spain could perhaps be placed in the same category as Italy and Ireland. Spain, however, also reports a low level of strikes. The strong increase in strike rates in recent years indicates that the low rate was probably due to legal restrictions.

[38] That the strike rate is not expected to follow the indicator of repression when the latter becomes extreme, indicates that the relationship between 'repression' and 'strikes' is not linear but curvilinear. For this reason rank-order correlation is used instead of linear regression.

[39] In the USA only about 28 % of the workers are organized (Schmidt p. 142) in comparison to 85 % in Sweden and 65 % in Norway (Olsson).

[40] The view of prison conditions as a reflection of the life situation of the lower strata *outside* the prisons is supported by the following 'basic rules' for Nazi criminal policy: 'The prisoner must be treated in such a way that he will envy the unemployed citizen with regard to food, clothing and housing conditions, even in the winter time' (Gløersen, p. 53).

[41] The total number of persons in prisons on a given day in the United States in 1970 was 413,000 or 213 per 100,000 inhabitants (Cahalan, Table 1). The proportion of Blacks was 47 % (p. 39), they numbered about 200,000 and computed for the total Black population of 22.5 million, the prison population rate for Black Americans was over 900.

[42] *Statistical Yearbook of South Africa 1970*, Table G-8.

[43] The reference is from Lenin, V.I. – 'Collected works', Moscow, Marx-Engels Institute 1960 – quoted from Conrad p. 157.

[44] The references are from Winter, E – *Red Virtue*, New York 1933, and Webb, S – *Soviet Communism: A new civilisation?*, London 1935. Quoted from Ranulf pp. 186–187. Another illustration of the attitudes towards punishment in the newborn socialist state is given in the following quotation from the same author (Webb): 'The infliction of physical suffering is frowned upon not only in the administration of justice, but also in education, and this goes so far that the parental slapping of disobedient children has actually been made a criminal offence'. A parallel development has also taken place in Sweden during the last decades, with legislation against physical punishment in education and child-rearing.

[45] Ranulf (1938) presented an explanation of 'disinterested tendency to inflict punishment'. According to the author, this tendency could be viewed as a function of the political influence from the middle-class values, which were supposed to be more punitive than the values of other classes. Ranulf's study was obviously triggered by the contemporary situation in Nazi Germany and did not try to trace the factors behind the middle-class values in Germany or elsewhere.

[46] This interpretation is in line with Lipset's (p. 219) notion that right-wing parties benefit from election topics of non-economic character, such as moral questions, etc. This is due to the necessity for such a party to get support also from voters of lower social classes. Because of the right-wing total domination of mass-media in most western countries (Lenke p. 91) it is also possible for the right-wing to push such questions for public debate.

[47] The vocabulary and tone used in the 'law-and-order' campaign in the USA in 1968 could have been direct quotations from the Nazi propaganda of the 1930s. While Nixon and others criticized the Democrats for 'coddling the criminals', the Nazis ironically criticized the Weimar government for its 'anxiety to harm the offenders, the tender-hearted efforts to enter his mind, the desire to understand his originality, the tendency to pity him as being a product of his milieu' (Holmgren, p. 80).

[48] Kutchinsky's study clearly showed the middle-class members in Denmark to be significantly more in favour of harsher forms of punishments like 'capital' and 'corporal' punishments. A Swedish study by Bondesson showed the public opinion to be much more 'pro-reform' than was expected.

REFERENCES

ALLART, E. *Att ha, att älska, att vara*, Lund 1975.
ANDENAES, J. In Ancel, M. & Strahl, I. (eds.) *Le droit penal des pays Scandinave*, Paris 1969.
ANTILLA, I. 'Åtgärder mot ungdomskriminaliteten', *NTfK* 1962.
ANTILLA, I. 'The trend of criminal policy', in *The Finnish Legal System*, Helsinki 1966.
ANTTILA, I. 'Crime problems in Scandinavia', in report presented to the Anglo-Scandinavian seminar in Bolkesjø, 1971.
ANTILLA, I. & TÖRNUDD, P. *Kriminologi i ett kriminalpolitisk perspektiv*, Stockholm 1973.
AROMAA, K. *Om jämförelser av fångtal*, 1977.
AULIE, A. *NTfK* 1952 p. 108.
BECKMAN, N. (mfl) *Brottsbalken, del 1*, Stockholm 1964.
BRÅ – Rapport 1977:7, *Nytt straffsystem*, Stockholm 1977.
BONDESSON, U. (ed.) *Rationalitet i rättssystemet*, Stockhom 1979.
CAHALAN, M. 'Trends in incarceration in the United States since 1880', Crime and Delinquency, 1979.
CARLSSON, G. 'Unga lagöverträdare', SOU 1972:76, Stockholm 1972.
CARLSSON, S. & ROSÉN, J. *Sveriges historia*, Del 2. Stockholm 1962.
CHRISTIE, N., ANDENAES, J. SKIRBEKK, S. 'A study of self-reported crimes', pp. 86–116 in *Scandinavian Studies in Criminology*, Vol. 1, Oslo 1965.
CHRISTIE, N. 'Changes in penal values', pp. 161–172 *Studies in Criminology*, Vol. 2. Oslo 1968.
CHRISTIE, N. 'Hvor tett et samfunn?', Oslo 1975.
CONRAD, J. 'Crime and its correction'. UCLA press 1965.
DAHL, T. S. 'Barnevern og samfunnsvern', Oslo 1978.
DANSTRUP, J. & KOCK, H. *Danmarks historie*, Band 12, Copenhagen 1965.
ERIKSSON, L. (ed.) *Varning för vård*, Helsinki 1967.
GLØERSEN, K. *NTfS* 1933–34, p. 41.
GLØERSEN, K. *NTfS* 1948, p. 53.
GRANFELT, O. 'Några straffrättsliga reformer och reformplaner i Finland efter allmänna Strafflagens tillkomst' in *Festskrift till Schlyter*, Stockholm 1949.
ILO – YEARBOOK OF LABOUR STATISTICS, 1972, 1976.
HATAJA, K. 'Förändringar i rättsåskådningen under senare tid', *SvJT* 1934 p. 1.
VON HOFER, H. 'Dutch prison population', Scandinavian Research Council for Criminology, 1975.
HOLMGREN, K. – 'Nationalsocialistiskt straffrättsförslag', *SvJT* 1934.
INTERNATIONAL CRIME STATISTICS, INTERPOL, PARIS 1968, 1974.
JANSON, C-G. 'The Handling of Juvenile Delinquency Cases', Department of Sociology, Stockholm 1977.
KALELA, J. 'Right-wing radicalism in Finland during the interwar period', *Scandinavian Journal of History*, 1976.
KORPI, V. & SHALEV, M. 'Strikes, industrial relations and class conflict in capitalist societies' *British Journal of Sociology 1979*, p. 164.

30   LEIF LENKE

KUHNLE, S. 'The beginning of the Nordic welfare states: similarities and differences', *Acta Sociologica* 1978, Supplement.

KUTCHINSKY, B. 'Knowledge and attitudes regarding legal phenomena in Denmark', *Scandinavian Studies in Criminology*, Vol. 2. 1968.

LAHTI, R. 'Criminal sanctions in Finland: a system in transition', *Scandinavian Studies in Law*, 1977.

LAHTI, R. 'Idéutvecklingen beträffande kriminalitet och straffsystem'. Paper presented to the seminar arranged by Scandinavian Research Council for Criminology in Norway 1979.

LENKE, L. 'Criminal policy and public opinion towards crimes of violence', in 'Violence in Society', Council of Europe, Strasbourg 1974.

LIPSET, S. *Den politiska människan*, Stockholm 1969.

LORENTZ, E. *Arbeiderbevegelsens historie 1789–1930*, Oslo 1972.

LORENTZEN, H. 'Reinforcing the police – actors, interests and strategies', Institute of Sociology of Law, Oslo, 1979.

NOUSIAINEN, J. *Finlands politiska system.* Norstedts förlag, Stockholm 1966.

OLSSON, J. *Facklig horisont – Europa och Nord-Amerika*, Lund 1977.

PUNTILA, L. A. *Finlands politiska historia.* Helsingfors 1964.

RANULF, S. *Moral Indignation and Middle Class Psychology.* Copenhagen 1938.

RIKSÅKLAGAREN *Häktning och anhållande* Stockholm 1974.

RØSTAD, H. 'Landets første riksadvokat'. *Lov og Rett,* Oslo 1967.

SCHMIDT, F. – 'Organisationerna och arbetsstriden – en internationell överblick', in Brantgärde et al 'Konfliktlösning på arbetsmarknaden'. Lund 1974.

SJÖHOLM, E – 'Om politimakten och dess begränsningar', Stockholm 1964.

SOU 1971:74 – 'Kriminalvård i anstalt', Stockholm 1971.

SOU 1979:6 'Polisen', Stockholm 1979.

STRAHL, I. *NTfK* 1952, p. 137.

SVENSK JURISTTIDNING 1930, s. 480.

SVERI, K. – 'Straffsystemer i Norden', Nordiska rådet 1977.

THAM, H. – 'Brottslighet och levnadsnivå', Stockholm 1979.

UUSITALO, P. *British Journal of Criminology,* 1972, p. 211.

WERNER, B. 'Socialgruppsfördelning vid självdeklarerad brottshet', *NTfK* 1971:3.

VETERE, E. & NEWMAN, G. 'International crime statistics: An overview from a comparative perspective', *Abstracts in Criminology* 1977.

VIRTANEN, K. 'Polisen i historisk belysning', Report to the Scandinavian Research Council for Criminology, (Unpublished).

VANN WOODWARD, C. 'Blacks and poor whites in the South', in *The Underside of American History'*, by Frazier, T. (ed.), Hancourt Brace, 1971.

WREDE, R. A. *Finlands rätts- och samhällsordning,* Helsinki 1953.

Abbreviations:
NTfK – Nordisk tidskrift for Kriminalvidenskab.
NTfS – Nordisk tidskrift för Straffrätt.
SvJT – Svensk Juristtidning

Reinforcing the Police – Actors, Interests, and Strategies

BY *Håkon Lorentzen*

During the last 10–15 years the police forces in Sweden, Norway, and Denmark have experienced a period characterized by reorganization and strong growth. Appropriations and manning have increased, patrolling has become more efficient, and a centralization of the decision-making power has taken place. Furthermore, paramilitary units for combating terrorists and social disorder have now been institutionalized. The general impression is that in its functioning the police has acquired a more military character than in the past.

These structural changes constitute the theme of this article. Using the Norwegian police department as the point of departure, I will discuss the process of implementing these changes: Who were the participant *actors?* What *arguments* have been utilized? and Which type of *arena* constituted the setting?

The purpose behind asking these questions is to problematize *explanations* regarding the growth in the physical apparatus of power. According to socialist theory, the police is an instrument of power in the hands of the bourgeoisie. In reality, however, the causal connection between the bourgeoisie and the police apparatus is often difficult to assess; changes in the organization and operations of the police can not always be directly connected to bourgeois interests. The collected material shows that while the main trends have remained the same, interest groups, types of arguments, and strategies behind the reinforcement of the police have changed. A satisfactory explanation of the police reinforcement thus requires an analysis of the relationship between the intentions and the consequences stemming from the participant actors' deeds.

1. THE GROWTH

In the 1960's and 70's most West European countries have experienced a large growth and reorganization of what is called the state's domestic apparatus of power: the traditional and civil (secret) police forces as well as militarily functioning troops for domestic use. During the rising unemployment and political unrest of the 70's, the growth has become especially visible to the public. In *Sweden* some years ago approx. 1500 policemen turned the small town of Båstad into an impenetrable fortress during the tennis match between

Chile and Sweden. In *Denmark* police forces have intervened progressively more often in strike actions and political demonstrations.[1] In *Norway* demonstrators faced the military-style 'anti-terror-police' while taking part in the Hammersborg action in Oslo – an incident in which hundreds of demonstrators protested against a city council decision to tear down one of the oldest schools in town.

It is no coincidence that now – in the 1970's – police activities receive more attention than in earlier days. During the last decade in Sweden, Denmark and Norway, changes that probably have no counterpart in this century have occurred in respect to personnel, material, and organizational structure. Some numbers illustrate this growth:[2]

Table 1. Appropriations to police tasks; converted into fixed crowns on the basis of the cost-of-living index of 1970:

| Year | Total in millions of crowns[3] | | |
	Sweden	Denmark	Norway
1965	590	489	296
1970	914	628	338
1975	1262	778	507

The table shows that in all three countries a huge growth has occurred in the 10-year period between 1965 and 1975. Expressed as a percentage, the growth in Sweden is 113 %, in Denmark 59 %, and in Norway 71 %. The largest growth in Sweden took place between 1960 and 1965 (54 %), while both in Denmark and Norway the major appropriation increases were granted in the latter period between 1970 and 1975 (23 % and 50 %, respectively).

In relation to population figures, the appropriations (fixed crowns) to the police have also risen.

Table 2. Number of crowns to the police per capita

Year	Sweden	Denmark	Norway
1965	75	103	79
1970	113	127	87
1975	153	155	127

Per capita every Swede's contribution to the police has increased by 104 % and every Dane's by 50 % in the 10-year period 1965–75, while every Norwegian in 1975 paid 60 % more to the police than a decade earlier. Compared to the level of general economic activity, the police has increased its share, too.

Table 3. Position of the gross national product allocated to the police, in percent.

Year	Sweden	Denmark	Norway
965	0.42	0.39	0.32
1970	0.58 (1971)	0.42	0.32
1975	0.64	0.54	0.45

It can be noted that among the three countries, Sweden allots the largest portion of the gross national product to police tasks (0.64 % in 1975), and in addition has had the biggest increase (0.22 %) from 1965 to 1975. Both Norway and Denmark have experienced less growth, but much information indicates that increases in police appropriations are accelerating in these countries.

During the relevant time period we have encountered – and still do – a far-reaching *structural rationalization* of the police department, which can not be observed from the figures given above. For example, in Sweden the number of the police districts has been reduced from 554 to 119. In Norway, to be discussed later, the local county police department is being rationalized, while simultaneously overlapping and coordinating administrative units, police regions, have been introduced. In Denmark policemen in administrative positions are being transferred to operational police work, while at the same time the organization is enlarged with civilian office staff. The *operational efficiency* of the police has been increased through increases in manpower but also through an extensive *technical improvement* of the department. Increasing use of patrol cars, electronic supervision and communication equipment, EDB-operated archives and registers, as well as military-style repressive devices (helicopters, water cannons, teargas, armored cars and the like) are well known phenomena in one or more of the above-mentioned countries.

In short, the development in Sweden, Denmark, and Norway can be characterized as follows:

a. *The relative independence of local police units has been weakened.* Decisions that used to be taken locally or regionally are now handled regionally or centrally. Power is being centralized – and the local population loses control over the controllers.

b. There is a continual shift from what can be called a *persuasion-oriented* way of solving conflicts toward a *coercion-oriented* conflict resolution. Simultaneously the direct contact-area between the public and the police is being reduced through the increased use of technical aids.

c. *Resources* granted to the police are steadily rising. By means of additional personnel, material and administration, the police is a growing organization, and this growth seems to be continuing in the late 1970's.

2. PHASES OF GROWTH, ACTORS AND ARGUMENTS

Certainly in Norway, the development sketched above has clearly strengthened the functioning of the police as an instrument of power. The question
is, can this development be seen as a 'conscious' response to political unrest
and economic crisis tendencies? Is there a group of rationally acting individuals who intentionally seek to strengthen the repressive police functions?
Or must the structural changes and the reinforcement be seen as an uninten-
tional consequence of a process in which the actors do not respond on the
basis of changes in the economic system? Or, as a third explanatory approach,
are we witnessing a development that via several transforming intermediate
levels can be traced back to economic structural changes?[4]
   On the basis of the extensive changes implemented in the prevailing system
and operation of the Norwegian police between 1965 and 1977, I will attempt
to illuminate below this question of effectuation. Within the time period
discussed and in relation to public scrutiny, the development presented can
be divided into three phases: the *latent,* the *parliamentary,* and the *political*
phase. Each of these phases can be distinguished on the basis of who the
participating actors are, the arguments they use, and the strategies they apply.

2.1. The phase of latency

During the phase of latency, the first meagre foundation was laid in what later
became the police-reinforcement of the 1970's. This phase is marked by two
groups of participant actors. On the one hand we have the interest organizations of the police, represented by the union officials and the police
commissioners, both in turn representing the interests of the police department, and on the other hand the *Ministry of Justice,* acting in the capacity
of final authority within the department. For years the first two groups
mentioned put pressure on the Ministry of Justice in order to enlist sympathy
for their understanding of the departmental problems and their demands for
increased resources.
   In this phase two parallel running conflict-themes occupied these groups
of actors. Firstly, discontent with the working conditions of the employees
led to a focussing on the problems regarding an effective *interest organization.* Secondly, a rising frustration emerged with respect to the material
conditions of the department in relation to what was felt to be an increase
of work tasks.
   In this section I will discuss the development of these two conflict-themes
– labelled the struggle for *police-union interests* and the struggle for a
reinforced department. For a long time these themes ran their separate
courses, but a common solution was found in the suggested *model of a
directorate* (a central police board).

The latent phase can be traced back to 1958 or possibly even further back in time. In that year 900 policemen at the Oslo police-office undertook an illegal work stoppage. By then the police force had already endured many years of frustration:

> For two years our representatives have persistently but hopelessly fought for the legal rights of our organization, and again and again our employer was warned not to demand unlimited loyalty from a police corps whose trust – owing to an uncommonly clumsy treatment of our case – was quite frayed.[5]

The reason for this strong dissatisfaction was the feeling among the employees that they had been left behind as regards wages, holiday regulations, over-time compensation and other working conditions. Since the second world war, the interests of policemen had been taken care of by the organized *Norwegian Police Union*. However after the conflict in 1958, a group of policemen broke with this union and founded the independent *Central Organization of the Police*. The break was justified by three arguments: 1. The Norwegian Police Union had not been able to take care of policemen's interests sufficiently; 2. The police's lack of a legal right to strike placed them in a unique position within LO (the Federation of Norwegian Trade Unions), thereby necessitating another type of organization and other pressure tactics; and 3. The police ought to be a politically neutral organization, positioned above all political association and the class struggle. Membership in LO was conceived of as incompatible with this goal.

The question of organization only reached its final solution in 1975. After many years of struggle, the Norwegian Police Union and the Central Organization of the Police then merged into one independent organization, the *Police Association*. The advocates for neutrality had won.

The shifting forms of organization obviously contributed to weakening the trade bargaining position of the police vis-à-vis the central authorities. One can notice a rising sense of powerlessness over the fact that no decisive breakthrough occurred, despite the declared good-will of several different governments. In 1963, it was said that:

> It seems as if the police department in our country does not have the same importance as it does in other countries. For more than 14 years the country – particularly the capital – has suffered from having a constantly shorthanded police force. The Minister of Justice, Jens Haugland, who was responsible for the Ministry of Justice and Police for 8 years, did not try to find a solution. One might ask the question: did he do anything during his long career to solve the crisis?[6]

In 1971, eight years later, the tone was even sharper:

> At the Rogaland Police-office our colleagues have started a serious and inspiring struggle. The talking has come to an end. The trust is impaired. How long is it

permissible to make the police department into a joker? A 'wild-cat strike' has been mentioned in order to gain something.'[7]

In sum, only to a small extent during this phase, did the police meet with sympathy regarding their union demands. Among union officials, the lack of success was seen as due to a disintegrated organizational structure and an inadequate bargaining position, but also as a result of deficient good-will on the part of the political authorities.

In the period 1958–65, changes also took place in what the police consi-dered their work area. Urbanization and consequences of the welfare devel-opment, the cues being rising crime rates, drug abuse, and increasing car traffic, created new work tasks for the department. But neither in these areas, was the Ministry of Justice willing to accommodate the new needs of the police.

> Even though they have the same relevance today as in the past, we will not bring into the picture the old arguments such as the *satellite towns,* the *steadily increasing traffic* or the juvenile delinquency. But let us take a look at our neighbouring country where they seriously talk about a *civil guard.* Ultimately the *ostrich-like* policy shows its results![8]

> News about muggers who assault old ladies or about young men who are being knocked down and robbed in 'Studenterlunden' have become everyday stuff – symptomatic of the conditions in our capital . . . In other areas as well, one can notice remarkable things. While in 1950 the assembly of cars in the capital totalled approx. 50,000 vehicles, today the number has risen to more than 108,000 requiring additional efforts by the traffic section – which still has close to 100 vacancies.[9]

During the latent phase, the two related conflict-themes – the demand for reinforcement and for better working conditions – did not reach a final solution. In 1964, however something happened that had a decisive impact on the further comprehension of the problems.

In that year we find the first dispositions toward the 1970's reorganization of the Norwegian police department, when the *Government Institution of Organization and Management* published its policy study. The purpose of this report, commissioned by the Ministry of Justice, was to present a proposal concerning a *rationalization* of the police department – a reconstruc-tion of the internal structure motivated by economic saving. In other words, the criteria of the report are concerned with measures that would reduce the state's expenditures. Based on these criteria, the report contained three major conclusions:

1. *The police ought to be organized into a separate detached directorate.* From being included in the parliamentary/political responsibility of the Minister of Justice, the central police leadership ought instead to be transferred to a detached directorate, managed by a national police chief.
2. *Coordination and planning of police tasks ought to be centrally conducted.* With a view to obtaining maximum administrative effectivity, the Government Institution of Organization and Management found that the planning ought to take place as far up as possible in the organizational structure. Until then, the main thrust of the planning had occurred in a flexible and local manner at the nation's 53 police-offices.
3. As a continuation of the conception of a centralized and coordinated police force, we also find the view stating the necessity for a *strong police leadership*. The report proclaims that once the police is organized into a detached directorate . . . 'the central leadership will acquire a marked independent status, offering an increased outward professional authority'.

The directorate idea received wide support from the police. At the meeting of trade union officials in 1966, the Central Organization of the Police favored the establishment of a committee whose task it was to investigate the need for, among other things, the introduction of a unified police force under the leadership of a police directorate. Such a committee was nominated in the fall of the very same year.

The introduction of the directorate model entailed an important turning-point in the struggle by the police. Indicatively, this solution was seen as a way to build a new and better platform for a stronger bargaining position – *both* with respect to trade demands and the demands for additional resources. With a detached directorate, it would no longer be necessary to pass through the detailed and often slow channels at the ministry, since the national police chief would be able to contact the Minister of Justice directly, or possibly even forward the relevant proposals to the authorities responsible for financial grants. Accordingly, the idea of a directorate meant that the police found a new outlet – or a new *channel* – for its discontent. Endless years of disappointments regarding unsuccessful negotiations with the central government were now followed by a belief in an effective unified organization that would be able to promote departmental demands.

Thus an important merger took place: both trade demands and reinforcement demands found a mutual expression, thanks to the idea of a directorate. In other words, the interests of the department received an organizational expression.

2.2 The parliamentary phase

In this phase the character of the question of reinforcement changed. From being considered an internal administrative issue, the matter became part of the parliamentary/political problem-solving mechanisms. Thereupon a new set of actors enters the decision-making arena: the 'professional' experts permanently positioned in the administration and frequently employed in examining problems of different kinds. They include in their investigations organizations and institutions that are viewed as legitimately concerned parties. Thus, a relatively closed 'police-segment' has been established that internally defines the relevant problems and possible solutions.[10] The official police-segment was stamped with what can be called a *liberal police-ideology*. That is, the police is primarily looked upon as a service and administrative institution, having no independent power or political importance. The main task of the police is to uphold the laws made by parliamentary and democratic organs, and thereby the police is made into a neutral tool in the service of public security and common safety.[11]

The parliamentary phase began when the Ministry of Justice made a significant step on the basis of the conclusions reached by the Government Institution of Organization and Management. In 1965 an official committee was formed ' . . . to study a possible reorganization of the central police administration'[12] The committee consisted of four jurists and one military officer, and later became known as the 'Aulie committee', named after its chairman, Attorney General Andreas Aulie. The committee finished its report in 1970.

The Aulie report put forward three main conclusions. Firstly, the central authority of the police ought to be in the hands of a detached directorate. Secondly, a national police chief, appointed for a specific term, ought to be in charge of the directorate. Thirdly, five regional police districts ought to be established, and all the local police commissioners be subordinate to a regional commissioner.

In comparison to the solution offered by the Institution, the Aulie committee added a new dimension to the argument for the reinforcement demand. Namely, while the former solutions were based on economic rationalizing premises, the reinforcement now received a *legal-juridical frame of reference*. Again one finds the influence of the liberal police-ideology:

> It is not the business of the police to analyze the problem. Instead, the duty of the police is – as promptly, efficiently and tactfully as possible – to handle all the situations mentioned – both the peaceful and the turbulent ones.[13]

The position of the police as an independent instrument of power was also analyzed from a legal point of view. By and large the committee only found positive effects in organizing the police department into a separate detached directorate. Potential opponents to such an arrangement were dismissed.

> It is possible that some, partly for reasons concerning public security and partly on emotional grounds, harbor the fear that a reorganization of the police in this country, whereby the departments are guided by a directorate, might entail the risk of a power concentration that could easily lead to abuse.
>
> The committee has considered the importance of this objection against the directorate arrangement, but is not convinced of the validity of the argument.
>
> The committee does not know of any country in which the democratic order has been at stake as a result of plots by the police department, whereby this organ has initiated or participated in the planning of measures leading to the overthrow.[14]

However the Aulie committee's resolution of the legal-juridical problem was based on an analysis of society of a clearly political nature. Several times in the report the committee point to the trends in the societal development that necessitate a reinforced police.

> When attempting to evaluate the status and future development of the police it is also necessary to take into account certain current tendencies that might not only require a certain increased activity but a real structural rationalization of the police as well. Among these tendencies one has noted an *epidemic-like world-wide spreading of certain periodic outbreaks of disorder* . . . When an incident of a more dramatic nature takes place in a country, the world at large is immediately confronted with the event in living pictures with comments. A cultural conflict, political outburst, disputed trial, is followed by the emergence of emotional high-pressure centers in near and distant areas. It happens that thereby situations are triggered which might be directly dangerous, in part alarming or troublesome. Much time does not elapse between annoncements of bombings in public buildings, attacks on or threats against embassies, highjackings, street riots or demonstrations of a legal or illegal kind; all of them with a more or less epidemic character. (p. 48).

About these phenomena it is further stated that:

> Seen in relation to the police's future state of preparation, the examples mentioned are not passing phenomena. Rather, it is a question of massive social problems that in the foreseeable future will be likely to mature fully in all countries. (p. 48).

These quotations are probably representative of the way problems were conceived of in the Aulie report. Evidently, political phenomena from the end of the 1960's constituted fundamental premises supporting the committee's wishes to reinforce the police. It looks as if the student protests all over Europe, the hippie movement, rising drug abuse, and an alleged crime wave resulted in a reactionary demand for a strengthened police force.

Furthermore, the quotation shows that the legal expertise of the administration's jurists was built on political assumptions of a highly dubious nature. Firstly, symptoms of basic structural changes were superficially interpreted as 'disorder' or 'riots'. Secondly, the connection between these phenomena and the police reinforcement was not problematized. More use of power was regarded as an adequate response to the problems under consideration. And thirdly, legal as well as political and organizational side-effects of a rationalized and more effective police force were not taken into account. Undoubtedly, however, the political premises of the Aulie committee were shared by a great part of the right-wing in Norwegian politics. The jurists of the committee can be viewed as carriers and exponents of political trends – and thus political interests – in society. Accordingly, without representing formal interest groups, the committee partook in converting political demands into apparently neutral administrative legal problems.[15]

In turn, the issue of reinforcement and reorganization as presented in a legal conceptual framework created the further premises for participation in the police-segment. The Ministry of Justice referred the Aulie report to various bodies for consideration. In the main and with few exceptions, the commenting bodies agreed that the time had come for a strengthening of the police department, and that the conclusions reached by the Aulie committee represented good solutions.[16]

Only a limited selection of interested parties, however, were asked for their comments. Most of them were associated with the state or local administration. The most important ones were: the 53 Norwegian police commissioners, all the ministries, the interest organizations of the police, the High Command of the Defense Forces, the Norwegian City and District Association, and the Norwegian Association of Jurists.

Thus, by limiting the police-segment to these relevant groups, the Ministry of Justice secured a high degree of ideological and political consensus behind its proposals. Moreover, since there also seemed to exist great agreement in the political parties regarding the Aulie report, the time looked ready for the introduction of a detached police-directorate in Norway.

We have now reached the year 1972. That year another significant event took place in Norwegian politics. At the popular vote on membership in the European Common Market the majority said 'no'. That meant that the Labor Party, who had promoted the case of the directorate, had to hand over the reins of office to a liberal-conservative coalition government, which in 1973 put forward a bill favoring a directorate. But after the general election in the fall of 1973, the Labor Party returned to power and the bill was subsequently withdrawn for the time being. Half a year later the bomb exploded: an internal working committee in the ministry (the 'Ekanger committee') produced a report which concluded that the leadership of the police ought to remain within the ministry, and that consequently one regarded the directorate-model as abandoned. At the same time this committee presented a plan suggesting two different organizational models with respect to the ministry's police leadership.

The left-wing considered this decision a victory. To KROM (the Norwegian Association for Criminal Reform), who had written a long 'anti-report' to the Aulie committee report and in other ways had actively worked against the plans for a directorate, this was good news.[17] The supporters of the directorate were greatly annoyed. 'The shelving of the police-directorate means a loss to public security', the Conservatives' Jan P. Syse stated in *Morgenavisen* (the paper of the Conservative Party). 'The proposal must be seen as a concession to the left-wing in Norwegian politics', *Morgenbladet* noted (independent conservative paper). 'A mistake to reject the police-directorate' commented *Aftenposten* (independent conservative paper).

At this point the parliamentary phase comes to an end. The definitive shelving of the directorate plans again showed the opponents of reinforcement as apparently triumphant in the arena. But only apparently. Later it would become clear that the supporters would renew their attacks in order to secure the reinforcement of the power-apparatus. By then the struggle had moved into the political phase.

2.3 The political phase

After the directorate-model had definitely been rejected, there were probably many, especially within the police department and the political right-wing, who feared that the plans to make the department more effective would also be shelved. Therefore the struggle for additional appropriations continued – but in this phase in another arena than earlier on.

The supporters of reinforcement now found it especially important to secure public support for their demands. Accordingly, the political phase became marked by an open public debate – but a debate in which the advocates controlled the premises by dominating the media of the arena. Through mass media, and particularly via the press, current events were often linked in a misleading and suggestive way to the issue of reinforcement. The main pattern was the following: by looking at isolated crimes and general societal trends from the perspective of the police's situation, both phenomena could be explained as a *result* of the police's (supposedly) low manpower and lack of adequate equipment.

During this phase we also find the beginning of *alliances* between various groups among the supporters of reinforcement. Representatives of the police department openly began to cooperate with representatives of political groups in a mutual effort to place public pressure on the appropriating authorities.

Apart from a series of separate references, particularly two discussions received prominence in the public debate. These will briefly be described. In July 1975, a trade-union shop in Bergen made the first move in a discussion that later came to be called 'the violence-wave debate'. After two members of the shop had within a short period of time been assaulted in the middle of town, the shop initiated 'a sharpened fight against the spirit of violence'.

The initiative was warmly supported by five other trade-union shops, the bourgeois press, and the police's own representatives. At a public meeting including trade-union delegates and the police commissioner of Bergen, the latter stated:

> We in the Bergen police are very happy over the initiative that has been taken. Nothing could be better than the support we here have received regarding our demands for increased resources to counteract the downtown violence. Because the development within this sector has been alarming during the last couple of years.[18]

The violence-wave debate quickly spread. Within a few months, this theme appeared in most of the nation's major papers. And the conclusion was basically the same: the police department has to be strengthened in order to be able to handle the violent tendencies in society. A quotation from *Agderposten* (the New Liberal Party) represents a commonly used way of reasoning:

> At police and county offices in our part as well as in large parts of the country, policemen despair and do not know what to do in order to curtail the enormous problems of order. The police are short-handed, and since they are forced to investigate cases instead of preventing them, naturally their work is burdensome.
>
> But despite these steadily aggravated problems, it does not look as if the Ministry of Justice, with the Minister of Justice, Valle, at the top, is willing to initiate measures that can strengthen the police department and thereby master at least one of the problems.[19]

Within a few months the violence-wave debate managed to create a widespread impression that: 1) violence and crimes were rapidly increasing in society, and 2) the police department ought to be heavily reinforced in order to counteract these tendencies.

It did not help much that representatives of KROM were able to refute the basis of the original debate in Bergen. They documented – in a heated discussion with representatives from the police and the conservative press – that the main increase in the statistics on violence in Bergen stemmed from the rather recent incorporation of a neighbouring community with the city. The *real* increase was so small that it could hardly be labelled a 'wave'.

The second important debate during this phase centered around the question: *Does an increase of policemen lead to reduced criminality?* The starting point of this debate, which went on in the nation's largest newspaper – *Aftenposten* – was a statement by the police commissioner in Trondheim:

> In spite of all scientific knowledge, most people still believe that patrolling police-constables have a strong moderating effect on people who assault peaceful citizens, snatch bags from old ladies, destroy all kinds of property, and so on.[20]

KROM strongly opposed this statement. After having referred to a major American study in which no relationship could be found between police manning and criminality, the representative of this association continued:

> But perhaps it is not the *real* possibility of being assaulted that Harkjerr wishes to reduce. Perhaps it is the *risk* people feel of being victimized, which is much higher than the real risk, that he wants to influence.
>
> Thus one might ask: where does people's fear of being assaulted stem from? Most of them acquire their fear of violence from frequent and sensational press reports.
>
> A study made at the Institute of Criminology and Criminal Law in Oslo shows that in the month of August 1974, the crime material made up 24.1 % of the total front page coverage of *VG*, 17.4 % of *Dagbladet*, and 15.2 % of *Arbeiderbladet*. It should also be mentioned that this month was an average month with respect to criminality.
>
> Why wonder over the fact that people are scared?

In the debate following this article, a number of leading policemen opposed KROM's representatives. The main line of their reasoning went like this: an increase in the number of policemen will offer the public increased protection against crimes and ameliorate the working conditions of the police. As long as Parliament decides the guidelines for the department and makes the appropriations, the Norwegian Police will never become an independent powerful factor. KROM answered: the crime increase is due to structural changes in society, and can not be reduced by additional police manning. There exist examples from a number of countries where the police department has become an independent factor with power to act on behalf of its own vested interests, and contrary to political directives.

As far as the arguments went, KROM seemed to win this debate. The police representatives did not manage to secure valid arguments for the view that increased police supervision would bring a reduction in the crime rates.

But behind the curtain a process had started which it was difficult for the opponents of reinforcement to cope with. The political decision to reject the police-directorate had brought the Ministry of Justice into a dilemma. On the one hand, the police and the political right-wing exerted a strong unceasing pressure. On the other hand, the opposition and the open debate had presently increased the political/ideological burden of the Labor Party – as a workers' party – by strengthening a department that traditionally was conceived of as an oppressive apparatus of the bourgeoisie.

The political phase – possibly as a consequence of this dilemma – became characterized by what can be called 'the strategy of small-step advances'.

This strategy primarily entailed two tactics. Firstly, important measures with broad and far-reaching consequences were introduced to the public as *technical* and therefore unproblematic minor changes. Secondly, large and visible reform plans were split up and implemented *step by step* as separate decisions which were disconnected from their context and spread over a long time. These disconnected decisions were simultaneously presented in such an order that every single step was built on the earlier one and legitimated the next. A development of the police which in a total perspective would appear as undesirable was subdivided and implemented piece by piece in a manner that made political opposition difficult.[21]

The first sign of the step-like advancement came when the Ekanger committee had finished its work. Its working document was only printed in a small number of copies and was very difficult to get hold of. Thereby the public was cut off from an open discussion about these new premises regarding the future of the police department.

The Ekanger committee's working document was not referred for consideration. But the police commissioners were consulted about their view of it. Regarding any report from this meeting between the police commissioners and the ministry, the evening paper *Verdens Gang* wrote:

> The Secretary of State, Ekanger, himself stated that he did not want any reports, since he considered the meeting an internal orientation about the ministry's first draft concerning an organizational form replacing the Aulie committee report, which the Minister of Justice had turned down.

The newspaper concludes:

> Why on earth is it not possible to inform the public about the new results reached by the Ministry of Justice, and on which yesterday the police commissioners were briefed?[22]

At this veiled meeting, and probably at several others of the same kind, the new foundation of the police organization was laid. The Ekanger committee report was never subjected to public debate – neither in Parliament nor by the general public. Thus, the basis of the development of the police during the 1970's rests on an internal xerox note that only a few people have had the opportunity to get acquainted with.

Another example of the step-like advancement is the establishment of the so-called 'anti-terror police'. This police unit is trained according to a military pattern of command and specializes in physical conflict resolution.

The immediate reason behind establishing this police unit was the so-called 'Lillehammer incident' in 1973, when Israeli terrorists shot and killed a person who they believed was a Palestinian agent. As a result of this episode, a special corps to combat terrorists activities was established at the Oslo police-office. Gradually the corps has been enlarged, and when finalized it will consist of approx. two hundred men, stationed at the nation's six largest police-offices.

The *mandate* of the anti-terror police has gradually been enlarged, too. From originally being a safeguard against terrorists, the corps is now handling 'individuals who are dangerous to the public safety' and social unrest. Much public attention was aroused, when a while ago it became known that the anti-terror police was mobilized against disorderly conduct at the Oslo subway.[23]

Moreover, perhaps the development within the *organizational structure* of the police offers the best example of the step-like advances during the political phase.

The *first step* in the change of the organization structure entailed a slight strengthening of the ministry's central leadership by ten new positions. The first task given to these ten persons was to investigate the future organizational structure and to assess the need for planning, cordination, inspection and training.

The *second step* meant a further strengthening of the central leadership – concurrently with a reorganization of the police section at the ministry. Practically speaking, this new police administration, divided into sections I and II, was constructed in the same way as suggested by the Aulie committee in its original proposal of a directorate.

The *third step* appeared as a relatively innocent legal revision. In the fall of 1976 the Parliament passed proposition No. 6 – 'On a legal revision of the Act of 13 March 1936 concerning the police'. This minor and apparently innocent revision cleared the way for considerable structural changes in the Norwegian police.

The 53 police-offices in the country, which today have equal status and are coordinately positioned, are to be merged into *five regional police-offices*. In each region, one police chief commissioner is placed above the others and given more authority in comparison to the old arrangement. In special cases, or with respect to specific areas, the regional police chief commissioner is given the authority to deprive the local commissioner of the command in his own district and to take over the work.

This legal revision also brought changes in the police's operational approach. While earlier departmental permission was required for the police in one district to cross district-borders when needed in another district, now the regional chief commissioner, if *he* finds it necessary, can order policemen to serve anywhere within the region.

In section 8 of the bill it is stated:

The Government will make further provisions relating to the organization of the police, and the division of authority and the cooperation within the police. These provisions can encompass the county offices as well.'

Thus the road is open for a long-range reorganization of the police and county departments. Through this legal provision any further reforms will take the form of *administrative* measures. It will no longer be necessary to involve Parliament – and the public – in order to institutionalize new proposals.

That is the current situation. To the public the question of reinforcement and reorganization has lost news-value. Only tiny press items offer now and then the interested reader any insight into the fact that the step-like advancement continues – through minor and on the surface insignificant moves, a large and encompassing structural change is being implemented.

SUMMARY AND RETROSPECTION

In the introduction it was suggested that, from a theoretical perspective, the structural changes of the police department during the 1960's and 70's posited a problem of effectuation. In a simplified and compact form this problem can be posed as follows: How is the prescribed economic development transmitted into political structures and processes? Stated differently, how can we reach an understanding of the relationships between, on the one hand, economic structural changes and, on the other hand, the reinforcement and reorganization of the police?

A *functional approach* can confirm the existence of a positive structural relationship.[24] In the light of the growing economic crisis tendencies of the 1970's, it seems obvious that the present police – as the power apparatus of the state – is significantly better prepared than in the past to protect and maintain the economic system against manifest political protests. On the basis of the data presented earlier, one can thus state that there exists a functional relation between the requirement of political stability in the economic system and the form and operations of the physical apparatus of power.

Such a functional model of explanation, however, has limited explanatory value. The implementation of abstract requirements at the system-level does not throw light on the *ways* in which changes are carried out. A functional analysis offers insufficient confirmation for one to be able to declare that the police department was reinforced *because* nowadays the economic crisis tendencies are rising. Such an explanation would imply what Elster calls 'intentions without actors', and thereby overlooks the fact that abstract system-requirements can not be implemented except when actors experience and translate them into specific required actions.[25] Thus it is necessary to uncover the relation between latent system-requirements, on the one hand, and their manifestation as problems by the groups of actors, on the other.

Below I attempt to further illuminate the ways in which the material presented can deepen the understanding of relationships between, broadly conceived, economic structural changes and changes in the power apparatus. These links between *abstract system-requirements, subjective intentions,* and *objective consequences* offer an inroad to an understanding of selective mechanisms between the economy and politics.

The description above distinguishes three main sets of actors as supporters of the police-reinforcement. The *first group* consists of the actors within the police organization. In turn, this group can be subdivided into two: 1) the police trade-union organizations and 2) the leadership of the local police units – both representing the interests of the department. The *second set* of actors is the professional problem-solvers in the administration, and the *third set* includes an unspecified public opinion as well as actors who in this context tried to influence that opinion.

The primary interest of the police trade-unions has clearly been to improve their members' general working conditions. The material frame of reference behind this demand has been the general rise in prosperity, and the discontent among the employees due to a feeling of being left behind compared to other groups. In a work situation with no right to strike and minimal opportunities to openly voice demands, dissatisfaction and frustration matured. Through the introduction of the idea of a directorate, a new orientation emerged: from then on the police organizations viewed the directorate as an opportunity to improve their bargaining position. In other words, these organizations did not regard the directorate idea as a *fulfilment* of their demands but as a strategically better starting point for voicing them.

In a general perspective it is reasonable to assume that society moves toward a symmetry between the organizational structures and functioning of the police, on the one hand, and societal geographical processes and events, on the other. To a certain degree the structures and operations of the police mirror the external social system. This reflection is not mechanical but is woven together by ideological bonds and legal rules.

Within the police department the leadership acquires an important linking function at a time of incongruity between the social system and the police organization. The leadership *experiences* the fact that geographical structural changes (centralization) and changing patterns of conduct (criminality, private transportation, strikes, and the like) 'materialize' inside the police organization in the form of commonly held expectations of increased police efforts. One can hardly observe specific class interests behind these expectations. But it looks as if *ideological premises*, that is, implicit assumptions about the police as a neutral problem-solving agent, play an important role. The local police leaderships feel these expectations, and subsequently articulate them in a compact form as demands for better equipment, material and organizational system.

The local police leaderships thus emerge as a set of actors who respond to and transmit expectations of action. These action-expectations can be seen as expressing general widespread views of the police as a problem-solving – and not repressive – institution.

As a group of actors the problem-solvers in the administration also make up two sub-groups – connected to the Aulie committee and the Ekanger committee, respectively. The Aulie committee seemed to anchor its reinforcement and reorganization plans to the *political consequences* of the economic development. As shown earlier, this committee traced an explicit and direct link from the 'disorderly tendencies' of the time to the reinforcement need of the police department. Seldom does one come across a more pregnant expression of the fact that, on the basis of a specific ideological understanding, the police is regarded as a protection against socially threatening tendencies.

The Aulie committee's value-laden analyses can be regarded as an overstepping of the mark within a state apparatus with a pluralistic self-understanding. In the Ekanger committee's working document these value-laden analyses were replaced by the popular police-populist tendencies of the time. By replacing the *visible intentions* behind the reinforcement, the state apparatus could acquire more legitimacy for a plan that mainly contained the same substance as the earlier report.

What then were the administration-actors' real intentions with regard to the reinforcement? A definitive answer is difficult to arrive at. A possible explanation would be that uncontrolled and visible developments, in the form of traffic-chaos, criminality or blow-outs in the North Sea, always entail diminishing legitimacy for the governing party. Thus a more or less explicitly expressed wish to prevent specific events in order to maintain the political legitimacy can be an important partial explanation of the large police appropriations during the 1970's.

The development during the political phase must be understood as a consequence of the defeat experienced by the right-wing forces regarding the case of the directorate. During this phase a mobilization of specific ideological attitudes took place in the public sphere. It looks as if a latent feeling of insecurity and fear among the people found expression in a form of anxiety vis-à-vis criminality and violence. This anxiety, in turn, was being connected to the need for a strong and reinforced police.

These connections can hardly be seen as accidental. In the public arena the bourgeois press emerged as a *connecting actor,* interlacing latent feelings, concrete events and solutions. By selectively presenting single incidents and exaggerating their significance and thereafter by relating them to the police's inadequacies, a strong pressure of opinion was soon created demanding a reinforced police department.

Accordingly, the next question is: With what basic intentions did the press act? Several motives seem to have played a role. Evidently, on several occasions direct influence was exerted by the representatives of the bourgeois parties to make the newspapers focus attention on the police. And generally speaking, sensational crime stories are good sale-products for the press. Thus the mobilization of fear against criminality and violence is partly a side-effect of the market mechanisms of the press.

In sum, the police's present form and mode of operation can not be viewed as a deductive 'response' to the economic structural changes. Different groups of actors – on the basis of their experienced problems and interests – have submitted various political and organizational contributions to the reinforcement process. At any one time the favored alternative solution can be considered the smallest common denominator – a *core solution* that formed an acceptable answer to the interests of the different groups of actors.

These concrete-historical connecting links have probably specific validity in the case of Norway. In the *USA* it seems as if the market needs of the armament industry constitute an important force in the reinforcement of the police.[26] In *West Germany* the conception of a 'domestic enemy' presents an ideological theme for mobilizing that is being used against different groups in different historical phases.[27] But despite various historical premises and political developments, these countries also seem to end up with a structural change of the police department following the pattern described above. In other words, the core solution becomes the same even when the contextual conditions differ.

NOTES

[1] See Jørgen Jepsen: Policing Labour Conflicts. pp.177–206 in this volume.

[2] These and subsequent data on the resources of the police are taken from the following three publications: Engström, et.al: *Om polisväsendets organisation i Sverige* (On the Organization of the Police System in Sweden). Stockholm, 1977. Koch: Notat om politiets udvikling og effektivitet i de siste 10 år (Note on the Development and Effectivity of the Police during the last 10 years). Copenhagen, the Institute of Criminal Science, 1977. Lorentzen: Noen bakgrunnsdata om norsk politi(Some Background Data on the Norwegian Police). Oslo, the Institute of Sociology of Law, 1977.

[3] The figures in Tables 1 and 2 are corrected with regard to the cost-of-living index of each country, using 1970 as the base year.

[4] On different analyses of effectuation of power, see Rød Larsen: 'Makt og herredømme' (Power and Domination), in *Sosiologi Idag*, No. 5/6, 1975.

[5] *Politimannen* (The Policeman) – organ of the Oslo Police Association, No. 1, 1958. This and subsequent quotations are from the *editorials* of the organ.

[6] *Politimannen* (The Policeman) – organ of the Police Association, No. 11, 1963.

[7] *Politimannen*, No. 4, 1971.

[8] *Politimannen* No. 12, 1960.

[9] *Politimannen*, No. 10, 1964.

[10] Egeberg, Olsen & Sætren: 'Organisasjonssamfunnet og den segmenterte stat' (The Organizational Society and the Segmented State), in *Kirke og Kultur*, No. 4, 1975.

[11] This ideology is clearly expressed in § 1 of the police instructions: 'The task of the police is to protect people, property and all legal activity, to maintain public order and peace and, to either alone or together with other official authorities, to guard against everything that disrupts the safety of society.'

[12] 'Innstilling om den sentrale politiadministrasjon' (Report on the Central Police Administration) of 20 November 1970 (The Aulie committee report).

[13] The Aulie committee report, p. 48.

[14] The Aulie committee report, p. 68.

[15] This circumstance became evident in the public debate that followed some years later.

[16] 'Odelstingsproposisjon' (Proposition to the Odelsting), No. 60, 1972–73.

[17] Politiets organisasjon og utbygging (The Organization and Reinforcement of the Police). Note by KROM, dated October 1th. 1974.

[18] Morgenavisen, 6. September 1975.

[19] Agderposten, 8. September 1975.

[20] Aftenposten, 12. July 1975.

[21] Bachrach and Baratz use the concept 'decisionless decisions' to describe this phenomenon. (Bachrach & Baratz: Power and Poverty. Oxford University Press, 1970.)

[22] Verdens Gang, 9. May 1974.

[23] Aftenposten, 5. May 1976.

[24] A functional analysis can briefly be described as follows: When a sub-system supports the maintenance of the basic structures of the main system to which it belongs, the relation can be described as functional.

[25] Elster: 'Statens rolle i marxistisk teori' (The Role of the State in Marxist Theory), in Tidsskrift for Samfunnsforskning, No. 2, 1977, p. 112.

[26] See The Iron Fist and The Velvet Glove, published by the Center for Research on Criminal Justice, Berkeley, 1975.

[27] See Lundbo, Levy & Nielsen: 'Den indre fiende' (The Domestic Enemy), in Hug!, No. 10, 1976.

The Proactive Police

BY *Henning Koch*

1. THE THEORETICAL FRAMEWORK

The labelling theorists originally started the debate concerning the process of selection by the police when registering crime. It was apparently this debate that formed the basis of theoretical interest in police research in the USA during the 1960s (Black & Reiss 1970, Bennett 1979).

Nevertheless, interest in this unofficial police function today seems to be lacking amongst leading criminologists in police science, and this in spite of the fact that the feasibilities of selection cannot be fairly said to have been subjected to sufficient empirical analysis. It is therefore pertinent to begin by defining what actually constitutes police selection and the theoretical opportunities open to the police.

It appears that there are two different kinds of police selection that have a decisive influence on the registration of crime. We shall call them: selection by detection and selection by decision (Fig. 1).

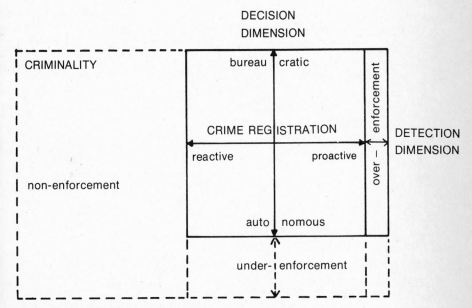

Fig. 1. Model of police selection in crime registration.

Selection by detection refers to the way in which criminal acts come to the knowledge of the police. As Black & Reiss (1970) have pointed out: 'For the police, as for most well-differentiated systems of social control, detection is largely a matter of organizational mobilization, and mobilization is the process by which incidents come to the initial attention of agents of the police organization. There are two basic types of mobilization of the police: citizen-initiated, or "reactive" mobilization, and police-initiated, or "proactive" mobilization . . .'[1]

The ratio of reactively detected crime to proactively detected crime differs with the type of crime and depends to a large extent on factors out of the direct control of the police, e.g. the fact that the citizens as primary agents of social control vastly outnumber the police, the degree of public willingness to report crime to the police, the limited police access to private places (Stinchcombe 1963), and the low predictability of crime occurrence (Reiss 1971).

But the actual distinction between detected and non-detected crime is also a direct result of police selection and dependent upon the police making use of its authorized or unauthorized discretionary power.

Proactive detection by the police may occur in one of two ways: either the police witness the crime being committed or they define a situation and a person as being suspect.

This selective process may consist in deliberately choosing times and places of patrolling likely to increase the probability of catching the criminal in the act, but it may also consist in a choice between the observance or non-observance of the rules of procedure, e.g. whether to employ 'agents provocateurs', or whether to employ the methods of stopping, arresting or frisking persons without there being a probable cause (Skolnick 1966, Reiss 1971, Feest 1971, Gamst-Nielsen 1973). When the police violate the citizens' civil rights in order to detect or seek to detect more criminal incidents than they are authorized to, we will use the term 'over-enforcement' (Skolnick 1966, Feest & Blankenburg 1972).

Also when the police reactively detect the existence of a criminal incident i.e. after a citizen's complaint, a selection can be made which will influence the crime registration. This selection is effected by a redefinition of the citizen's complaint, e.g. by defining what would be assault according to the penal code as public disorderly conduct according to the municipal code, assault as domestic disturbance, or theft as the recovery of lost property. It is a question of classifying one criminal act in terms of another, as well as defining a criminal act as being non-criminal. The re-definition may be reversed: from a non-criminal to a criminal incident. Of course the re-definition often suggests a citizen's uncertainty as to whether or not a law has been violated, and if so, which, but this is far from always being the case (Coleman & Bottomley 1976, McCabe & Sutcliffe 1978).

The police can also directly influence the number of reactively detected crimes by changing the method of patrolling, e.g. by introducing or increasing patrolling on foot (Schnelle et al. 1975).

One must distinguish the type of selection that consists in uncovering and defining the criminal incidents from the other type of selection, which consists in deciding how the detected incident is to be dealt with. This latter type of selection we shall call: *selection by decision*. By decision we mean the actual decision – whether the incident should result in an arrest and/or a report (or any other formal reactions), or whether the case should simply be 'cleared on the spot' by means of an informal caution or the like (Cressey & Elgesem 1968, Steer 1970, Koch 1973, Støkken et al. 1974, Nelken 1976, McCabe & Sutcliffe 1978). When police selection is exercised in this way, violating procedural rules of the proper authority to withdraw charges and the principles of equality (Sjöholm 1978), we will talk about 'under-enforcement' (Banton 1964).[2] In these situations the police choose to report on fewer incidents than they are authorized to.

That this type of selection is at all practicable is due to the non-bureaucratic structure of the lower levels of the police organization (Støkken 1974, Manning 1977). Field work, in particular, is liable to escape control from superiors. This applies especially to cases that are 'cleared on the spot'.

Control is almost impossible when the police proactively detect a criminal act and clear the case on the spot, and even in situations where the station's duty officer has received a complaint, there is a certain scope for selection. This scope is only to some extent due to the technical difficulties of effective supervision. Although he could check up by personally contacting the complainant, the duty officer often refrains, because of his knowledge of the complex character of police work and a respect for his colleagues' judgement in the field, gained from his own experience as a patrolling officer.

Thus the police officer on patrol can, and does, make autonomous decisions. If he solves the case by an arrest and/or a report, his decision will be bureaucratic, i.e. subject to superior control.

Several studies of the police have shown that the police, especially in the case of minor offences, try to avoid 'putting pen to paper' to the greatest possible extent (Parnas 1967, Feest & Blankenburg 1972, Manning 1977). In an earlier Danish study (Borg et al. 1973), the police officers often used the expression: 'The matter is not worth the paper on which it is written'. McCabe & Sutcliffe (1978) have established that this is also common practice both when complaints reach the police station in the form of telephone calls, and when complainants turn up in person. Feest & Blankenburg express it in a more general way by saying: 'Die Subkultur der Polizei ist eine schriftfeindliche Kultur . . .'[3]

Criminological research is particularly lacking in empirical analyses of police selection in connection with *under-enforcement of proactively detected major offences.* This study will focus on drunken driving (cf. Hauge (ed.) 1978) and thefts of vehicles (automobiles, motorcycles, mopeds, bicycles, etc.) for use only ('joy-riding'). The penalty for the first type of offence ranges from fines to imprisonment up to 1 year. In practice the penalty for a first offence varies from a fine of D.kr. 1000, per D. kr. 25,000 annual pre-tax income (maximum fine D.kr. 40,000) to 10–40 days' imprisonment with possible suspension of the driving licence (Due et al. 1979). The possible penalties for the other type of offence are the same, apart from the fact that the maximum imprisonment is 2 years. If the charge is not withdrawn by the prosecution, the penalty will in practice be a fine or a suspended sentence (for a first offence).[4]

2. REACTIVE OR PROACTIVE POLICE?

After the publication of Black & Reiss' article, 'Police Control of Juveniles' (1970), introducing the terms reactive and proactive policing, Anglo-American criminology has considered it almost an axiom that the police has a reactive function (Reiss 1971, Manning 1977, McCabe & Sutcliffe 1978).

Black & Reiss characterized the work of the ordinary uniformed police thus: 'Although some specialized divisions of municipal police departments, such as traffic bureaus and vice units, do depend primarily upon proactive mobilization for their input of cases, in routine patrol work the great majority of incidents come to the police' attention through the citizen-initiated form of mobilization.'[5]

In Reiss's own work, the now classical *The Police and the Public* (1971), he states that, excluding traffic violations, only 6 per cent of the time in service, i.e. performing actual tasks, is spent on incidents initiated by the patrolling police, and 7 per cent of all incidents, criminal as well as non-criminal, are initiated by them.[6]

Although Reiss modifies his view of the police's work thus in his book: 'The major divisions of a police department usually engage in both proactive and reactive work', his statistics lead to the conclusion that the citizens' 'discretionary' power is of greater importance than the discretionary power of the police. The citizens' 'discretionary decisions to mobilize the police are a principal source of input into the system, and these decisions profoundly affect the discretion exercised by the police'. Using a study by Black based on participant observation of police-citizen encounters, he concludes by saying: 'Examining all such encounters where a complainant indicated a preference for police action in the situation, Donald Black discovered that the police tended to act according to the preferences of the complainants for police action.'[7]

Thus Reiss's results apparently exclude the possibility of police selection, or at least they divert interest from a further examination of proactive policing and police selection by minimizing the problem.

The general lack of interest in these matters that seems to have been the consequence for Anglo-American criminology is foreign to German and Scandinavian police research. The excellent theoretical and empirical studies by Brusten (1971) and Feest & Blankenburg (1972) have analysed a number of various determinants in connection with police selection. In Scandinavia, Hauge & Stabell (1975) have established that drunkenness and drunken driving in a Norwegian rural district are mainly detected by proactive policing, and Lorentzen (1977) has examined the demands and expectations with which the police are confronted in traffic control and how these factors influence police selection.

3. THE PROACTIVE FUTURE

With regard to the future of policing it is no doubt important to focus on the proactive police functions, if not for quantitative then for qualitative reasons.

As a consequence of the realization that police patrolling (in cars) lacks effectiveness with regard to crime deterrence as well as detection and arrests (Kelling et al. 1974, Kelling & Fogel 1978), it is likely that police administrators will in future suggest a change in principle in the framework of procedural law. This will, for example, allow for an extensive use of field interrogation and infiltration with the purpose of increasing the amount of information about the community that the officers police (Kelling & Fogel 1978, Sherman 1978). The lack of information is today considered to be the main obstacle to an increase in crime detection. Similarly it is to be expected that the legal criteria for search and seizure procedures will be 'lowered' from a probable cause to a vaguer suspicion.

This development has in fact already started in Europe. At a meeting in the Council of Europe in November 1977, police administrators from France and Germany suggested a new concept of the police: *the social police* (Féraud 1978, Steinhilper 1978). In the French version, which was a fully elaborated organizational model, this police force would engage in 'preventive police action' at a 'pre-delinquency stage' and towards 'potential delinquents'. The 'pre-crime prevention' is described thus: 'Therefore, whilst continuing to use a system of prevention after the offence on the grounds that it might save a limited number of individuals from relapsing into crime, one is led to believe that one might make simultaneous use of methods of prevention before the offence, . . .'. The 'pre-delinquency stage' is described as: '. . . social maladjustment among young people, . . ., a vagrant or parasitic way of life, membership of asocial or anti-social groups, deviant behaviour etc., . . .'. The powers of the police are according to the proposal 'limited' in this way: 'The role of the preventive police should be limited to identifying such cases, without attempting to undertake remedial treatment. After possibly spending a short time in a police reception centre, the young persons concerned should be placed in the care of welfare services for observation and medical and psychological treatment'. This work should to a large extent be carried out with the help of local voluntary auxiliaries.[8]

The German version seems to be less radical. This may be due to the fact that the organizational proposals are less concrete. Steinhilper as an introduction says: 'Police preventive work must be extended beyond merely technical prevention to include social intervention. Preventive efforts must start at very early stages'. He continues: 'Police officers capable of integration into the juvenile milieu must take care of the minors in good time in order to avoid their becoming criminals. One of the main chances that the police have is to provide the juveniles with the guidance that they are missing. The police can play the part of the "older friend" and . . . become acquainted with the problems and difficulties of the minors and obtain information and insights which may be utilized for preventive strategies. The officer can recognize the formation of endangered and criminal groups at the beginning; . . . It appears to be of importance in this respect that the police officers concerned do not perform any executive functions themselves (e.g. that they do not make any arrests). It is their primary task to isolate, at the origin of concentrations of a criminal nature, the criminal member of a group from his hangers-on or to remove non-criminal members gradually from criminal groups'.[9]

In order to become effective this proactive social police function, with or without physical powers, presupposes legalization of some hidden repressive control measures on the basis of an *anticipation of future guilt* by 'potential delinquents'.

A development in principle in the same direction is actually taking place, both in Germany and in Denmark. According to West German federal procedural law, the police may now frisk people and search their houses if they are staying in a certain area, and if it is of importance to the investigation of terrorist activity (which is very broadly defined) or armed robbery. It is not a condition that the investigated persons are suspected of any criminal act. A proposition of a federal police law gives the police even greater authority (Zabern et al. (ed.) 1978 and 1979).

In Denmark, the police administrators are at present working hard to get a new section in procedural law through Parliament. It will authorize the courts to keep suspects in custody for up to 7 days if the suspect has been caught in a criminal act and the police have a vague suspicion that he has committed other similar acts (in situations where there are no other legal grounds for taking him into custody for the detected crime).

Since a crime has been committed (by somebody) the German and Danish legal conception might be defined as: *anticipation of (existing) guilt,* which indicates the fact that no probable cause is needed and only a vague suspicion, if any, will suffice (Koch 1975, Zabern et al. (ed.) 1978).

4. A DANISH STUDY OF THE EFFICIENCY OF THE POLICE

By a change in the law the geographical areas of Denmark's police districts were altered from 1 April 1973, so that 18 police districts outside Copenhagen were abolished. The aim was to rationalize the Danish police: a more efficient police without additional expense. This plan was to be implemented by concentrating a sufficiently large police force in each police district, enabling a 24-hour alert to be established in all districts, unlike previously. The preventive patrolling was also to be increased in order to compensate for this centralization and, because of the demand often made in public discussion during the 1970s, for more police on the streets. The alert should be in the form of a patrol.

The efficiency of patrolling would be improved mainly by an increase in the number of patrolling hours (in cars), while only a few lines were given to a more qualitative improvement e.g. in the form of a foot patrol.

It should be noted that this part of the patrolling does not primarily seem to serve as a prevention, but aims at creating contact and security in relation to the population, especially as patrolling on foot will not take place in areas with a high crime rate, but 'at times and in places where streets are more crowded than usual, e.g. after cinema hours, when restaurants are shutting up, during busy shopping hours, and generally where crowds gather . . .'[10] (cf. Kelling & Fogel 1978).

From 1 April 1974 to 31 March 1977 motorized patrolling (by car and motorcycle) rose in man-hours by about 20 per cent compared to patrolling on foot, which increased by about 4 per cent.[11]

The purpose of this research is, in the light of the official quantitative efficiency measure, to illustrate:

1. Does the increase of the total number of patrolling hours influence the number of registered offences, irrespective of whether these are registered reactively or proactively?
2. Does the 'individual' increase in the number of patrolling hours per man per day influence the policeman's use of under-enforcement?

If rearrangement of the general organization of the work and a rationalization of the written work are not effected simultaneously, the officer will have fewer hours at the typewriter for making reports. Thus he might be tempted to clear more cases on the spot.

Aarhus police district was chosen as the research area.[12] Aarhus is Denmark's second largest town, and, with regard to criminality, has several characteristics of the big city. As to the number of inhabitants, Aarhus police district is the largest police district of the country (outside Copenhagen), with about 275,000 inhabitants.

In order to have a certain margin of time before and after the administrative decision of 1 April 1974 on an increase of the patrolling, the research period chosen was from 1972 to 1976. The consequence of this was, however, that a practical and theoretical difficulty arose, since the geographical structuring of the police district was changed in 1973. The former police district only included the city of Aarhus, but it now also includes the surrounding municipalities. The number of inhabitants almost trebled, and the geographical area increased by more than 20 times.

It is therefore evident that it will not be possible to use this research to describe the changes in the public need for police services from 1 January 1972 to 1 April 1973. During this period of time the complaints from the population outside the former police district of Aarhus were directed to other police districts, which are not included in this research.

The appearance of the new geographical areas has only resulted in a 20 per cent increase in inquiries resulting from complaints. The usual patrolling and consequent police initiative continue to be concentrated in the town of Aarhus.[13]

The research is based on registration, by means of optically readable data records, of a representative section of every third operation in the police district. A 24-hour log taken from police station records gives not only a list of all the complaints received during that period, but also the greater part of the inquiries started on police initiative, thus giving all the cases that result in some form of apprehension, most of the cases that result in a report, and many incidents cleared on the spot (with the exception of minor traffic offences in the latter two).

It is of course not possible with a retrospective, longitudinal study to register any development in 'the proactive under-enforcement', because this type of policing is not registered. In order to get an understanding of this practice, participant observation on patrol and unstructured interviews (Filstead (ed.) 1970) with police officers of different ranks were undertaken during a 9-week stay in Aarhus police district.

5. THE EMERGENCY SQUAD

First and foremost the research covers the uniformed police, who are on duty day and night, either patrolling or remaining at the station *to deal with exigent incidents,* whether they are registered reactively or proactively. This section of the uniformed police, which is by far the largest, will in this research be called: the emergency squad. This theoretical construction is made up of the ordinary emergency squad, which covers all emergency cases, and the special emergency squad, which, owing to a particular resource, the police dog, is sometimes used for special tasks such as arrests and searches, but which normally participates in inquiries and ordinary patrolling. It is characteristic of the emergency squad that it turns out irrespective of which police department is to follow up the case, e.g. in the form of a report. Since nearly all police divisions in Denmark patrol, we have chosen not to use the more well-known names: patrol and canine division. Instead we have tried to find similarities in their functioning: solving all immediate problems. By this definition all other police divisions, including traffic divisions, are excluded.

6. INQUIRIES

The reaction to the immediate criminal or non-criminal incidents will be termed inquiries, irrespective of the initiative (police, citizen or other).

This study distinguishes primarily between positive and negative inquiries. A positive inquiry is an inquiry into a matter which, irrespective of who took the initiative to inquire, proves to be of police interest, although they may not necessarily define the incident in the same way as the possible complainant. This will, however, usually be the case. A negative inquiry is one which proves to be of no interest to the police and may be caused by a complaint,

Table 1a: Positive inquiries (incidents requiring police involvement)

Index %	1972	1973	1974	1975	1976	Total (N-%)
Non-criminal incidents	100 31 %	117 32 %	126 31 %	141 31 %	163 33 %	5 217 32 %
Domestic disturbances	100 6 %	107 5 %	131 6 %	139 6 %	139 5 %	925 6 %
Penal code violations	100 17 %	104 16 %	126 17 %	127 16 %	127 14 %	2 619 16 %
Municipal code violations	100 19 %	112 19 %	139 21 %	160 22 %	177 22 %	3 488 21 %
Traffic violations	100 7 %	101 7 %	131 8 %	164 9 %	168 8 %	1 294 8 %
Road accidents	100 15 %	107 15 %	91 11 %	105 12 %	116 12 %	2 090 13 %
Other violations	100 2 %	172 3 %	188 3 %	165 3 %	195 3 %	467 3 %
Searches for wanted persons	100 2 %	126 2 %	167 3 %	184 3 %	188 3 %	436 3 %
Total	100 99 %	112 99 %	126 100 %	140 102 %	152 100 %	16 536 102 %

or by an alarm going off, which, on the arrival of the police, turns out to be false.

The registration material used in this study of police inquiries is for the most part based on the police's definition of the situation. However, this does not apply to negative inquiries resulting from complaints, where the citizen's definition of the circumstances has been registered with the purpose of illustrating the erroneous conceptions of police work on the part of the population. We are not here thinking of deliberate false alarms. Here we only include negative inquiries resulting from wrongly defining a situation as criminal or somebody's behaviour as 'suspect'.

The positive inquiries account for 85 per cent of the total number of police inquiries while the negative inquiries (including false automatic alarms) account for 15 per cent (Table 1a and 1b).

A relatively large proportion of the work carried out by the Aarhus emergency squad concerns non-criminal incidents. Thirty-two per cent of positive inquiries consist of looking for missing persons, providing social relief service (advice and assistance), assistance in connection with illness, injury, persons found dead, suicides or fires, as well as carrying information, transportation of prisoners and persons generally to various authorities. A remaining unspecified category is the enforcement of general order, such as the regulation of traffic and other preventive tasks. The largest single category is the one including transportation of prisoners, which constitutes 22 per cent of all non-criminal incidents.

Assistance in connection with illness and assistance to injured persons (either in homes or in public places) adds up to 10 per cent, more or less equally distributed on both categories. Presence at accidental fires likewise accounts for 10 per cent, while the bringing of persons before various authorities constitutes 13 per cent, persons brought before the bailiff being the most common of these.

Domestic disturbances are here classified under a special category, which represents 6 per cent of all inquiries. Non-criminal incidents and domestic disturbances do not usually require a report.

The second largest category of inquiries is the one concerning violations of the municipal code (disorderly conduct, breach of the peace, drunkenness, etc.) which total 21 per cent of all positive inquiries. Penal code violations constitute 16 per cent. The fourth largest category concerns road accidents, which represent 13 per cent of all inquiries. These latter tasks are very time-consuming with regard to the time spent in the field (interrogation, measuring etc.) as well as the time used for the writing up of reports.

It has not been possible to distinguish accurately between road accidents and traffic violations. Minor 'Road Traffic Act' offences, which typically occur in almost all road accidents, are not always described with the accuracy necessary in order to trace them to the pertinent sections of the law. We have therefore made the distinction as follows: less serious Road Traffic Act offences, which are not connected with road accidents, and more serious Road Traffic Act offences, which will typically be described in detail (whether or not they are committed in connection with a road accident), have been registered as traffic violations.[14] This means that all incidents concerning drunken driving are registered here.

From 1972 to 1976 the total number of positive and negative inquiries increased by 66 per cent. A relatively steady rise can be seen during this period. While the positive inquiries rose by only 52 per cent, the negative inquiries rose by 204 per cent.

Table 1b: Negative inquiries (incidents not requiring police involvement)

Index %	1972	1973	1974	1975	1976	Total (N-%)
Complaints	100	121	134	200	224	748
	38 %	27 %	21 %	25 %	28 %	26 %
Alarms	100	200	310	374	354	2 087
	62 %	73 %	79 %	75 %	72 %	74 %
Total	100	170	243	308	304	2 835
	100 %	100 %	100 %	100 %	100 %	100 %

The automatic alarms, alone, constitute three-quarters of all negative inquiries. These have also increased the most (by 254 per cent), while the negative inquiries resulting from complaints have increased by 124 per cent. The fact that an automatic alarm has been released is often established sooner than the fact that a citizen has been mistaken in placing a complaint with the police.

Negative inquiries never result in a report, but it would be wrong to assume that positive inquiries always result in a report.

From the earlier mentioned studies on the willingness to write a report we know that it is of considerable importance for the officer's decision about under-enforcement, especially in cases of proactive detection, whether or not the case in question demands a report, and if so how exhaustive that report should be. The officer's decision will also be influenced by the existing work load.

It is therefore necessary, when estimating the increase in the number of inquiries carried out by the emergency squad, to make a qualitative as well as quantitative estimation. In other words, we must find out how great a share of the increasing number of inquiries requires a report.

If we consider the relative distribution of positive inquiries, we can establish the following facts:

There has only been a minor increase in the number of inquiries concerning non-criminal incidents. Concerning domestic disturbances the number has remained proportionately constant over the years. Both categories of inquiries will typically not require a report. The number of penal code violations, which normally do not require reports by the emergency squad, is decreasing. The number of road accidents, generally considered to be very time-consuming and requiring the preparation of reports by the emergency squad, has, however, also been decreasing.

Violations of the municipal code and traffic violations are offences that have increased above the average by 77 per cent and 68 per cent respectively. Whereas the first type of offence for the most part is cleared without a report, the increase in traffic violations adds to the work load of the police, since they usually require a report.[15]

7. NEGATIVE COMPLAINTS

The largest group of negative inquiries resulting from complaints, 52 per cent (Table 2), concerns penal code offences and violations of the municipal code. The citizen believes that a certain crime ('suspect behaviour' is here excluded) has been committed, but on the arrival of the police the incident proves to be of no interest at all. In 31 per cent of the incidents the citizen has informed the police of a non-criminal incident or a domestic disturbance. Only 13 per cent of the negative inquiries are based on complaints concerning road accidents or a traffic violation.

Table 2: Negative complaints

Index	1972	1973	1974	1975	1976	Total (N-%)
Incidents defined by citizens as:						
non-criminal incidents (incl. domestic disturbances)	100	104	143	170	304	189 31 %
Violations of the penal code and the municipal code	100	143	129	188	186	313 52 %
Traffic cases (road accidents and traffic violations)	100	15	123	192	192	81 13 %
Others	100	250	200	400	200	23 4 %
Total	100	114	134	189	221	606 100%

During the 5-year period we have seen a rise of 121 per cent in the number of negative complaints.

The conclusions to be drawn are: 1) *that* the citizens (and public authorities) to some extent misinterpret the relevance of the situation to the police, and especially the criminal content (this happens in 4 per cent of all complaints), 2) *that* they to an increasing extent mobilize the police in these situations, and 3) *that* the main increase in these mobilizations is in situations which they themselves define as non-criminal.

8. THE INITIATIVE FOR THE POSITIVE INQUIRIES

The private initiative constitutes 65 per cent of all initiatives; 21 per cent emanate from public authorities (e.g. courts, prisons, hospitals, but also doctors, ambulance men, watchmen, etc.), while the police (the patrols and the station together) take the initiative in 12 per cent of all positive inquiries. The patrolling police alone initiate 7 per cent of these (Table 3).

Since the proportion of official initiatives constitutes almost a fourth of all initiatives, it gives a somewhat different picture of the reactive character of police work than could be expected on the basis of the American studies (Reiss 1971).

The citizen's overall dominance and resulting discretionary influence on the amount of, and outcome of, police work seems less clear in Denmark. A general discussion of Danish police work must take into account the proportion of initiatives issuing from public authorities, whose motives for engaging the police, and whose expectations of the police, might be entirely different from those of the ordinary citizen.

The private initiative is distributed with about 28 per cent on non-criminal incidents (incl. domestic disturbances), 23 per cent on violations of the municipal code, 18 per cent on penal code violations, 18 per cent on road accidents, and 9 per cent on traffic violations. In Reiss's study 83 per cent of all private initiatives concerned non-criminal incidents.

This seeming discrepancy is mainly due to methodological differences between the two studies. Apparently what we have registered as penal code violations is equivalent to Reiss's category: criminal incidents, which constitutes 17 per cent of the initiatives.

This does not mean, however, that Reiss did not register public disturbances, drunkenness or minor traffic violations. But he included 'many minor violations' in the non-criminal incident category on the basis that they did not result in citations or arrests.[16] When one is studying the discretionary power of the police, it does not seem obvious to register any violations as non-criminal matters, because the police's definition then is referred to the result arrived at rather than the actual content of the situation.

Table 3: The initiatives resulting in positive inquiries

% / %	Non-criminal incidents	Domestic disturbances	Penal code violations	Municipal code violations	Traffic violations	Road accidents	Other violations	Searches for wanted persons	Total (N-%)
Private initiative	20% / 41%	8% / 98%	18% / 75%	23% / 74%	9% / 69%	18% / 92%	3% / 64%	1% / 31%	10 786 / 100% / 65%
Official initiative	73% / 49%	0% / 2%	5% / 7%	13% / 13%	2% / 4%	4% / 6%	3% / 20%	1% / 6%	3 466 / 101% / 21%
Alarms	2% / 0%	0% / 0%	97% / 5%	0% / 0%	0% / 0%	0% / 0%	1% / 0%	0% / 0%	145 / 100% / 1%
Patrol initiative	6% / 2%	0% / 0%	25% / 12%	32% / 11%	26% / 24%	4% / 2%	4% / 11%	3% / 8%	1 228 / 100% / 7%
Other police initiative	53% / 9%	0% / 0%	5% / 2%	8% / 2%	4% / 3%	1% / 0%	3% / 5%	27% / 55%	881 / 101% / 5%
Total (N-%)	5 203 / 32% / 101%	924 / 6% / 100%	2 616 / 16% / 101%	3 479 / 21% / 100%	1 293 / 8% / 100%	2 090 / 13% / 100%	465 / 3% / 100%	436 / 3% / 100%	16 506 / 102% / 100%

The official initiative mainly concerns non-criminal incidents (73 per cent). These are, for example, requests to bring people before the bailiff, or the transportation of prisoners. Regarding inquiries into criminal incidents, the initiative is principally taken in cases of violations of the municipal code.

In Denmark police initiative, although 40 per cent of it comes from the station, definitely is of greater importance than in the USA. Whereas the non-patrolling police initiative typically concerns non-criminal incidents (e.g. searches for missing persons) and searches for wanted persons, 83 per cent of the patrol initiatives relate to criminal incidents. According to Reiss, criminal incidents account for only 14 per cent of the initiatives taken by the patrolling police. This considerable disparity cannot be explained by methodological differences alone. Twenty-five per cent of the patrol initiatives concern penal code violations, 32 per cent concern violations of the municipal code, and 26 per cent concern major traffic violations.

Out of all traffic violation inquiries, 24 per cent result from patrol initiative. Patrol initiative represents only 12 per cent and 11 per cent of violations of the penal code and of the municipal code respectively.

Proactive policing concerning these three categories is directed mainly towards drunken driving (90 per cent), theft of vehicles for use (61 per cent), and drunken and disorderly conduct in public places (99 per cent).

9. PROACTIVE POLICING

It might be expected that an increase in the number of patrolling hours would show a similar increase in the number of incidents detected via patrol initiative. The State Commissioner of Police's patrol-statistics only cover the period 1 April 1974 – 31 March 1977. Patrolling by car is predominantly carried out by the emergency squad. By applying the data of the statistics to the years 1974–76, it can be established that time spent patrolling in the police district of Aarhus has increased by 13 per cent.

Patrol-initiated inquiries, during the same period, show an increase of 23 per cent. In other words, patrol initiative increases more than the increase in the number of patrolling hours would suggest. This is probably due to the fact that the number of patrolling officers increased by approximately 20 per cent from 1974 to 1976 (see note 13). There are no statistics on the number of patrolling hours before 1 April 1974, but on the basis of statistics for the financial year 1974, the police in Aarhus estimated that, compared with the previous period, 'patrolling had increased considerably and had been made more effective.'[17]

As illustrated in Table 4, patrol initiatives during the investigated period have increased by 74 per cent, while non-police initiatives (private or official initiative) have increased by 47 per cent.

Table 4: Patrol initiatives and non-police initiatives

Index %	1972	1973	1974	1975	1976	Total (N-%)
Patrol initiatives	100 8%	91 6%	142 9%	150 8%	174 9%	1 228 8%
Non-police initiatives	100 92%	113 94%	122 91%	137 92%	147 91%	14 252 92%
Total	100 100%	111 100%	124 100%	138 100%	149 100%	15 480 100%

In relation to the total increase in the number of inquiries, however, the number of the patrol-initiated inquiries has not risen, in spite of the increased size of the force. In other words, the suggested connection between the number of patrolling hours and the number of inquiries by proactive policing cannot be established on this general level.

10. PROACTIVE DETECTION AND UNDER-ENFORCEMENT OF DRUNKEN DRIVING.

When we consider the positive inquiries concerning drunken driving (whether or not involving traffic accidents), we find that 36 per cent of these are patrol-initiated.

If we now look separately at whether these cases involve accidents or not, we find that as many as 70 per cent of cases without accidents are patrol-initiated, whereas in cases involving accidents 90 per cent result from private initiative. In other words, proactive detection of drunken driving only achieves practical importance in cases not involving accidents.

Since an important change in the Road Traffic Act with regard to drunken

Table 5: Arrests for drunken driving (with motor vehicles and mopeds) not involving accidents

N	1972	1973	1974	1975	1976	1977	Total (N-%)
Patrol initiative	43	34	40	76	73	106	372 72%
Non-police initiative	14	21	16	33	30	34	148 28%
Total	57	55	56	109	103	140	520 100 %

driving was introduced on the 1 July 1976, this part of the study has been extended to also include the year 1977.

Patrol initiatives during this 6-year period show a total increase of 147 per cent (Table 5).

The trend in the total number of arrests remains constant from 1972 to 1974, then in 1975 we see a rise of almost 100 per cent, and in 1977 a further increase of 36 per cent.

Both types of initiative increased from 1974 to 1975, while only those cases detected on patrol initiative increased significantly from 1976 to 1977. The number of patrolling officers kept constant during the latter period.

With regard to the increase in patrol initiatives from 1974 to 1975, it is, of course, tempting to associate this with the increase in patrolling hours implemented in 1974.

There are official statistics available which cover this topic in relation to all of the country's 54 police districts. These statistics are drawn up so as to separate cases involving accidents from those not involving accidents (presumed to be police-initiated). There are, as earlier mentioned, also statistics covering the number of patrolling hours. By comparing these two sets of statistics (from 1974 to 1976) we can test the above hypothesis. Using Spearman's correlation coefficient, it turns out that there was no connection at all between the two variables.

As sufficient information is not available at the present time, this study cannot explain the increase in the cases of drunken driving, not resulting in accidents, from 1974 to 1975, but it is a fact that the increase was common throughout the whole country. Since no large organizational change took place other than the increase in time spent patrolling, the increase could be actual.

The expansion in cases resulting from patrol initiative from 1976 to 1977 can, however, be explained. This increase was also common to the country as a whole, since cases not involving accidents rose by about 30 per cent from one year to the next (three times the increase in cases involving accidents). The trend continues, though to a lesser degree, from 1977 to 1978 (Koch 1979).

Participant observation and interviews with police officers have revealed that the increased initiative on the part of the police is closely connected with the fixing of punishable alcohol levels in the blood (at 0.8 and 1.20 pro mille) which were introduced in the new Road Traffic Act of 1976. This consequently made it easier for the police to deal with cases concerning drunken driving, especially those detected proactively.

Previously, the suspect in addition to the blood test had to undergo a clinical test by the doctor, but normally in the presence of the officer who was to write the report. Thorough and lengthy interrogation of suspects and possible witnesses had to be carried out after the medical examination before allowing the suspect to go free.

Today it is sufficient to take the blood test and the officer who is to write the report does not now have to be present; he only has to bring the suspect before the duty officer and write an initial summary report, giving the suspect's data and the times and places of the actual driving, the number of drinks, etc. The duty officer then notifies a doctor and arranges for surveill-ance. The officer is then free to go out and 'pick up the next'. The report will be supplemented by a short interrogation of the suspect, when the result of the blood test is known, at a time which is more convenient to the officer.

The reason for this change in procedure is that since the change in the Act, the evidence of the blood test is in practice sufficient in the majority of cases.

The simplification of the procedure has both a quantitative and a qualitative influence on the increasing patrol initiative. The new procedure is time-saving and leaves the officers with more time to make arrests, but most importantly it stimulates the initiative, because the officers are now in a position to investigate serious offences (i.e. those more likely to result in imprisonment) with a minimum of report-writing.

A Norwegian study (Lorentzen 1973) has shown that a simplification of the procedure, e.g. in the treatment of cases of speeding, similarly has an important influence on the patrol initiative. The simplification, which enabled the police to fine on the spot by handing the offender a giro transfer form, was introduced in connection with standard fines corresponding to fixed speed limits. The change in the law resulted in a drastic increase in the detection, especially of minor speed violations. When interpreting these results one has to take into consideration, though, that even for these violations the level of fines was raised considerably.

Gardiner pointed out in his study on traffic enforcement (Gardiner 1969) that a complication of the case by the courts had the effect that the police were less likely to write tickets or to bring ticketed violators into court. If it is common practice that the courts require the officer to be present when his traffic case is scheduled to be heard, irrespective of whether the motorist will plead guilty or not, the police officers often feel that they are wasting their time.

There is another plausible explanation of the increase in cases. With the introduction of the new Road Traffic Act, any driver (irrespective of verifiable suspicion of driving under the influence of alcohol) could be submitted to the breathalyser test. It had been expected by legislators that this rather radical change of the means of investigation would result in a higher risk of discovery (Waaben 1978). Therefore it has been suggested that the increase in arrests of drunken drivers, not involved in accidents, since 1976 could be a result of, or at least partly due to, a procedural simplification of this kind.

On the basis of this study, however, it is not apparent that this change in the legal criteria for police intervention has had any direct influence on police practice. The practice of proactive detection of drunken driving was, before the new Road Traffic Act came into force, that a driver who acted strangely was stopped and asked to produce his driving licence (the police have always had the right to ask to see it). If voice, movements, smell, or eye expression supported a suspicion of intoxication, the driver was requested to inflate a balloon. It is unlikely that a large percentage of the drivers thus questioned would have refused to do this. It would most probably result in arousing further suspicion, and contribute towards justifying a medical examination at the station. Thus the judicial requirement of a well-founded suspicion has hardly hampered investigation in practice.

Experience obtained during observation of police patrolling in Aarhus police district shows that the procedure is largely the same today. There is no question of the officer, immediately on having stopped the driver, asking him to inflate a balloon – in spite of the fact that the law warrants such a procedure – not even in connection with spot checks. Suspicion will more often than not be present even according to the new Road Traffic Act.

While, no doubt, simplification of the procedure through rationalization of reporting has resulted in an increase in the proactive detection of incidents of drunken driving, thus enforcing the rules on drunken driving more effectively, it is of course, in retrospect, more difficult to establish whether the previous more time-consuming and complicated procedure resulted in under-enforcement.

One can get an impression of this by comparing the police initiative in proactively detected incidents where they apprehend the offender while driving, with the incidents where they have to call on the supposed offender at his home subsequent to a complaint and often after a certain lapse of time. In the latter cases it is much more difficult to collect evidence.

To illustrate the significant difference in work load deriving from these types of situations, I will give two examples[18] concerning this issue. One resulted in a report, the other did not.

There was a complaint that a car had gone off the road into a field. We could not tell when it had happened. It had turned a somersault. The driver had left it. It was impossible for us to find him. His wife, who was contacted by telephone, had not heard from him. Later the couple called the station and told the police that he had now arrived home safely. He had sworn to the duty officer that there was no question of drunken driving, and that he had not been drinking at all. We were ordered over the radio to drive out and take a look, anyway. The officers spontaneously shook their heads. Three hours had passed since we had become aware of the incident and they considered it quite hopeless to make a case out of it. So instead of driving out there straight away, they went all the way to the station to discuss it with the duty officer. One of the officers said that he had recently written a 28 page report about a drunken driver and that it had been shelved simply because some friends of the driver had stated that they had been drinking with him after he had left the car, and therefore his case was lost completely. The officer could not of course prove that they were 'very good' friends (i.c. that they were willing to lie), but he was sure of it and convinced that the man was guilty. Therefore, he was not very keen on writing a report in such a situation. The duty officer was in no doubt at all. He said: 'It is quite possible that you are right. But we'll have to drive out there and have a talk with him.' He was a quiet, sensible sort of man. When asked how much he had to drink, he said that he had had six beers since 2 o'clock p.m. and that he had had had the accident at 10.30. p.m. They then breathalysed him, it showed a positive result, and they arrested him. He stated that he had not been drinking after he had got home. Nevertheless, to make sure that he did not change his statement later, they asked for permission to search his house to see whether there were any bottles which were wet at the neck and to measure the contents of each bottle. First they examined a few bottles of alcohol and some beer bottles in the kitchen; they then went through the bar which contained about 30 to 40 bottles. They went into the bathroom, sniffed at the basin and the toilet and examined the bedroom, the balcony and the nursery. There was mould in some bottles in the garage, but these were nevertheless examined. The exaggerated thoroughness was due to the fact that if the officers had to work on 'such a bad case' at all, they wanted to make sure that it did not 'slip through their fingers'. The search itself took over an hour. The next day the man called the station and said that on account of the shock from the accident, he had forgotten to tell them that just before we had arrived, he had been out in the garden to get some fresh air and had had a strong beer which he had left out there.

In this example the officers were compelled by the duty officer, who knew that the alleged offender and his wife would be at home, to follow up the case. In the following example it was more or less up to the officers to decide whether or not to follow up the case.

We got a message over the radio that some guy had seen another man drive away drunk from a cafeteria. The complainant had seen the car parked outside the driver's house. The officers immediately swore about this case, because they thought it was hopeless. The offender had been at his address for some time. First we went to the supposed offender's address. We could not see 'the god-damned car', we did not have its exact registration number, only some possible figures. A green Marina was parked close by and the car was supposed to be green. However, the number of the green car did not look right, but on the other hand the complainant might have got it wrong. Outside No. 7, which was where the offender was supposed to live, a red Marina was parked, but its number had nothing to do with the supposed number of the car. As they did not know the exact registration number and in spite of the fact that a green Marina was parked near this entrance, they decided to drop the matter. They did not call over the radio for the name and address of the driver of the green Marina, which can be normally ascertained by means of the registration number. They then cancelled the case over the radio, saying that it was useless, as it was, to try to contact the complainant, which is the normal procedure when you have nothing to go on. But we were told over the radio to go on with it. We arrived, and rang the bell, it was quite dark inside. The officer did not ring the bell very enthusiastically and was soon heard saying: 'Let's leave.' We reported back that the complainant was not in. The complainant called the police again later, and it turned out that we had got the wrong address. We drove to the right address and talked to the complainant. He was drunk and could not remember exactly when he had last seen the supposed offender at the cafeteria. But he himself had been at the address, which was nearby, and had seen the car there. We got the impression that he went out with the offender's mother-in-law. We could sense some family discords. When he was asked directly why he was so keen on 'having that guy nailed for drunken driving', he said: 'Well, there are so many who want to get at me.' We said that we would go over there and have a look, but he did not believe us. When we arrived, the car was not there, so we dropped the case and drove on. The officers might at least have rung the bell at the address. As one of the officers said: 'As a matter of fact, we don't know whether the man has driven drunk. We only know that the other one was drunk and that they probably disapprove of one another. It looks as if it might be an act of revenge.' He did not think that you could possibly, on such a vague foundation, wake up people in the middle of the night.

There is of course no doubt that the police would have been within their rights if they had rung the bell of the supposed offender's house, because they had had a complaint (otherwise only a few cases of investigation subsequent to a complaint would be legal) even if the person in question turned out to be sober, or at least not drunk.

As the officers, on the other hand, could not be certain that he was a drunken driver, the case is of course not an obvious example of under-enforcement. In the light of their exclamations, their statements, their actions, and specially their omissions, there is not much doubt that their behaviour was characterized by a desire not to have to report on this troublesome case.

The reason for this attitude was that the case might be just as time-consuming as the former example, and that the officers still could not be sure that it would be accepted in court. As the two examples have indicated, the risk of under-enforcement seems to grow with the degree of complication.

Even in cases of proactive detection that can be handled by one of the 'easy reports' resulting in a conviction, officers have been known to use under-enforcement for different reasons.

Early in the evening during our patrol, we were following a car that was being driven rather poorly and also a tail light on the car was broken. We followed the car and tried to make it stop at the side of the road. At first the driver reacted neither to our horn nor to the 'Stop' sign (which is not all that unusual). We had to try again and the car then pulled in to the side and the driver got out, somewhat confused. The officer went over to him and asked who owned the car and was told that it belonged to the driver's mate. The officer asked him how many beers he had had during the day. He had had two or three, he sai . He was then asked to get into the police car to take a breathalyser test. He sat down and inflated the balloon. It showed some discoloration. The officer then addressed the man and said: 'You told me before that you had had three beers. It is not true, you have had more according to the breathalyser. You have certainly had more than three beers.' 'Oh well, but I had something to drink at work as well. I cannot remember now how many I had. It might be about four.' 'Well, first you told me two, then three, and now four. How many did you have? That's what I am asking you. Did you have so many that you lost count?' The officer then asked if he had a driving licence. He was asked when he had passed his driving test. It was about 15 years ago. The officer said: 'What rules in the Road Traffic Act concern speeding?' (The driver had not driven too fast, but a new Road Traffic Act had just been passed, and according to this the police were to a larger extent to control e.g. the drivers' knowledge of the law with regard to a possible re-examination, which, if not satisfactory, might lead to a withdrawal of his licence). 'Well, you are allowed to drive at 60', the driver replied. 'If we disregard the speed limit, what rules are then applied?' The driver was a little uncertain but began to talk about 'according to circumstances' etc. He then said: 'You are not allowed to drive faster than circumstances permit!' The officer looked at him and said: 'Did you ever hear that you are only allowed to drive at a speed which gives you time to slow down within the light range, when it is dark?' The driver had hardly had time to reply before the officer went on: 'Let's have a look at your driving licence.' I could tell that he would let him go, and when we were back in the patrol car he said: 'Well, yes, we cannot really pin him down on anything. He is a spray-painter and they do walk around in those steams and may become a bit "drunk" from them.' But he told him to get a new driving licence (the one he presented was torn) and to have his head and tail lights repaired. He told him to have it done soon and that he would not take his name and address this time. The officer said, he figured that the driver would then probably be better able to afford to have his lights repaired if he was not fined. We then left.

It is certain that working in chemical fumes can cause bloodshot eyes, one can become dizzy, etc., but this driver actually did admit that he had been drinking. Even though the breathalyser might be misleading, a blood test could have shown whether or not the man was intoxicated. As seen in the example, the officer interrogated the driver in a very authoritative way partly about things not concerning the matter. That was the officer's only reaction, since he did not choose to charge him with any violations, although minor violations had been committed apart from the suspicion of drunken driving. In this case police harassment was considered a sufficient deterrent which made punishment unnecessary. The next incident is an even more striking example of under-enforcement as the officers were certain that there was an illegal level of intoxication.

We were following a car. It was being driven almost in the middle of the road and the driver looked very tired. He pulled in to the side of the road, and the police officers supposed that he lived there. They asked for his driving licence and as he had obviously been drinking, he was asked to get into the patrol car. Before asking him how many drinks he had had and when he had had the last one, the officer said: 'You do not have to tell us' (which is correct procedure). Well, he did not mind. He had had the last beer a quarter of an hour ago and he had had four or five during the evening. He was asked to inflate a balloon and he agreed. He seemed very dull. When they had made the test, they explained to him: 'If we make a little effort it looks as if you have had it!' The man said: 'Well, I might as well be completely honest.' The officer said hurriedly: 'Yes, but don't say more than necessary.' But the man insisted: 'No, I'll tell you the whole story.' He had been to a party for post office employees – he worked at the Post Office – and he had been drinking a lot. He had had about six to seven beers that evening and in his own opinion he had had too much to be driving a car properly. They watched him for a while and one of the officers said: 'Well, if that is so, I think that you have had quite enough for tonight. Quickly to bed!'

Afterwards we discussed it together, and they were all sure that the man had had an alcohol level of at least 1.20 in the blood. But they were not very keen on arresting him. The reason they gave was that the degree of intoxication did not influence his driving too much.

But as the very reason why we had noticed him was that he was driving in the middle of the road, this is hardly sufficient explanation of the under-enforcement. As in the former example the driver did not contest the authority of the officers, but even showed penitence and a will to co-operate with the police. All this combined with the fact that he had now reached his destination, is the most likely explanation that a formal reaction was not considered necessary (Feest & Blankenburg 1972).

11. DETECTION AND UNDER-ENFORCEMENT OF THEFT FOR USE.

With regard to the inquiries into thefts of vehicles for use only, we note that a majority of 56 per cent result from patrol initiative. There is no clear trend in this initiative during the investigated period. Despite the fact that the number of patrolling hours increased from 1974 to 1976, there is no indication of a correlative increase in the number of proactively detected incidents of this kind of theft.

These incidents differ from those concerning drunken driving not involving accidents in that some directly concerned individual, who wants his stolen property recovered, will sooner or later place a complaint with the police.

The likelihood of under-enforcement will thus be limited and will, generally speaking, only occur with the victim's prior consent. The following example from a police log shows how the situation may arise in cases of theft involving near relatives, work associates etc.

Theft of car for use? Violation of the Road Traffic Act Section 18, subsection 1 – Officers (numbers) brought in the driver of a car, (name), whom they had stopped, in order to point out to him that a tail light was missing on the car. As the driver had no driving licence nor any other form of identification, he was taken down to the station. The apprehended had no licence (in fact he had never had one) and the car turned out to belong to (name), the apprehended's employer. The owner of the car was contacted by telephone and came to the station. He was made familiar with the situation and stated that he had not given permission to the apprehended to use his car. However, he did not wish his employee to be charged with theft and they left the station together. A report will be made by (officer's name) according to which the apprehended will be charged with violation of section 18, subsection 1 (driving without a licence).

During participant observation I came across another instance where the possibility of under-enforcing a theft, entered into the officer's assessment of the situation.

It was early in the morning and we were about to return to the station. A car had stalled and the driver was obiously drunk or at least something was wrong. He was a young man. He admitted that the car belonged to a friend of his and that he did not have a driving licence. The car had stalled where the road curves while he and his friend were driving along. The friend had gone home, but he thought it was a mess just to leave the car there in the middle of the road, obstructing the traffic, so he decided to move it further down the road. His explanation was somewhat incoherent, just as it also aroused suspicion that he had no keys for the car and that we found a screwdriver inside the car. He was arrested and the officers decided to drive over to where the friend lives. While we were driving, one of the officers suddenly said: 'I think we should go down to the station and get this straightened out.' Shortly afterwards the young man exclaimed: 'I may as well admit it. I took the car from my friend's place without asking, and I used the screwdriver to start it. What's the point of denying it, anyway?' He was taken to the station. Then we went to see the friend. As the friend might be involved in some way or other, the officers chose to present him with the case in a neutral fashion. They asked him where his car was. He seemed quite naturally surprised and said that one of his friends had been driving around looking for it, because it had suddenly disappeared. He became very angry when told that the other friend had 'borrowed' it. Afterwards I asked the reporting officer if he was accusing the young man of theft for use, drunken driving, and driving without a licence. He replied that this was what he was doing at the moment, but that he would reconsider the matter next week when he had talked to the owner again. The owner being fairly upset at the moment, there was no point in asking him if he wanted to report his friend for theft. The officer would wait and see how the owner felt in a week's time because it might well be that he wanted nothing done about the matter, and the officer would probably take this into consideration.

What determines the attitude of the police in these two examples is probably not so much the close relationship between offender and victim. What is important in these cases is that the drivers can be accused of several offences one of which will result in infliction of a real penalty, which in the officers' opinion means the effectuation of a fine or of imprisonment.

The following example serves to illustrate this interpretation (the example was given to me by the officers involved).

> The other day the station received a complaint of a car theft. Police cars from all police divisions were sent out to track down the offender. Some hours later he was arrested at the residence of the complainant who turned out to be his girl friend. She now wanted to withdraw the complaint. The duty officer doubted as to whether this could be done, while an officer from the CID was of the opinion that the complaint could not be withdrawn. Later when I raised the question in the night-canteen, it was generally agreed that it is not entirely up to the complainant to decide whether a complaint should be withdrawn or not. The question of theft, however, was not crucial, as there were witnesses to the man's drunken driving. The end result of the case was considered to be satisfactory. The man would receive a penalty for his drunken driving (the minimal penalty being a heavy fine), while he would not 'get anything' for the theft for use.

The police officers were hereby indicating that they believed that the theft would only result in withdrawal of the charge or a suspended sentence.

Later, while discussing similar cases, policemen have expressed the 'hope' that the driver is *also* drunk, when they suspect a car theft. Their job seems to them more meaningful when the inquiry results in some kind of penalty. It is unsatisfactory to catch criminals if others let them go.

A similar attitude can be seen among other kinds of law enforcer, i.e. among ticket inspectors on the Copenhagen suburban railway system. In 1976 the Danish State Railways wanted to criminalize travelling without a ticket, apparently so that the suggested fine, when inflicted, could be converted into imprisonment if the violator did not pay up. The unofficial reason for this was that the inspectors experienced problems with an increasing number of recidivists who were literally unable to pay the extra-charge. This was said to be 'a thorn in the ticket inspectors' flesh', i.e. a constant source of irritation to the inspectors, since they felt that nothing happened to the violators. The directors feared that the consequence of this feeling of frustration could be a less effective enforcement. Thus it became more a question of controlling the 'controllers' (Vestergaard & Koch 1979).

Not only in cases consisting of a combination of theft for use and drunken driving does the prospect of inflicting punishment have actuality for the police officers. According to the police officers, it is not unusual that when detecting other kinds of serious offence (which might otherwise lead to withdrawal of the charge or a suspended sentence), they will write an additional report on even less serious traffic law violations (that always result in a fine). It is not, of course, that the police officers invent offences, but rather that they prosecute offences that they might otherwise have ignored.

It is nearly always possible to find substance for a report on some defect on the vehicle or in the driving.

The interest shown by the police may even vary in the same type of offence. In connection with this research I was a participant observer in a minor police district in the provinces where police control seemed to be more efficient, due to a closer knowledge of the local population.

One day during a coffee-break the police officers were discussing some colleagues' provisional withdrawal of a driving licence belonging to someone known to them all. One said that he was sure the man in question would persist in driving although his licence had been taken away. Another officer went on to say that there was nothing much they could do about that. The man would need to be stopped and told that he was not allowed to go on driving, and he added: 'It won't be worth stopping him until he has his driving licence suspended. Then he'll get 10 days' imprisonment.'[19]

Police officers' inclination to 'make deals' with the complainant, or to under-enforce proactively detected incidents of theft of (old) mopeds or bicycles, may indirectly be provoked by doubt as to whether or not the offender is intoxicated. This has to do with the division of responsibility between the uniformed police and the CID. In Aarhus police district the rules governing which division is to carry out the actual treatment of a case (i.e. report-writing) are as follows: if it is a matter of drunken driving alone, the uniformed police write the report; this also applies to cases concerning drunken driving in connection with theft for use. If it is a question of theft alone, it is the CID who must write the report.

The following example (also reported to me by the officers involved) will serve to illustrate how the division of responsibility can create problems:

The canine patrol had stopped a driver and breathalysed him. The breathalyser proved negative whereupon the officers drew the conclusion that the driver was not intoxicated. They arrested him, however, because the car was stolen. When they arrived at the station the duty officer likewise judged the man to be sober (without the use of a breathalyser). The same estimation was given by four other police officers who happened to be in the office. The duty officer then notified the CID that he had a 'case' for them. A detective came over, looked at the man and breathalysed him for a second time. He then told the duty officer that the apprehended was drunk and that it was not a case for the CID to deal with.

The reaction of the CID in the latter example naturally places the uniformed police in an awkward position. The uniformed police will, of course, have to write a report on the theft for use and probably also have to request a doctor to take a blood test, the breathalyser being only advisory. As they disagree fundamentally with the detective in his judgement of the situation, they will regard their treatment of the drunken driving offence as a waste of time.

The fact that the nature of an offence is assessed differently by the CID and by the uniformed police is a manifestation of the kind of selection by detection which arises out of the organizational structure of the police (Coleman & Bottomley 1976).

If the theft happened to be of a less serious nature, as in the examples below, the division of responsibility may induce selection by decision in terms of under-enforcement, if the uniformed police would otherwise risk 'being stuck' with the offender. This would hardly apply to cases where the offender had already been taken to the station.

However, the police also make use of under-enforcement in incidents where theft for use is the sole offence. In these situations under-enforcement is often a result of a mixture of the cognitive processes of selection by detection and selection by decision. By making no particular effort to establish the existence of a crime (as in the first of the following examples) or, having recognized a crime, by refraining from acting upon this knowledge (as in the second example), they redefine the situation by registering the incident as non-criminal.

This way of under-enforcing can occur in incidents of less serious theft for use, also when there is no close relation between offender and victim.

The canine patrol were called out to a typical situation requiring dogs. Some youths, who had been beaten up by rivals from another club, were lined up in front of this youth club to take revenge. As we approached the scene, a number of the youths drove off on their mopeds. We drove around for a while looking for the ring leader. Not having any luck we returned to the square in front of the youth club. There was still a crowd of young people around. Suddenly some youths who were standing by a wall shone a bright light at us. One of them was holding a moped which he now flung down, and as the patrol approached him, he ran down some steps towards a gang-way under the road. The officer sitting next to the driver rushed out of the car, flung the boot open and let out his dog. He told me afterwards that he assumed the youth to be a moped thief, because he had started to run when the police came. (It is a widely accepted axiom amongst police officers that running away is safe indication of a bad conscience). Another youth now went up to the moped to lift it up from the ground. The other officer yelled at this youth in an extremely authoritative voice: 'If you touch it, you'll be accused of stealing it!' The supposed moped thief had emerged on the other side of the road but had been caught up by the police dog and its master. I noticed that the dog had snapped at the youth's leg. The officer then searched the youth and they both came back to the patrol car. The youth was then asked if the moped belonged to him. He said, it did not, but he had borrowed it. The policeman asked who he had borrowed it from. From a guy whose second name the youth did not remember. Neither could he remember the guy's address. It did sound fairly suspect. One of the officers called over the radio for the transport car to come and fetch a youth arrested for theft for use. The other officer told his colleague to take it easy and not to call the transport straight away. The youth, who was rather uncomfortable in the situation, now said that he had been about to take the moped placed by the tree next to the wall, back to the owner whose name he could now remember. That was what he had been about to do. But he did not know the name of the street, nor the number at which the guy lived. Suddenly some other youths joined in. One of the youths was known to the 'lenient' officer, who happened to live in the same housing area. This one said he was convinced that the supposed offender was innocent, and that he would never do a thing like that. The other youths agreed. He had just lost his nerve. Then the police officers decided to get the transport car to bring in the moped as a piece of lost property. The 'lenient' officer explained to me later: 'I'm sure they were right. Even if he *was* actually trying to steal the moped, let him go this time. The evidence against him is so weak that it would have been unreasonable if he were to have been branded and got a record on account of this accusation.'

The final example is a clear-cut case of under-enforcement.

On our last patrol yesterday we drove in a civilian car. It was late at night and we were driving through the centre of town. At a crossing, a guy was pushing a bike across the road. He looked at the car in a funny way. He went on to the pavement and we started to follow him. Then one of the officers said: 'Hey, stop a moment. Let's have a chat with that guy.' His hunch turned out to be right. The guy admitted straight away that he had stolen the bike. He had picked it up outside a restaurant nearby and he was not going far with it. The bike was very old and rusty. It was a lady's bicycle. The officer inspected the lock to see whether it had been forced. It had not. When he was asked why he had taken it, he said that he had been in a restaurant and because he was tired he wanted to get home quickly. He was rather drunk. He fully realized that it was wrong and he was very sorry about it. The officer then said: 'Well, so you know you are not allowed to do this. This is what we would call 'illegal possession of lost property'!' The officer told him that they could arrange it so that he took the bike to the station where he would be registered as a person bringing in lost property. As we got into the patrol car, the officer said quite spontaneously that it was in fact rather awkward that I had been present in this situation, because it was not quite in keeping with the rules.

CONCLUSION

The study describes the work of the uniformed police (excl. traffic division) in Denmark's second largest town, Aarhus, from 1972 til 1976.

Approximately 40 per cent of the total positive inquiries (i.e. requiring police involvement according to police definition) concern non-criminal incidents (incl. domestic disturbances). Forty per cent concern violations of the penal code (incl. searches for wanted persons) and the municipal code, by and large evenly distributed between both categories. Eleven per cent concern traffic violations and other violations, while road accidents contribute with 13 per cent.

Of the initiatives to these inquiries 65 per cent are taken by the public (citizens), 21 per cent by public authorities, and 12 per cent by the police themselves (7 per cent by the patrolling police alone).

Of the citizens' initiatives 28 per cent concern non-criminal incidents, 23 per cent violations of the municipal code, 18 per cent penal code offences, and 27 per cent traffic cases (i.e. road accidents and traffic violations).

These results differ from those obtained by a similar analysis of police work in the USA (Reiss 1971), partly in that the impact of the influence of the public on police work is not as clearly definable, and partly in that the public are less inclined to mobilize the police in non-criminal matters. The latter disparity is mainly due to a methodological difference in the registration of incidents.

At the same time, though, there seems to be a trend in the direction of the public calling for police assistance in matters which the police do not consider relevant to them at all, and that includes situations where the public themselves realize that it is not a criminal matter, but still want police assistance to sort things out.

The reactive character of the Danish police work thus to some extent differs from that of the American police.

During the investigated period the number of positive inquiries undertaken by the police increased, and there was an increase in the hours of car patrolling. The relative distribution of inquiries initiated by police patrols and inquiries initiated by citizens or public authorities keeps constant, however.

In Denmark proactive policing of criminal incidents has greater importance than in the USA. Here 83 per cent of the patrol initiatives relate to criminal incidents (penal code, municipal code, and traffic violations) whereas criminal incidents, according to Reiss, account for only 14 per cent of the initiatives taken by the American patrolling police. The disparity is significant even when the methodological conditions mentioned are taken into consideration.

The patrolling police's initiative is important, especially in connection with offences of drunken driving, not involving accidents, but also with regard to theft of vehicles for use only ('joy-riding') and incidents of drunken or disorderly conduct in public places.

There is no apparent connection between an increase in the number of patrolling hours and an increase in the number of proactively detected cases of drunken driving. A change in the Road Traffic Act which introduces fixed pro mille limits means that a blood test result typically is the only evidence required by the courts in cases of drunken driving. The change has resulted in a simplification of police procedure in that these cases, contrary to previous practice, require only a minimum of report-writing. This rationalization has further resulted in a considerable increase in patrol initiative. The fact that a probable cause for suspicion is no longer prerequisite to the use of a breathalyser test, has not in itself simplified the procedure.

The inclination of the police to under-enforce is stronger in cases of reactively detected drunken driving, where the offender typically has not been stopped while driving but arrested at his home, because the collection of evidence is complicated.

The increasing initiative of the patrolling police in the former cases of drunken driving seems stimulated not only by the reduction of report-writing, but also by the fact that the police officers can expect the accused to receive some unconditional, in their opinion real, penalty (i.e. either a (heavy) fine or imprisonment).

The significance of this attitude is also seen in other cases, e.g. theft of vehicles for use. The police seem more inclined to under-enforce such an offence when complainants who have some connection with the accused decide not to press charges, if the accused can be charged with a minor offence, the evidence of which is unquestionable and which is bound to result in an unconditional sanction (as opposed to withdrawal of the charge or a suspended sentence).

Thus there would appear to be two factors that are conducive to effective enforcement of an offence and that at the same time minimize the risk of under-enforcement: Firstly, an easily obtained and safe piece of evidence, and secondly, the probability of an unconditional (heavy) sanction.

It is important, however, to note that these two factors are contradictory in principle from a procedural point of view. Criminal acts possibly resulting in heavier unconditional sentences require greater juridical safeguards and a more thorough treatment of the case.

If the results obtained from this research can be said to apply to the work of the police generally, we have raised an ideologically challenging question, which in a democratic society constitutes something of a dilemma. This is especially so if we are moving towards a more proactively policed society, as presupposed by way of introduction.

On the one hand, a high risk of discovery and an equal enforcement in cases of serious offences is considered to be proof of justice. On the other hand, a thorough and meticulous treatment of these offences, allowing for the possibility of relaxing the penal sanctions when individual and extenuating circumstances speak in favour thereof, is also considered a proof of justice.

If effective detection of crimes, and equal enforcement, are dependent on a swift treatment of the case and the prospect of unconditional formal sanctions, we are up against a choice. We can hardly pretend that we can have it both ways. Effective detection and keeping the citizens' civil rights intact are ideals which at some stage become incompatible.

NOTES

[1] BLACK & REISS 1970, p. 66.
[2] BANTON 1964, pp. 131–133.
[3] FEEST & BLANKENBURG 1972, pp. 28–29.
[4] Cf. Directives from the Director of Public Prosecutions No. 1 1974.
[5] Op. cit., p. 66.
[6] REISS 1971, pp. 94–96.
[7] Cf. chapter II generally 'Policing Everyday Life', quotations from pp. 89, 114 and 83. The last conclusion was also reached in the later joint study by Black & Reiss (1970) on the basis of statistics that are highly debatable, if not inapplicable (in 41 per cent of the police-juvenile encounters it was impossible to determine the complainant's preference!) (p. 71).
[8] Cf. Council of Europe report of 2. June 1978 from the Third Criminological colloquium on the Police and the Prevention of Crime in Strasbourg 21–23 November 1977. The quotations from Féraud's report are taken from pp. 25–26.
[9] Cf. Steinhilper's report, pp. 91 and 108.
[10] Cf. circular of 3 April 1974 from the State Commissioner of Police to the local police chiefs.
[11] Cf. patrol-statistics of 20 September 1977 from the State Commissioner of Police. The total force of uniformed police and criminal police in Denmark was in 1978: 8,655. Eighty per cent of the force are made up by the uniformed police. The patrolling uniformed police probably make up about 6,000 men. This means that there are 12 uniformed policemen available for surveillance per 10,000 inhabitants. After a slight increase in the number of duty hours (excl. illness, training and education) since 1974, the number of hours has dropped from 1977 to 1978 (see the annual statistics from the State Commissioner of Police).
[12] This article is the first report of the efficiency study financed by the Danish Social Science Research Council and the University of Copenhagen. The study covers two police districts, Aarhus and Kalundborg (a minor police district in the provinces). The police districts were chosen for the research according to the following criteria: a high-patrolling police district where a considerable increase in the total number of patrolling hours (since 1974) were recorded, and which also had a high number of patrolling hours per man a day (more than 3 hours), and a low-patrolling police district which did not show any increase in the patrolling and which had a low number of patrolling hours (less than 2 hours).
[13] There are no directly accessible records of the exact number of police officers patrolling on the particular days included in this research, but a rough estimate by the Aarhus police of the average number of patrolling officers during the period investigated shows an increase of approximately 20 per cent from 1974 to 1976, whereas the number of officers from 1972 to 1974 and from 1976 to 1977 has been constant. At a later stage of this research the exact number of officers will of course be compared with the exact number of inquiries.
[14] This category primarily concerns major traffic violations (approx. 70 per cent). These violations are distributed with 83 per cent on drunken driving, 15 per cent on accidents with persons injured, violations of rights of way, reckless overtaking, driving over a red light, knocking over a pedestrian on a pedestrian-crossing, speeding and the like.
[15] With regard to public disturbance, 82 per cent of the incidents are cleared on the spot, whereas only 24 per cent of the incidents of public drunkenness are handled in this way. In most of the remaining 76 per cent the only reaction will be an administrative detention, typically for about 8 hours, which is not followed up by a report, even though

the violation is punishable. This is due to a directive of 5 January 1971 by the Ministry of Justice.

Reports on minor traffic violations detected on the patrolling police's initiative will most frequently be journalized directly, i.e. without entering into the police log. They include parking violations, turning left or right without signalling, driving without lights, driving without paying road tax, driving without crash helmet or without seat-belts on and the like. There has most probably been an increase in the number of such reports, but statistics are not, however, accessible with regard to the emergency squad alone. The figures available include the work of the traffic division, who detect the greater part of these violations.

[16] REISS 1971, p. 76.

[17] Cf. a schematic survey of 15 May 1975 from the State Commissioner of Police based on reports from the police districts.

[18] The following qualitative material presenting examples, discussions, and judgements is representative of the present theme of research, and constitutes extracts from the entire observational material of approx. 350 pages collected in two different police districts over a period of 12 weeks.

It is the author's strong conviction that it is almost impossible to describe unofficial, illegal, police practice by means of any kinds of questionnaire. In the earlier Danish study officers still in training (from their start in the police to six years of service) were asked their opinions about and attitudes to various aspects of their work including some controversial questions. The most significant conclusion to be drawn was that we received standard answers, in that the distribution of answers from the officers, irrespective of length of service (with the exception of those, who had been only one month in the force), was almost identical (Borg et al. 1974). In both studies it has also been attempted to ask police officers to let themselves be interviewed personally, the results of which have been meagre, since they feel restrained in this situation.

The best methodology, used in this study, seems to be spending all one's time with the officers, sharing the night watches as well, and primarily watching things as they develop. Very often issues crucial to the understanding of police work accidentally arise during an actual inquiry or during a coffee-break discussion. Having collected these issues the author presented the majority of patrolling officers in both districts with his interpretations, sometimes having them confirmed and at other times refuted. These confrontations of views were made e.g. in connection with a similar actual task or during the long hours of patrolling at night. With regard to the examples, key-words and citations of direct speech were written down in the patrol car or upon returning to the station directly after the incident had happened. The whole description was then dictated to a tape recorder within no more than 8 hours.

[19] The officers hereby indicated that even though driving without a licence is an offence in itself, it will not add much to the possible penalty to be inflicted for the main offence (drunken or reckless driving), which had resulted in the provisional withdrawal. Once the licence has been suspended by court decision, driving will be considered a new offence, which is regarded as one of the most serious offences according to the Road Traffic Act.

REFERENCES

BANTON, MICHAEL: *The Policeman in the Community*. Tavistock Publications, London 1964.

BENNETT, TREVOR: The Social Distribution of Criminal Labels. Police 'Proaction' or 'Reaction'? *British Journal of Criminology*, Vol. 19, 134–145, 1979.

BLACK, DONALD J. & ALBERT J. REISS, JR.: Police Control of Juveniles. *American Sociological Review*, Vol. 35, 63–77, 1970.

BORG, OLE, KIRSTEN GAMST-NIELSEN & HENNING KOCH: *Hvem(s) er politiet?* (Who(se) are the Police?). Institute of Criminal Science, University of Copenhagen 1973 (mimeographed).

BORG, OLE et al.: Resultater fra undersøgelser af ordenspolitiet i København (Results from research on the uniformed police in Copenhagen). *Tidsskrift for Dansk Politi* (i.e. the periodical of the Danish Police) 62–82, 1974.

BRUSTEN, MANFRED: Determinanten selektiver Sanktionierung durch die Polizei. In Johannes Feest & Rüdiger Lautman (eds.): *Die Polizei, Soziologische Studien und Forschungsberichte*, Westdeutscher Verlag, Opladen 1971.

COLEMAN, CLIVE A. & A. KEITH BOTTOMLEY: Police Conceptions of Crime and 'No Crime'. *The Criminal Law Review*, 344–360, 1976.

CRESSEY, DONALD R. & ELG ELGESEM: The Police and the Administration of Justice. pp. 53–72 in *Scandinavian Studies in Criminology*. Vol. 2. Universitetsforlaget, Oslo 1968.

DUE, OLE, BJARNE CHRISTENSEN, PETER LILHOLT, KIRSTEN SØRENSEN, PETER WIESE & BENT ØSTERBORG: *Færdselslov* (the Road Traffic Act with commentaries) Vol. 1, Juristforbundets Forlag, Copenhagen 1979.

FEEST, JOHANNES: Die Situation des Verdachts. In Johannes Feest & Rüdiger Lautmann (eds.) *Die Polizei. Soziologische Studien und Forschungsberichte*. Westdeuscher Verlag, Opladen 1971.

FEEST, JOHANNES & ERHARD BLANKENBURG: *Die Definitionsmacht der Polizei. Strategien der Strafverfolgung und soziale Selektion*. Bertelsmann Universitätsverlag, Düsseldorf 1972.

FÉRAUD, HENRI: The Social Role of the Police in the Prevention of Crime in a Modern Society. pp.23–49 in Council of Europe: *The Police and the Prevention of Crime*. Strasbourg 1978 (PC-CC (78) 3).

FILSTEAD, WILLIAM J. (ed.): *Qualitative Methodology. Firsthand Involvement with the Social World*. Markham, Chicago 1970.

GAMST-NIELSEN, KIRSTEN: Problemet: Retssikkerhed og effektivitet i forvaltningen (The Principles of Law and Efficiency in the Administration) in Ole Borg et al. 1973.

GARDINER, JOHN A.: *Traffic and the Police. Variations in Law-Enforcement Policy*. Harvard University Press, Cambridge, Massachusetts 1969.

HAUGE, RAGNAR (ed.) *Drinking and Driving in Scandinavia. Scandinavian Studies in Criminology Vol. 6*. Universitetsforlaget, Oslo 1978.

HAUGE, RAGNAR & HARALD STABELL: Politivirksomhet i et norsk landdistrikt (Police Functions in a Norwegian Province) *Nordisk Tidsskrift for Kriminalvidenskab* (The Scandinavian Periodical for Criminal Science) 269–286, 1975.

KELLING, GEORGE L., TONY PATE, DUANE DIECKMAN & CHARLES E. BROWN: *The Kansas City Preventive Patrol Experiment. A Technical Report*. Police Foundation, Washington 1974.

KELLING, GEORGE L. & DAVID FOGEL: Police Patrol – Some Future Directions. In Alvin W. Cohn (ed.): *The Future of Policing*. Sage Publications, Beverly Hills 1978.

KOCH, HENNING: Den patruljerende betjents arbejdsopgaver (The Patrolling Officer's Tasks) in Ole Borg et al. 1973.

KOCH, HENNING: Om anteciperet skyld (On Anticipated Guilt) *Juristen og Økonomen*, 419–432, 1975.

KOCH, HENNING: *Politipatruljering og spritkørsel* (Police Patrolling and Drunken Driving). Institute of Criminal Science, University of Copenhagen 1979 (mimeographed).

LORENTZEN, HÅKON: *Forenklet rettferdighet? Forenklet forelegg – målsetting og virkning* (Simplified Justice? Simplified Sanctions – Aim and Effect) Institute of Criminology and Penal Law, University of Oslo 1973 (mimeographed).

LORENTZEN, HÅKON: *Systemkrav og aktørtilpasning. En analyse av politiets arbeid i vegtransportsektoren* (System Demands and Subject Adjustment. An Analysis of the Police Work in the Road Transport Section). Institute of Sociology of Law, University of Oslo 1977 (mimeographed).

MANNING, PETER K.: *Police Work. The Social Organization of Policing.* The MIT Press, Cambridge, Massachusetts 1977.

McCABE, SARAH & FRANK SUTCLIFFE: *Defining Crime. A Study of Police Decisions.* Basil Blackwell, Oxford 1978.

NELKEN, DAVID: Extending the Use of Police Cautions: A Critical Appraisal. *The Criminal Law Review,* 360–373, 1976.

PARNAS, RAYMOND I.: The Police Response to the Domestic Disturbance. *Wisconsin Law Review,* 914–960, 1967.

REISS, JR., ALBERT J.: *The Police and the Public.* Yale University Press, New Haven 1971.

SCHNELLE, J.F., R.E. KIRCHNER, M.P. McNEES & J.M. LAWLER: Social Evaluation Research: The Evaluation of Two Police Patrolling Strategies. *Journal of Applied Behavior Analysis,* 353–365, 1975.

SHERMAN, LAWRENCE W.: Legal Issues in Law Enforcement. In Alvin W. Cohn (ed.): *The Future of Policing.* Sage Publications, Beverly Hills 1978.

SJÖHOLM, ERIK: *När og hur får polisen ingripa?* (When and how can the police intervene?) P. A. Norstedt, Stockholm 1978.

SKOLNICK, JEROME H.: *Justice without Trial. Law Enforcement in Democratic Society* John Wiley & Sons, New York 1966.

STEER, DAVID: *Police Cautions – a Study in the Exercise of Police Discretion.* Basil Blackwell, Oxford 1970.

STEINHILPER, GERNOT: Violence and the Police. pp. 91–117 in Council of Europe: *The Police and the Prevention of Crime.* Strasbourg 1978 (PC–CC (78) 3).

STINCHCOMBE, ARTHUR L.: Institutions of Privacy in the Determination of Police Administrative Practice. *The American Journal of Sociology,* 150–160, 1963.

STØKKEN, ANNE MARIE, MALIN BRATTSTRØM, NILS CHRISTIE, THOMAS HAALAND, DAG LEONARDSEN, GUNNAR LIND & TOVE LØVHAUG: *Politiet i det norske samfunn* (The Police in the Norwegian Society). Universitetsforlaget, Oslo 1974.

STØKKEN, ANNE MARIE: Power or Powerlessness – Social Control in a Suburban Environment. pp. 67–81 in *Scandinavian Studies in Criminology. Vol. 5.* Universitetsforlaget, Oslo 1974.

VESTERGAARD, JØRN & HENNING KOCH: *Kriminaliseringen af togpassagerer uden gyldig rejsehjemmel – noget om interesser og argumentation i en retspolitisk beslutningsproces* (The Criminalization of Train Passengers without a Valid Ticket – a Study of the Interests and the Argumentation in a Legal Policy Decision Process). Institute of Criminal Science, University of Copenhagen 1979 (mimeographed).

WAABEN, KNUD: Drinking-and-Driving in Scandinavia. The Legal Framework pp. 1–10 in *Scandinavian Studies in Criminology, Vol. 6.* Universitetsforlaget, Oslo 1978.

ZABERN, TH. V & F. WERKENTIN (eds.): *CILIP – Newsletter on civil liberties and police development no. 0*, Berghofstiftung für Konfliktforschung, Berlin (March/April) 1978.

ZABERN, TH. V. & F. WERKENTIN (eds.): *CILIP No. 2* (January/February) 1979.

The 1976 Police Strike in Finland

BY *Tuija Mäkinen & Hannu Takala*

INTRODUCTION

The strike by the Association of Finnish Police *(Suomen Poliisien Liitto)* began on 13 February 1976. The strike lasted 17 days.

The strike was nation-wide. High-ranking police officers, the Central Criminal Investigation Police, and the security police did not take part in the strike. In addition, the Association of Criminal Investigation Police – through which the criminal investigation police in the cities are unionized – did not participate in the strike.

According to the Ministry of the Interior, about 24 % of the total number of policemen remained on the job.

In principle, the strike affected police work generally. It is clear, however, that the strike did not have the same effect on police districts with but a few policemen as it did on the city police departments, with their highly developed administrative structure and division of labour.

The strike was popularly known as 'the uniformed police strike'. The uniformed police can best be described as the police who do the field work. According to a study carried out by the Helsinki Police Department, 40 % of the field work performed by the uniformed police involves public drunkenness. The second most important sector of field work in traffic control. The uniformed police are the police the public sees on patrol. It is this feature that most clearly distinguishes them from the criminal investigation police, whose work is primarily done out of public sight. It can be said that in Helsinki as well as in the other cities it was the traffic control and the maintenance of public order that were affected by the strike, in so far as the criminal investigation police, the social division police, or the high-ranking police officers were not able to perform these functions in addition to their normal work.

In the rural areas the strike had a more general effect on the activity of the police. In principle, during the strike all police duties were left to the local police chief and his assistant. Also, in the rural areas policemen have traditionally carried out some non-police duties; these, too, were affected by the strike.

It is impossible to say exactly how much the strike affected the police performance ability. Those policemen who were not on strike carried out their work almost without a break. Some police districts pooled their resources

to form areas of cooperation. These exceptional measures may have elimi-
nated part of the drop in operational readiness that the strike would have
otherwise caused.

According to the Police Act, tasks generally belonging to the police can
be assigned by governmental statute to the army, the frontier guard, or other
governmental authorities. These authorities already have some police duties
that were continuously carried out despite the strike. In addition, the army
forms a reserve force that can be called out to back up the police when
necessary. The Helsinki Fire Department, for one, operates to a degree
parallel to the police, since the Department has a general emergency centre.
The existence of these organs should be kept in mind, as they all formed a
reserve that in part replaced and in part – if it was believed necessary – could
have replaced the police on strike.

In addition to the official organs involved with the maintenance of order,
there are private guard agencies that are hired to perform some supervisory
and guarding duties. According to one study, at the beginning of 1975 the
number of approved guards was almost one-third of the number of policemen
in regular police duties (Komiteanmietintö 1976: 70, 5). These private guard
agencies replaced to some extent the police on strike.

The Research Institute of Legal Policy carried out a study of the police
strike and its effects. This paper is a summary of the more extensive research
report (Takala 1979).[1]

Disturbances in the normal activity of the police – such as a strike – may
bring to light features in the duties and character of the police that may
otherwise remain hidden. For this reason a police strike provides a good
opportunity to study the police. The police strike was studied as an extraordinary strike. Its reasons and background were studied, as was the way
that people reacted to a labour struggle on the part of the police.

We were also interested in studying how the strike affected behaviour.
People can change their behaviour in this regard in two ways. First, they may
adopt special precautions. Therefore, we studied what precautions were
taken, and how much insecurity was felt. Second, the risk of apprehension
and the ability of the police to prevent public disturbances was lessened
during the strike. For this reason, we studied the offences, public disturbances, and the general preventive effect of the exceptionally low risk of
apprehension.

BACKGROUND TO THE STRIKE

The background to the strike can be explained in part by the development
in the policeman's level of earnings and the conditions on the job, and in part
by the unionization of the police.

Apparently, the policemen's level of earnings has generally corresponded
to the development in the public sector.

Table 1. The average annual increase in the nominal income in the public sector and
of all wage earners 1948–74. (Source: TANDEM 1977, 489)

Years	Public sector	All wage earners
1948–55	18.5	14.8
1955–65	13.4	11.2
1966–74	8.9	11.4

Table 1 shows that since the mid-1960s the rate of growth of the income in
the public sector has slowed, when compared to the figures for all wage
earners. Without a doubt, during the past 10 years the police have had an
excellent reason to feel that they have been losers in the competition for
well-being, even if the same fate has been shared by the other professions
in the public sector.

Another 'official' reason for strikes is that the development of earnings does
not correspond to increases in productivity or the amount of work.

Table 2. The number of police per capita 1950–75. (Source: Törnudd 1978, 9)

Year	Police per 10,000 in population
1950	17
1955	16
1960	16
1965	18
1970	20
1975	22

Instead of the number of police per capita (see Table 2), the police have
preferred to use the development in criminality as a reason for dissatisfaction.
For example, figures can be produced to show that in 1950, 31 crimes were
recorded per policeman, while the number in 1975 was more than twice that,
72 per policeman. Even though these figures can be shown to be misleading
in many respects, their significance as far as criminal policy is concerned lies
in the fact that they show how the police have been able to use the crime
trends to help them in their struggle for higher wages.

The unionization of the police has been characterized by internal conflict
and splits between those working in different types of duties. The primary
conflicts have been between the criminal investigation police and the other
police, as well as between the police in Helsinki and the police elsewhere.
The Association of Finnish Police was established in 1923 in order to

represent all the lower-level policemen on a national basis (Ruotsalainen 1973). The criminal investigation police formed a splinter group in 1930, returned in 1946, and broke away again in 1976. The Helsinki Police Association, in turn, broke away from the Association of Finnish Police in 1957 and returned in 1972. The Association of Finnish Police joined the largest trade union association, the Association of Finnish Trade Unions, in 1946. The general strike of 1956, during which the police were assigned the task of maintaining order in the face of the strikers, gave rise to police bitterness against the Association of Finnish Trade Unions. The police broke away, to return again in 1969.

In 1945, the Association of Finnish Police consulted its membership for permission to go on strike. The post-war inflation had put the squeeze on pay. However, the common front necessary for a strike was not attained. The police did not participate in the strike by government officials in 1955, as the Association of Finnish Trade Unions had not granted permission, and as the Cabinet members had given their assurance that the interests of the police would be looked after just as well as the interests of the government officials on strike. In 1962, the police threatened a mass walk-out. The threat was not carried out. In 1973, all police sergeants, senior and junior constables, and women constables threatened to go on strike. The strike was avoided through negotiations. However, the rank-and-file did not accept the solution presented by the Board of the Association of Finnish Police.

Before and during their unionization, the police have generally remained satisfied with wages over which other groups of workers would have gone on strike. The Government, on the other hand, lulled the police force into moderation through, among other methods, groundless promises.

A feature that may be mentioned is that the police force is definitely more right-wing than the other professionally unionized government official groups. (Paukku 1978).

LEGAL ASPECTS OF THE STRIKE

Government officials received the right to go on strike in 1970. It has been said that the police received this right coupled with 'devout hopes that the police would, notwithstanding, never go on strike'.

The collective bargaining system for government officials sets very strict limits on strikes by such officials. In addition, the arrangements even make it difficult to go on a legal strike on allowable grounds.

The professional government officials' unions had given notice on the termination of the wage settlement relating to officials as of the last day of January, 1976. At the end of January, the Association of Finnish Police announced that it would go on strike on 13 February 1976. The threat was carried out. The employer – the State of Finland – took the matter to the

Labour Court even before the strike began. However, at that time the Labour Court in part refused to deal with the case and in part threw the case out of court.

The State Board on Government Labour Conflicts declared that the strike was a danger to society. On the second day of the strike, the Association of Finnish Trade Unions agreed to a new wage settlement. Having taken the matter to the Labour Court once more, the employer stated that the new wage settlement, having been signed by the central trade association, also obligated the members of the association, even though the Association of Finnish Police had not yet accepted the settlement. If this was the case, the police too were obliged to refrain from strikes aimed at the wage settlement. The employer demanded the highest possible renumerative fine. The Association of Finnish Police, on the other hand, stated that in accordance with the general principles on proxy, the Association had the right to withdraw from an agreement reached between central organizations.

On 25 February 1976 the Labour Court held that the strike was illegal, and sentenced the Association of Finnish Police to a 25,000 mark renumerative fine. At the same time it confirmed for the first time the legal rule that has been called the basis of collective agreements: once central organizations have agreed on a principal agreement, this obligates the member associations, even if these associations have followed the proper procedure in giving notice of the termination of a collective agreement for government officials.

Pressured by the decision of the Labour Court, and following lengthy negotiations chaired by the state arbitrator, the assembly of the Association of Finnish Police decided on 29 February to declare the strike at an end on 1 March.

THE ATTITUDE OF THE POPULATION TOWARDS THE STRIKE

In connection with a market research survey carried out in late February and early March by the Finnish Gallup, a sample of the population aged 15 years and over was asked their opinion about the police strike, the duties of the police, feelings of insecurity, and precautionary measures. The sample consisted of 516 people.

The sample was first asked: 'In your opinion, should strikes by the police be prohibited by law?' and 'Should strikes in general be prohibited by law?' Table 3 shows the answers.

A clear majority of the population was in favour of the right to strike in general, and also in favour of the right of policemen to go on strike. A somewhat larger part of the population was in favour of prohibiting strikes by the police by law than was in favour of prohibiting strikes in general by law. Those most in favour of an unlimited right to strike were office

Table 3. Opinions of the public on whether or not strikes, and especially strikes by the police, should be allowed.

	Men (N=243)	Women (N=237)
In favour of prohibiting strikes by the police (%)	28	34
In favour of prohibiting strikes in general (%)	19	27

employees, followed by workers. Farmers were least in favour of such a right. The attitude of the different groups was the same towards the right of the police to go on strike. The larger the income of the respondent's household, the more favourably he was disposed towards an unlimited right to strike and also towards the right of the police to strike.

In all, 20 % of those who did not accept the prohibiting of strikes by law were opposed to the right of the police to go on strike. These respondents were to be found among the workers and the employees to a greater degree than among the farmers. This attitude was most apparent among the low-income households in small cities in the countryside.

Various precautionary measures were adopted by the group that favoured prohibiting police strikes by law only to a slightly greater extent than among those who did not favour such a prohibition. Therefore, the negative attitude towards the right of the police to go on strike cannot be explained by a serious concern for personal safety. In the same way the respondents' opinions on whether the number of uniformed police should be increased, decreased, or kept the same did not appear to be related to any great extent to the opinions on the right of the police to strike.

About one half of the population believed that the present number of police was suitable. Very few were in favour of lessening the number of police. Even though similar figures are not available from earlier years, it would appear that earlier there was a more unanimous demand for more police. It may be that the strike lessened the force of these demands.

THE POLICE STRIKE AND THE MEDIA

The police strike was widely featured in the media. The articles in the press on the strike were analysed through content analysis in order to ascertain the picture that the press was giving of the strike and of occurrences during the strike.

In a previous study of the press coverage of a metal workers' strike, the conclusion was reached that the attitude of the press towards the strike was clearly connected with the party the newspaper represented: left-wing newspapers were in favour of the strike, right-wing papers were opposed (Salmela 1972). The attitude towards the police strike was not as clear-cut. On the basis of an analysis of a total of 859 articles taking a stand on the strike, it was noted that the difference in the attitude of the newspapers over time – before the strike, during the first and second week of the strike, and after the strike – was almost more marked than the differences between newspapers representing the different parties. In general, the press had a negative attitude towards the strike before it, but during the strike the attitude became more favourable. After the strike ended, the attitude became most negative. The Communist and the People's Democrat press took a more favourable attitude towards the strike all along the line than did the other newspapers. Almost one half of the articles on the strike consisted simply of press releases from the parties to the strike (47 %). The next largest groups consisted of coverage of the behaviour of the public during the strike (19 %) or of the activity of the leaders of the strike or the individuals on strike (19 %). In these figures, statements published in the press count as one unit each.

Of the views published in the press, over one half were press releases issued by the employers (59 %). The picture that the press gave of the behaviour of the public during the strike can be seen from Table 4.

Table 4. Statements in the press on the behaviour of the public, by period (%)

	Feb. 1– Feb. 12	Feb. 13– Feb. 20	Feb. 21– Feb. 29	March 1– March 15	Entire period
Citizens remained law-abiding	25	67	60	41	59
Victimization risk increased	50	25	23	14	25
Willingness to commit an offence increased .	25	3	17	45	16
Total %	100	100	100	100	100
(N)	(12)	(96)	(39)	(22)	(160)

Over one half (60 %) of the statements on the behaviour of the public was published during the first strike period. Especially then it was emphasized that the public had remained law-abiding; this theme was repeated in general during the strike. Before the strike began anxiety was expressed over the safety of the public should the police go on strike. This anxiety received less attention after the strike. At that time, more attention was given to the increased willingness to commit offences during the strike.

According to a study carried out at the University of Tampere, the strike increased the newsworthiness of crimes committed during the strike (Kallio 1977).

BEHAVIOURAL CHANGES DURING THE STRIKE

Changes in behaviour were studied on the level of attitudes, and simple empirical methods were used in order to uncover actual behavioural changes. A Gallup survey was used to study feelings of insecurity among the public.

As the official crime statistics became unreliable owing to the strike, we tried to gather information on events that were easily observable. Three different aspects in changes in behaviour were studied. First, we studied the precautions taken during the strike by the public and by certain crime-prone shops and offices (precautions taken by the public during the strike were studied through a Gallup survey, and precautions taken by apartment houses, cafés, goldsmiths, photography supply shops, grocery stores and liquor stores in the Helsinki area were studied through telephone interviews; questionnaires were also sent to private detective and private guard agencies). Precautions taken by some state officials were also studied to some extent.

Second, we studied changes in criminality and criminal behaviour. The study included not only homicides but assaults, which were studied on the basis of the data of a Helsinki clinic that takes care of patients who have injuries caused by violence. Damage to property in Helsinki was studied on the basis of damage caused to telephone booths and damage of premises guarded by private guard agencies. Property offences were studied: thefts and robberies of premises guarded by private guard agencies, as well as thefts and robberies directed at department stores and shops, were included. Changes in traffic behaviour were also studied: material on drunken driving was obtained through observation and through questionnaires administered in front of certain restaurants and at some petrol stations. Speeding and other minor traffic violations in Helsinki were studied: these data included information on violating the rules on using traffic lanes intended for public transport, as well as information on how often pedestrians crossed the street against a red light. Information on traffic accidents was also obtained.

Our third interest on the behavioural level was in changes in public disturbances. In Helsinki we observed public disturbances along one street, in the railway station and its immediate surroundings, and in some parks and squares. Through telephone interviews we obtained information on disturbances in apartment houses, cafés, and certain shops.

FEELINGS OF INSECURITY

During the strike we asked a sample of the population whether they felt insecure, and, if so, what were their reasons for this. Such subjective insecurity can also reflect actual objective insecurity. Changes in the feeling of insecurity are difficult to point out; there is only one previous study on the subject from the year 1972 (Suhonen & Suhonen 1972), and even this cannot be generalized to cover the entire population. In addition, the research methodology for the study in 1972 was different from the Gallup survey technique that we used. Even so, some conclusions may be drawn from the changes. Table 5 shows reasons for insecurity in our study and the 1972 study.

Table 5. Reasons for insecurity: the reason first mentioned by the respondent

Reason for insecurity	1976 Gallup survey		1972 study	
	rank order	(%)	rank order	(%)
Financial resources	1.5	(16)	1	(23)
Illness	3	(13)	2	(14)
Unemployment	1.5	(16)	3	(13)
War	8.5	(2)	4.5	(8)
Traffic	10.5	(1)	4	(11)
Human relations	6	(5)	5.5	(8)
Agriculture-related problems	12	(0)	8	(3)
Future of children	7	(3)	10.5	(1)
Violence	4	(11)	7	(4)
Pollution	10.5	(1)	9	(2)
Other social insecurity	5	(6)	10.5	(1)
Housing conditions	8.5	(2)	..	(..)

Financial resources, illness, and unemployment were the three major reasons in both studies for feelings of insecurity. Financial resources (lack of money, increase in prices, small income and pension, taxes) were mentioned by 24 % of those interviewed as causing them some insecurity. In the earlier study violence (being afraid to go out alone, drunkenness, crime) caused relatively little insecurity, while in our study violence was experienced as the fourth leading cause of insecurity, after matters concerning income, work, and health. The difference in the ranking of insecurity caused by violence may be due in part to the fact that the 1972 study was carried out in areas where crime is not regarded as such a big problem. The difference may also reflect an actual change in the feeling of insecurity.

Our study showed that people with higher education and a higher social status regarded violence and crime as more threatening than did the other social groups. Violence was also experienced as more threatening in the Helsinki area than in other towns and in the countryside. When all statements on feelings of insecurity are taken into consideration, violence ranked second in the Helsinki area as a reason for insecurity. A quarter of the people residing in the Helsinki metropolitan area felt insecure because of crime and violence.

There was no clear relationship between the attitudes on the number of policemen and the reasons for feelings of insecurity. Nor was violence as a reason for insecurity clearly connected with a wish for an increase in the number of policemen.

PRECAUTIONS TAKEN BY THE POPULATION

Feelings of insecurity may lead people to take some precautions. How much the police strike increased feelings of insecurity is not quite clear, but according to our findings there apparently was an increase. Four per cent of the population avoided going out alone. Of those belonging to this group, one-third were people living alone. Further, elderly women seem to have avoided going out alone to a greater extent than the population on the average. During the strike 0.8 % of the population had safety chains installed on their doors. This can be regarded as important, since these were permanent measures that were not removed after the strike: when the strike ended, households had a stronger defence against crime than before. In all, six out of the 420 interviewed had taken precautions either already some time before the strike or during the strike. Among those who felt most insecure (those avoiding going out alone), the same ratio was 4 to 27.

One measure of the precautions taken was the avoidance of walking alone on the streets. If people think that the presence of the police increases the safety on the streets, it is presumable that they avoid walking alone if the police are on strike. We observed the number of people walking alone along some streets in Helsinki and in two areas near the city centre. The control period was the period immediately following the strike. The results are shown in Table 6.

Table 6. The proportion of those walking alone during the strike and after the strike (%)

Period	Men			Women		
	under 20	20–40	over 40	under 20	20–40	over 40
During the strike	27	58	48	20	33	53
After the strike	33	40	57	24	36	61

The proportion of those walking alone among both men and women under 20 or over 40 was somewhat smaller during the strike than it was after the strike. A clear exception is men in the 20–40 age bracket: their proportion was larger during the strike than after. Our measures of the precautions taken by the population seem to have been too rough. It may be that insecurity is a stronger factor when one has to make decisions over the safety of others: fathers go on errands instead of their children, guests are advised to take a taxi rather than walk. Asking questions on these matters might have produced a clearer picture of the subjective insecurity during the strike.

PRECAUTIONS TAKEN BY SPECIAL GROUPS

In interviews of janitors representing our sample of 65 apartment houses in Helsinki, we found that 7 % of the apartment houses had taken some precautions because of the police strike. These precautions included: increased guarding of the apartment house, changing the closing time of the doors, and changing the locks. The taking of precautions in apartment houses was not a common phenomenon, but more precautions were to some extent taken in disturbance-prone city areas than in other areas.

It was rather common that certain shops and cafés took precautions. Table 7 describes this.

Table 7. Precautions by certain shops and cafés

	No precautions	Precautions	Examples of precautions
Cafés (N=32)	28	4	Doorman hired, restrictions on serving beer, extra locks
Appliance shops (N=22)	16	6	Extra locks, expensive articles removed from the window for the night, sales personnel given special instructions, iron bars installed in the windows, extra guarding
Camera and photo supply shops (N=20)	7	13	Extra insurance taken out, supply of weapons, extra locks, expensive articles removed, sales personnel given special instructions, lights on at night
Goldsmiths' shops (N=37)	24	13	Expensive articles removed from the window, more male sales personnel, extra guarding, sales personnel given special instructions
Grocery shops (N=27)	8	19	Sales personnel given special instructions, extra guarding, supply of weapons, money and expensive material removed to safer places, more care taken as to customers, security material was obtained

In shops that usually have small, tempting articles and where shoplifters are commonly found, precautions were taken because of the strike. Nearly one half of the shops that took precautions because of the strike retained these precautions permanently. Liquor stores were instructed to keep their lights on all night. Of a sample of 12 liquor stores in Helsinki, four mentioned that, in addition to this, they also took money to a safer place more often than usually. Six liquor stores mentioned that their guarding was more intensive during the peak hours, as they hired private guards.

Different department stores all over the country had taken precautions because of the strike: resources for guarding were increased (this is not based on a systematic sample). After the strike, the precautions returned to normal.

PRECAUTIONS BY PUBLIC OFFICIALS

The activity of different officials during the strike can be characterized as wary rather than as having involved any concrete measures. As far as is known, the army cut down on the number of leaves, but the Prison Administration did not cut down on the number of prison furloughs. Amusement licenses were refused to some extent during the strike.

The official releases on criminality during the strike were centralized and handled by the Ministry of the Interior. The Ministry strongly emphasized the peacefulness of the situation, and the degree to which matters were under control. This certainly prevented general restlessness, which would have furthered crime and public disturbances.

PRECAUTIONS TAKEN: SUMMARY

Precautions were taken during the police strike by the public and by officials. However, these precautionary measures were not harsh. Only a small proportion of the population did something to improve their safety during the strike, although they had been aware of the risks because of the interest that the mass media directed at the strike. A certain awareness of possible risks is in itself a form of precaution that can increase personal safety. We know that the victims of crimes are not 'selected' accidentally. Among those with a high risk of becoming victims of property crimes, precautions were rather common. Because of this, the precautions should be considered more important than their amount would indicate.

CHANGES IN CRIMINAL BEHAVIOUR

One point of departure in examining the effect of the strike on criminality is the theory of the deterrent effect of the system of punishments. In this theory, the risk of apprehension – and thus the activity of the police – has a central role: it is hypothesized that when other factors are constant, the willingness to commit offences increases or decreases along with the risk of apprehension.

Some prohibitions have been internalized to a great degree. The ordinary citizen is generally law-abiding through sheer force of habit. The behavioural norms and customs prevalent in the immediate surroundings prevent the

temptation to commit an offence. Because of these reasons, among others, we cannot suppose that even a radically diminished risk of apprehension would lead to an increase in all crimes and in all social groups. The immediate assumption was that the low risk of apprehension during the strike would affect criminality
– in social groups that often transgress the boundaries of legal behaviour
– to a greater degree the less other factors prevent crime,
– to a greater degree the more planning the crime involves, and
– to a greater degree the lower the subjective risk of apprehension and the greater the subjective change in this risk.

It is, of course, a question of the subjective risk of apprehension. It is clear that this may differ from the actual risk. In the following we describe how our data reveal the effect of the lowered risk of apprehension on criminality.

VIOLENT CRIMES

As serious crimes were investigated by the criminal investigation police, the police records on homicides are reliable for studying the number of homicides during the strike. There were a total of 16 homicides or attempted homicides in Finland during the strike, 50 % more than could be expected. The homicides resulted in the death of 12 persons (in one act the perpetrator killed himself). In two cases there were no bodily injuries. Towards the end of the strike the acts tended to be more violent than during the beginning of the strike. Most of the acts took place indoors, and only two happened out of doors: one on the street and one in a yard.

The police reports give the impression that the police were called in immediately after the crime had been discovered, and there seems to have been no uncertainty as to whether or not the police should be informed, regardless of the strike. Nevertheless, the number of homicides during the strike is high, but the relationship between the police strike and the number of homicides is not clear on the basis of the data.

Table 8. The daily mean of patients entering a Helsinki clinic because of violent injuries

	Jan. 2–31*	Feb. 1–12	Feb. 13–29	March 1–31
Monday	3.3	2.5	6.0	3.8
Tuesday	5.0	4.5	8.5	4.0
Wednesday	3.5	4.5	3.5	5.6
Thursday	4.0	5.5	6.5	4.5
Friday	10.0	3.0	9.0	5.3
Saturday	12.4	10.0	12.0	14.3
Sunday	7.5	9.0	10.0	6.3

* New Year's Day is not included, owing to its exceptional features.

Our data on assaults were taken from the records of patients taken to a clinic in Helsinki because of injuries resulting from violent acts. These data describe changes in assaults more reliably than the police statistics. Table 8 presents the daily mean of patients in this clinic in January, February, and March 1976.

The daily mean of patients is generally higher during the strike than during the control periods. In the mean, there were 22 % more assaults during the strike than during the other periods. Especially violence out of doors increased. Regardless of whether we compare assaults during the strike with the surrounding time periods or with the corresponding period in 1975, there were more patients than usual at the clinic during the strike.

PROPERTY OFFENCES AND VANDALISM

According to our study, appliance shops and camera shops were not subjected to larcenies either during the strike or during a control period immediately following the strike. Larcenies had taken place in two goldsmiths' shops out of the 37 shops questioned; these took place after the strike. However, there had been larcenies in two out of three food shops after the strike, and in somewhat more during the strike itself. The differences between the shops are natural, as in food shops and especially in self-service shops articles are more easily obtainable than in other shops. In general, larcenies did not take place any more than usual during the strike, with the exception of the food shops.

Robberies of shops were more common during the strike than afterwards. Every tenth shop had been subjected to a robbery or an attempted robbery during the police strike. During the control period following the strike two shops had been robbed, while attempts were made in three. Thus, there were 50 % more robberies of shops during the strike than afterwards.

In the premises guarded by private guards robberies were somewhat more common during the strike than during the control period before and after the strike. The average number of robberies per day in these premises was 1.3 before the strike, 1.8 during, and 0.5 after the strike.

Thefts from telephone booths in Helsinki were more frequent during the strike, and vandalism of these booths was 50 % more common during the strike than either before or after. Acts of booth vandalism averaged 22.0 per week in January, 15.0 per week in February before the strike, 32.5 per week during the strike in February, and 23.2 in March.

Damage done to apartment houses was a more frequent occurrence during the strike than after, and damage to premises guarded by private guards was more frequent during the strike than either before or after.

The data on property crimes were limited. Each small datum alone does not describe changes during the strike, but when examined together the data support the conclusion that property offences and vandalism increased during the strike.

TRAFFIC OFFENCES

The police strike had the clearest effect on traffic control. Police not only control traffic, they also guide traffic. These functions were affected by the strike. In Helsinki, municipal officials take care of the supervision of parking, and so this function continued normally during the strike. The importance of the police in causing a decrease in traffic crimes or accidents has been studied by increasing the control of traffic. The number of policemen in traffic control duties has been doubled or tripled, and the effect on accidents and crimes has been studied. Various studies appear to prove that improved police control decreases the number of traffic offences and accidents. On the other hand, there have been indications that these effects are only marginal. The visibility of police in traffic calms traffic, but its effect is not permanent. Should the police, however, control traffic through cautions or fines, the effect on drivers and traffic is more permanent (e.g. Syvänen 1969 and the studies mentioned therein). During the police strike, drivers had good reason to believe that the police would be absent from traffic control, and thus the risk of apprehension was minimal. The situation was an excellent one in which to study the effects of such a non-existent risk.

On the basis of the data on blood alcohol tests made on suspected drunken drivers, we found that drunken driving was no more common during the strike than during control periods before and after the strike. However, those who drove under the influence of alcohol tended to have more alcohol in their blood than was the case during the control periods.

Drunken driving during the strike was also studied on the basis of data that were not dependent on the activity of officials. We studied persons who entered restaurants after having parked their car in front of one of three restaurants. Before leaving the restaurant with their car, they were handed a card asking whether or not they had drunk alcohol. Observations on their behaviour were also made. Seven out of ten drivers before and after the strike stated that they had not drunk any alcohol. The number of those who refused to answer was somewhat larger after the strike than during it. The number who admitted having drunk some alcohol (usually one drink) was somewhat larger during the strike than afterwards. According to more or less unsystematic observations of the patrons of restaurants, drivers were more drunk during the strike than after, but the number of sober drivers was the same both during and after the strike.

We handed questionnaires to drivers coming to 12 different petrol stations in Helsinki during and after the strike. We asked whether the drivers had driven their car under the influence of alcohol during the preceding weekend. The response is described in Table 9.

Table 9. Self-reported drunken driving

| | Question: 'Did you drive the car under the influence of alcohol during the preceding weekend?' | |
	During the strike (N=955) %	After the strike (N=891) %
Yes	3.4	3.9
No	92.7	92.4
Refused to answer or no answer	3.9	3.7
Total %	100.0	100.0

Both our restaurant data and the petrol station data are somewhat unreliable. However, the proportion of 'yes'-answers is nearly the same as the proportion that one would get on the basis of data on drunken driving tests administered at police roadblocks.

The effects of the police strike on other traffic behaviour were clear: the strike led to an increase in speeds and also in speeding violations (Summala & Roine 1976). Private cars used the traffic lanes reserved for public transport to a greater degree during the strike than afterwards. However, the laxness in traffic discipline did not worsen traffic safety: accidents resulting in death did not increase in number. Pedestrians did not cross against a red light more often during the strike than afterwards; however, this is a violation that the police seldom control.

The accidents that the Helsinki public transport vehicles were involved in were investigated separately. Their number did not increase because of the strike. A clear change in traffic discipline should be noticeable in traffic accidents. The effects of the strike on traffic behaviour can also be explained by the drivers taking greater precautions when driving, as they possibly did not trust other drivers, or they intentionally avoided situations where they would have to take risks. Also, the period was too short for permanent changes in traffic behaviour. In sum, traffic safety did not decrease during the strike, nor did drunken driving increase, although drunken drivers had a greater amount of alcohol in their blood. Violations of the speed limits and other traffic offences increased clearly during the strike.

PUBLIC DISTURBANCES

One of the functions of the police is to maintain order. Only part of the behaviour that is considered disturbing is composed of criminal acts. For example drinking alcohol in public places is more or less regarded as a public disturbance or as unseemly behaviour rather than as criminal. City ordinances set out certain acts as public disturbances: the most commonly fined acts are drinking alcohol in public or semi-public places (such as hallways) and urinating in public. The nature of the disorder is very much dependent on whose point of view defines what is order and what is not. What is disturbing to the police is not necessarily disturbing to the ordinary 'man in the street'. The same mode of behaviour may at times be disturbing and at other times not disturbing, depending on the situation or even on the person. The measurement of disturbances and their changes, independent of police activity, is problematic. In our study, we have concentrated on drunkenness and on some minor infractions of municipal ordinances and alcohol legislation. We also studied the formation of groups in public places.

A group of people is not in itself a public disturbance, but it can easily be considered as such (as this is a rather strange phenomen in Finnish society). Especially if the group is composed of young people or alcoholics, the police is apt to break up the group. The police strike took place at a time when there were no special places for disturbances or no special forms of groups. In Helsinki only the railway station and its immediate neighbourhood had a reputation of harbouring people who are inclined to disturb public order.

During the strike, the number of drunks taken into police custody decreased. The police jails were nearly empty. About 150 drunks who would normally be found in jail on Saturday nights were out on the streets of Helsinki.

Twelve parks and squares near liquor stores in Helsinki were observed (we took photographs in order to improve our observations). The median of members in groups during the strike was 27.5 and after the strike 20.5 The groups were somewhat larger during the strike than after it. The drinking of alcohol was more open in the parks during the strike than after it. According to observations made along one street in Helsinki known to be a gathering place for idlers and 'vagrants', the state of order in the street did not seem to worsen during the strike.

The railway station in Helsinki and the nearby subterranean shopping area are places likely to become centres of disturbances. We observed these premises for a 30-day period during and after the strike. One purpose was to study the groups and gangs in this area. A group of young people can threaten public order through its form, even though no single person acts in a disturbing manner. In certain places the fact that a group of people merely hangs around creates unpredictable situations. Table 10 describes the results of studying the size of groups on 10 days during the strike and after it.

Table 10. The size of groups in the area of the Helsinki railway station

Size of group	Subterranean shopping area		Railway station	
	during the strike	after the strike	during the strike	after the strike
Over 10 members ..	1	3	2	3
7–9 members	5	1	4– 5	1– 3
4–6 members	26–30	9	18–21	29–30
2–3 members	32–38	12	37–51	28

The groups tended to be larger during the strike than after it. The larger the group, the more likely its members were to be young people (13–17 years old). These groups were mainly responsible for the damage to property in the subterranean shopping area (wall panels torn down, windows broken, and so on). The railway station was guarded during the strike by private guards, whose work was effective and at times even violent. There were on an average, 15.0 guards each evening during the strike and 6.2 guards (including policemen) after the strike. The guards mainly pushed those who were hanging around in the station out of doors, and so the groups kept moving in and out of the station. We observed an average of 10.0 drunks per evening during the strike and 12.3 after the strike. The station was kept 'tidy' during the strike; however, drinking was somewhat more evident in the tunnel during the strike than it was afterwards.

One indirect measure of the illegal sale of alcohol that we used was the number of people standing on the steps leading to the station itself. Of course, this is a rough measure, but the steps are known as an area of illicit sale of alcohol, and the observers came across such situations personally a few times. The number of people standing on these steps at various times during the evening was:

	9:30 pm	10:30 pm	11 pm
during the strike	7.6	8.0	8.4
after the strike	3.6	3.1	2.4

During the strike, the number of people on the steps increased as the evening wore on; after the strike, the trend was the opposite. Our data support the conclusion that the selling of alcohol was livelier and more open during the strike than it was afterwards.

At the bus station two blocks away from the railway station, the guarding was more effective during the strike than after it, and as a result there were fewer drunks to be seen than afterwards.

SUMMARY AND CONCLUSIONS

Our study as a whole supports the general impression that public order remained fairly good, and criminals did not go on a spree. On the other hand, certain 'strategic' measurements demonstrated that the police strike led to an increase in violent crimes, property offences, and traffic offences, and in public disturbances. The changes were not dramatic but they were evident.

Various precautions may have prevented some of the effects of the strike.

The effects of the strike differed from those of some well-known and studied strikes, such as those in Boston and Liverpool in 1919, Montreal in 1969, and Baltimore in 1974 (see e.g. Russel 1977 and Sellwood 1978). With some exaggeration, it can be said that while experts spent their time counting the economic and other losses of the short-term terror brought on by these strikes, Finnish experts calculated the savings in police salaries during the Finnish police strike. The strike was a very calm one, even though there was an increase in crime.

The following reasons can be given for the calmness:
- as a whole, the social situation in Finland at the time can be regarded as extremely stable;
- Finland appears to lack effective organized criminality that could have taken advantage of the extraordinary strike situation, just as it appears to lack disturbance-prone population groups or a tradition of restlessness;
- the cold weather during the strike did not favour disturbances out of doors, and possibly even the winter Olympics that took place at the start of the strike may have had an even greater effect on the leisure-time activity of people, and thus also of disturbance-prone people, than the police ever could.

In general, it is apparent that the strikes mentioned above that have led to 'anarchy' are used as arguments to prevent the unionization of the police and the granting of strike privileges. The many apparently calm police strikes are forgotten (Reiner 1978). The Finnish police strike can scarcely be regarded as having led to exceptional results.

The concrete outcome of the strike from the point of view of the police was slight. However, the police themselves believe that the strike was beneficial: it has been revealed as a weapon, and quite soon promises were made that it would be used again. The willingness of the police to go on strike, as demonstrated in many countries during the 1960s and the 1970s, reveals the radicalization of the police (see Robinson 1978). However, it does not appear that the strike has led to any great solidarity of the police towards the strikes of other professional groups: soon after the police strike, the police were again protecting strike-breakers during the foodstuff workers' strike.

The strike study itself is an experiment in measuring the significance of the police in preventing crime and maintaining order, utilizing sources of information independent of the police.

NOTE

¹ In addition to the authors of this article, Kauko Aromaa, Matti Joutsen, Jukka
Kekkonen, Seppo Leppä, Martti Mäki, Kevät Nousiainen and Reino Sirén have
participated in the writing of the report. All of the above have in one way or another
participated in the planning of the study, the gathering and processing of the data and
in the writing of the final report.

REFERENCES

KALLIO, HEIDI: Poliisiuutisten määrän muuttuminen tamperelaisissa päivälehdissä poliisilakon aikana 13.–19.2 1976 (Changes in the amount of crime news in the press
published in Tampere during the police strike 13.–29. February 1976). Tutkielma
sanomalehtiopissa. Tampereen yliopisto 1977.
Komiteanmietintö 1976: 70. Yksityisetsivä- ja vartioimisliiketoimikunnan mietintö
(Report of the state committee on private detective and guard agencies). Helsinki
1976.
PAUKKU, OSSI: VTY:n järjestötutkimus (An organization study on the Union of Officials
and Public Sector Workers). Helsinki 1978.
REINER, ROBERT: Striking facts. New Society, Vol. 44. N:o 818 (1978).
ROBINSON, C. D.: The deradicalization of the policeman: a historical analysis. Crime
and Delinquency 2/1978.
RUOTSALAINEN, VEIKKO: Suomen Poliisien Liitto ry 1923–1973 (The Association of
Finnish Police 1923–1973). Hämeenlinna 1973.
RUSSEL, FRANCIS: A City in Terror. The 1919 Boston Police Strike. Westford 1977.
SALMELA, MARJA: Vuoden 1971 metallilakko ja lehdistö (The metal workers' strike in
1971 and the press). Pro gradu-tutkielma Helsingin yliopiston valtiotieteellisessä
tiedekunnassa 1972.
SELLWOOD, A.V.: Police Strike 1919. London 1978.
SUHONEN, PERTTI and SUHONEN, LIISA: Turvattomia suomalaisia. Tutkimus turvatto-
muuden kokemisesta (Insecure Finns. A study on feelings of insecurity). Rauhan-
ja konfliktintutkimuslaitos. Tutkimuksia n:o 4/1973.
SUMMALA, HEIKKI & ROINE, MATTI: Liikenteen valvonnan poikkeustilanne: Ajoneuvo-
jen nopeudet poliisilakon aikana (An exceptional situation in traffic control: speeding
during the police strike). Tie- ja vesirakennushallitus. Helsinki 1976.
SYVÄNEN, MATTI: Näkyvän valvonnan vaikutus kuljettajien ajotapaan (The effect of the
visible control on the way of driving). Tampereen yliopiston psykologian laitoksen
tutkimuksia n:o 31/1969. Tampere 1969.
TAKALA, HANNU (ed.): Poliisilakko (The Police Strike): Oikeuspoliittisen tutkimuslai-
toksen julkaisuja 30. Helsinki 1979.
TANDEM Tasa-arvon ja demokratian tutkimus: Demokratian rajat ja rakenteet. Tutkimus suomalaisesta hallitsemistavasta ja sen taloudellisesta perustasta (The limits and
structures of democracy. A study on the Finnish way of ruling and its economic
base). Juva 1977.
TÖRNUDD, PATRIK: Crime Trends in Finland 1950–1977. Research Institute of Legal
Policy. Publication 29. Helsinki 1978.

Police Investigations and the Personal Integrity of the Suspect in Scandinavia

BY *ANDERS BRATHOLM*

I. THE LEGAL RIGHTS OF THE INDIVIDUAL AND EFFECTIVENESS

In many areas conflicts prevail between a proper regard for the legal rights of the individual and the demand for effectiveness. Perhaps this conflict is especially manifest in the work done by the police to clear up criminal acts. If the police were not bound to observe various regulations protecting the legal rights of the individual, the possibility of solving cases would probably be much better than in the present situation. Nevertheless, in most countries a general opinion exists to the effect that concern for individual rights must carry a lot of weight in the work done by the police. An investigation must not be carried out in a manner that violates the legal rights of the individual.

An important aspect of individual rights is the need for protection against violations of personal integrity. In their work the police can, for instance, harm the personal integrity of the victim or the witnesses. But violations against the integrity of the suspect are the greatest danger, since such infringements can provide particularly good opportunities for solving the case.

The subject matter of this thesis is the protection of the integrity of the suspect during police investigations.

II. ARGUMENTS FOR THE PROTECTION OF THE PERSONAL INTEGRITY OF THE SUSPECT

Limitations

Various considerations lie behind the protection of the suspect's integrity. We can divide these into six categories.

1) The suspect may be innocent. Thus the methods of investigation must not be more extreme than is defensible vis-à-vis suspects who are in fact innocent.

2) Some investigation methods cannot be defended, since they may lead to faulty information, and thereby enhance the risk of incorrect court judgements. For example, torture may easily lead to incorrect confessions. (But there are also other, and more important, objections to torture; see below.)

8. Policing Scandinavia

3) A third objection to investigation methods that are an affront to personal integrity is the harm they do to public confidence in the administration of criminal justice. Public opinion does not accept that all methods are admissible in order to clear up a criminal case. If the methods used offend the common sense of justice, people might become sympathetic to the delinquent. This sentiment might in turn result in a greater reluctance on the part of the public to report criminal acts to the police or to be witnesses in such cases; there will be more unwarranted acquittals and so on.

4) A fourth objection is that the use of investigation methods that are an affront to personal integrity brutalizes the users of these means. This impact might create the atmosphere of a police-state, and in the long run contribute to undermining democracy and human rights in general.

5) Without regard to whether the effects are assumed to be good or bad for society, a fifth objection is the immorality inherent in treating a human being in a degrading or personally insulting manner. This view originates in the belief that the individual – including the criminal – has certain inviolable human rights.

6) Finally, against the use of investigation methods that are an affront to personal integrity it can be said that they infringe international conventions which the Nordic countries, among others, are bound to observe: foremost the U.N.'s declaration on human rights and the European declaration on human rights. But in turn, these conventions rest on considerations mentioned under points 1–5.

So far the inquiry is perhaps not very problematic. Difficulties only arise when one asks *which* methods of investigation are, or ought to be, regarded as violating personal integrity.

A historical retrospective glance shows that opinion on permissible investigation methods has altered greatly. By and large the development has moved in a humanizing direction; today far more consideration is paid to the integrity of the suspect than in the past. For example, torture, which for long was an accepted method of investigation, has been banished in most countries. However, that does not mean that one has in practice succeeded in eliminating this method. Brutal methods of investigation are still used in several countries, but now more secretly. Amnesty International, among others, has convincingly documented such usage.

In some areas it is not possible to make a historical comparison, because the process of technological development has given us a number of new investigation methods. Particularly in these new areas doubts prevail concerning what ought to be allowed. Technical progress in some fields is so rapid that legislation and legal theory experience difficulties in keeping up with the new developments.

Even though doubts arise regarding the acceptability of an investigation method, these doubts should not be exaggerated. The starting point is the fact that there must be authorization in the written law permitting one to encroach upon the individual. Norwegian law entails a rather strict principle of legality, not least with respect to the activity of the police. However, here as in many other areas a certain friction prevails between 'the law in the books and the law in action'.

The following account will to some extent also cover legal conditions in Denmark and Sweden in addition to Norway. In the pertinent area there are great judicial similarities between the three countries, but interesting differences as well.

III. CORPORAL ENCROACHMENTS ON PERSONAL INTEGRITY

One can distinguish between external and internal corporal encroachments against a suspect. The internal ones are the most extreme from the point of view of personal integrity, since they will normally be experienced as more indiscreet. Often they also entail a greater amount of pain or discomfort.

1. On external encroachments (examinations)

The Nordic laws on criminal procedure contain provisions which stipulate that an individual who is suspected of a crime that carries a certain minimum penalty can, among other things, be bodily searched if there are reasons to believe that this search will bring about, e.g. the discovery of evidence against him.

Primarily the provisions on body search aim at acquiring material things which the suspect carries, such as clothing with traces of blood, stolen goods, weapons, and so on. But these regulations are also applicable in order to find traces or marks on the body of the suspect which are related to the crime, e.g. scratches in connection with the suspicion of rape.

Taking the suspect's fingerprints is a form of external examination that is allowed upon suspicion. But according to Norwegian law this suspicion must concern an act which carries a stricter penalty than a fine (the law on criminal procedure *(strpl.)* § 227 a). Similar limitations exist in the other Nordic countries as well.

Because of the requirement of suspicion of a criminal act of a certain seriousness, the police cannot take fingerprints at random – indiscriminately, in the hope of thereby finding the guilty person. But if the individual voluntarily submits to fingerprinting, this must be legally acceptable. However, what if an individual, when asked, refuses? Is it then possible to conclude that his refusal now makes him a suspect and that the law's requirement of suspicion is thus met? If so, in that case the police can take fingerprints at random when it is important to clear up a crime. A whole neighbourhood, for instance, may be asked to furnish fingerprints, and if a few refuse a suspicion thereby arises which may provide a basis for enforcing the taking of fingerprints. Such an approach can probably not be endorsed. A person who refuses cannot thereby be said to be legitimately suspected of being guilty. If so, additional elements must be available that make it possible to say that such a suspicion is present.

According to Swedish law, suspicion is not necessary in order to take fingerprints (or photographs).

According to further rules in the various countries' laws, photographs of a suspect can also be taken, and the pictures can be kept for a shorter or longer period. If a criminal case has ended without establishing the guilt of the accused, the person concerned can, according to Norwegian law, demand that his fingerprints and photographs be destroyed.

It may very well be maintained that all of these *external* examinations of a suspect – including taking his fingerprints or photograph – do not go beyond such conditions as he should reasonably endure, once he is suspected of more than a totally petty criminal act. Examinations of this nature normally do not entail either pain or discomfort, beyond the uneasiness that the examination might result in evidence against him. In other words, such encroachments cannot naturally be regarded as violations against the individual or his integrity.

The Norwegian law on criminal procedure does not give distinct legal authority to the effect that a person charged with an offence must partake in external examinations or tests other than the ones included in the provisions on searching and fingerprinting. What is the situation with respect to, e.g., footprints, tooth-impressions, and similar external examinations which aim at acquiring evidence against suspects?

Since such examinations can hardly be said to be much more radical than those positively admitted, by analogy one may conclude that there is power to carry them out. Neither in Denmark does there exist clear authorization for such examinations, but it is nonetheless assumed that they are allowed. The solution is probably the same in Sweden.

2. On internal encroachments

Encroachments on the body of the suspect can probably be undertaken only when there is distinct legal authority. This assumption must follow from the kind of principle of legality on which the public law in the Nordic countries is founded. It can be said that the concern here is with such extreme encroachments that the presumption is that the police are prevented from making such examinations without the existence of an explicit legal rule.

In one area of police examinations there exists in all the Nordic countries legal authority for undertaking an encroachment on the suspect's body in order to obtain evidence against him: blood samples can be taken from a person who is suspected of having driven a motor vehicle, an aircraft, etc.

while intoxicated, or from someone who has violated the rule on obligatory abstinence. The latter provision concerns professional drivers and airmen, among others. At present in Norway no authorization exists for taking blood samples in the case of suspicion of *other* criminal acts. In Sweden, however, there is a general permission to take a blood sample from anyone who is suspected of having committed a criminal act that can lead to imprisonment.

In Norway authorization is lacking for undertaking other encroachments on the suspect's body than a blood sample in the above-mentioned cases. For example, a woman suspected of infanticide does not need to endure a gynaecological examination. Before World War II – in 1936 – the Norwegian Supreme Court had to deal with the question whether a gynaecological examination was permissible in a suspected case of illegal abortion. The court decided that such an examination could not be carried out without the woman's consent *(Norsk Retstidende (Rt.),* 1936, p. 204). An examination of the contents of a suspect's stomach must probably be similarly viewed.

According to Swedish law, corporal inspection can be undertaken of a person suspected of a criminal act which can entail imprisonment. At the corporal inspection examinations that can take place without appreciable harm may be carried out. For example, one may examine the suspect for hidden jewels or for traces of venereal disease.

In Norway it has been discussed whether one ought not to have further access than is the case today to undertaking encroachments on the body of the suspect. A committee, which some years ago presented a proposal for a new Norwegian law on criminal procedure, arrived at the conclusion that a suspect ought not to be able to oppose corporal inspections that go beyond the external examination of the body. According to the committee report: 'It is not very reasonable that a person who is charged with a criminal act – perhaps of a more serious nature – shall be able to prevent the solution of the case by opposing a bodily examination that usually can take place without inconvenience or discomfort. To take a blood sample or an X-ray, or to perform a common medical examination of the individual charged is a minor encroachment in comparison to other procedures which he must endure for the case to be cleared up, e.g., pre-trial detention or placement in a psychiatric hospital' (p. 223). The committee refers to the fact that several new laws contain authorization for bodily examinations, such as the Swedish law on criminal procedure.

As a result the committee proposed a provision that legally sanctions both external and internal bodily examinations of the suspect when the act committed can, according to the law, lead to deprivation of liberty, provided that the examination does not represent a disproportionate encroachment or involve danger or significant pain.

The reservation with regard to danger means that one cannot take a blood sample from a haemophiliac, for example. It follows from the proposal that an examination can cause pain as long as the pain is not significant. Accordingly, one would presume that this provision authorizes, e.g., forcible pumping of the stomach of a suspect. This measure can be painful, or at least very unpleasant, but normally it does not cause significant pain. Furthermore, there is an important restriction in the denial of a *disproportionate* encroachment. Accordingly, the encroachment must be reasonably proportionate to the suspicion at hand. For example, according to the proposal there is hardly permission to undertake examinations of the stomach or rectum in the case of suspicion of minor offences. (Since the writing of the above, this law proposition has been adopted by Parliament.)

IV. THE USE OF TECHNICAL, CHEMICAL OR SIMILAR AIDS IN ORDER TO OBTAIN THE TRUTH FROM THE SUSPECT

The oldest method to make a refractory suspect tell the truth is torture. (As mentioned, torture is still used in many countries, especially during political cases in states subject to a dictatorship.)

In the Nordic countries torture was employed as late as the 17th and 18th centuries. In Norway it was forbidden by the constitutional law *(grl.)* of 1814, § 96. There it states that 'painful Interrogations' must not take place. The other Nordic countries have similar prohibitions.

The primary reason for banning torture is the unwillingness to utilize such an inhumane investigation method in order to have the case cleared up. It is important to clear up crimes, especially serious ones, but not at any cost. Torture, in addition, affects the users of the method in a brutalizing way and, furthermore, it can easily lead to wrong confessions.

A few methods of interrogation lie on the borderline of what is permissible, or according to the actual situation even cross the boundary, e.g., particularly long interrogations, interrogations at night, or interrogations without giving the examined individual a reasonable amount of food, liquid, breaks, and so on.

From time to time charges are directed against the police for using improper interrogation methods, but as a rule such charges are met with counter-charges, and it is seldom possible to fully elucidate what has happened. Much can be said for allowing the person under questioning to demand the presence of a witness during the interrogation. According to Swedish law, a 'trust-worthy witness' shall, if possible, be present at the police hearing. Commonly a policeman is used. The argument for this practice is generally the very difficulty in finding other persons who are willing to spend time at these often long and tedious hearings. That objection is hardly decisive. It could be made a citizen's duty to be a police witness in the same way as an individual is obliged to serve as a court witness. Since 1957 such an arrangement has been introduced in Gothenburg, Sweden, i.e. a system that utilizes paid examination witnesses, who serve at the police station during interrogations in criminal cases. The question whether this arrangement shall be introduced elsewhere is now under deliberation in Sweden.

An individual who as a suspect (or a witness) is questioned by the police cannot demand to be accompanied by a lawyer. Exceptions apply if he is *charged,* that is, if the investigation is directed against him (cf. *strpl.* § 97). The person who is charged, e.g., because he is arrested, can require to have a lawyer present during all stages of the investigation (*strpl.* § 99). In practice it happens that some time passes before a charged and arrested person's wishes to contact a defence lawyer are met. For the police to cause such a delay is unlawful.

The question of the suitability of an applied examination method is seldom brought to court. But there is one such instance (*Rt.,* 1948, pp. 46). The case involved some men who were charged with co-operation with the Germans during the occupation. They were also charged with having liquidated a person who worked for the Norwegian home-front. In order to possibly obtain a confession, the police decided to bring the persons charged one by one nightly to the place where it was thought the liquidation had occurred, and under conditions similar to the ones prevailing during the night of the liquidation. This approach resulted in confessions. At the hearing of the appeal, the Supreme Court sharply rejected the approach. It was said that the action gave an impression of an administration of criminal justice not in accordance with Norwegian law, and which could not be tolerated. There was, however, no question of setting aside the evidence obtained in this illegal manner, and the penal convictions were upheld. Besides, other evidence against the persons charged was available, whereby the correctness of the judgement did not stand or fall with the acceptance of the evidence obtained through the use of unlawful means.

In some countries the police use technical or chemical aids which are particularly suited to getting a truthful explanation, or for disclosing lies during the investigation.

The so-called lie-detector is most widespread. It is an instrument with some wires connected to the legs, arms etc. of the person who is under questioning. In this way one can with help of the instrument measure such a person's blood pressure, breathing, etc. during the interrogation. One can by studying these reactions estimate whether the person being questioned is telling the truth or lying when he answers the various questions.

The effectivity of the lie-detector is somewhat disputed. To some degree the effectivity depends on the personality of the individual being questioned and – not least – on the examiner's expertise in applying the detector. It has been maintained that the reliability of the lie-detector is over 90 per cent when used by qualified staff.

Today the lie-detector is utilized in police hearings in countries like USA,

Japan, and Israel. The results from these examinations cannot be presented as evidence in a possible criminal case against the person charged. The lie-detector is only used as an internal police aid. The argument is partly that the lie-detector is not sufficiently reliable, and partly that the use of such material in a criminal case would go against the fundamental rights of the accused. In a decision by the Supreme Court of Nebraska (USA) the results from a lie-detector were rejected on the ground that the instrument could not be cross-examined! This decision must be seen against the background of the great weight placed on cross-examinations of witnesses, experts, and others in the American trial (see further Bratholm, 'The Right to Lie' in *Legal Essays: A Tribute to Frede Castberg,* Oslo, 1963, pp. 531–46).

It must be assumed that in the Nordic countries the lie-detector cannot be utilized as an investigation method. This tool deviates too much from common methods, and such large uncertainties are connected to its usage that it ought not to be used except on distinct legal authority. Such authorization does not exist in the Nordic countries.

The solution must be the same regarding the use of the so-called truth-serum (narcosis-analysis) in the investigation. (Truth-serum is a medical drug which lends itself to loosening the tongue of the individual being questioned.) Nor can hypnosis be used.

Several years ago in some investigations in Sweden, the truth-serum was utilized with the consent of the suspect or on his request, because he in this manner wanted to prove his innocence.

The former Swedish Attorney General, Maths Heuman, discusses in an article *(Svensk Juristtidning,* 1955, p. 255) the legitimacy of the use of the truth-serum in investigations. He concludes that anaesthethic or intoxicating means ought not to be used in the questioning of a person charged with an offence, not even with his consent. To make exceptions in the latter instance can in practice easily entail an illusionary voluntariness. A refusal to consent could easily produce a stronger suspicion, and this knowledge might pressure the person charged into agreeing to the test.

Some countries explicitly prohibit the use of such investigation methods as are here referred to. Against the background of the experiences during the last world war, West Germany has adopted a ban against the use of the truth-serum, the lie-detector, and similar investigation methods which can influence the suspect's faculties of recollection and appraisement. If such a method has notwithstanding been used, the evidence cannot be presented in court. That rule applies even when the suspect himself asks for its presentation (see *Strafprozessordnung* § 136 a).

V. SECRET MONITORING BY THE USE OF TECHNICAL AIDS

In all the Nordic countries the police have a limited power to intercept telephone conversations. In Norway this permission applies to cases concerning the security of the state and cases of illegal dealing in narcotics. In the other Nordic countries interception can also take place on suspicion of some other serious crimes.

The power to monitor telephone conversations is in all the Nordic countries surrounded by strict formal rules. For example, the court's permission must normally be obtained in advance.

The Norwegian law committee on criminal procedure has proposed a rather substantial extension of the power to intercept telephone conversations in Norway. When the proposal was presented, authorization to intercept in drug cases was lacking, but such legal authority was introduced in 1977.

Regarding the power to secretly monitor personal conversations by the help of technical means other than telephone interceptions, the legal conditions differ somewhat in the Nordic countries.

Several technical methods are available for this purpose, but the most common one is the use of a secret tape-recorder or other concealed listening devices.

In Denmark authority exists to secretly utilize listening devices in investigations. Such eavesdropping can occur to the same extent as the use of telephone interceptions. The court's ruling is always required before the monitoring can take place.

The Norwegian criminal provision covering the secret use of tape-recorders and similar technical aids (*strl.* § 145 a) does not make any exemption for the police. But one can hardly totally exclude the possibility that the police's use of secret tape-recordings, though formally against the rules of § 145 a, might in certain circumstances be accepted as legitimate, at least in the case of preventing serious crimes. The judicial argument will in that case be that secret monitoring in such instances is not contrary to law (illegal) (cf. § 47 on necessity in the Norwegian penal code). Illegality, as is known, is a general requirement for an act to be punishable.

In Sweden there is a statutory enactment which, along the same lines as the Norwegian penal order, prohibits secret monitoring by tape-recording and the like. This prohibition also encompasses police investigations (see *Sveriges offentliga utredningar* (SOU), 1970:47, Protection against monitoring, pp. 96–7). The reason for this provision is that the possible advantage attained through the use of such investigation methods does not compensate for the threat such methods constitute to the individual's integrity. The Swedish national police administration has expressed the view that in this area there is no desire for rules exempting the police, since thereby the public's confidence in the police might be weakened.

Even if a monitoring method is not in direct conflict with any statutory enactment, nonetheless, it might according to circumstances be regarded as illegitimate. An example from Norwegian practice will be mentioned.

For the purpose of obtaining evidence, the police in a small town had hidden a microphone in a room where the person charged was to have a conversation with a partner, also charged, who had confessed his participation in the crime in question – a theft. The microphone was attached to a tape-recorder in another room. According to the plan the one who had confessed was to get the other person to expose himself in the course of the conversation. As a precaution, a policeman was also placed in a listening position in an adjacent room. In this case the monitoring with the help of a tape-recorder did not infringe § 145 a of the penal code, since one of the participants in the monitored conversation had given his *consent*.

By chance the accused discovered the arrangement, and the police did not get the confession they had hoped for. When the case came to the attention of the Attorney General, he clearly disapproved of this investigation method. He expressed the opinion that even though the method was not explicitly forbidden, nevertheless, it conflicted with the prerequisites of the law on criminal procedure and could not be permitted.

In this instance the Attorney General probably reacted to the fact that the police had led the person charged into a trap. But if the charge had involved a more serious act, e.g., manslaughter, there is some question as to whether this investigation method might not have been accepted.

VI. SECRET SURVEILLANCE BY THE USE OF TECHNICAL (VISUAL) AIDS

To observe a suspect through shadowing and the like is one of the police's oldest working methods, and if it is used with discretion and sense, decisive objections can hardly be raised against these means. If the method is utilized in a gravely undue manner, it could according to circumstances constitute a ruthless violation of an individual's privacy – a situation which is covered by the Norwegian penal code, § 390 a.

The situation is more unclear when the observation occurs by means of the use of technical aids.

There is a wide variety of such aids, which are constantly becoming better developed. One can think of, e.g., cameras with telephotographic lens, film cameras, TV-cameras, etc.

In Denmark a definite ban exists against the use of such technical aids. The Danish penal code's § 264 a is directed against any person 'who unauthorized takes photographs of persons who find themselves in a not freely accessible place'. It is further stated: 'The same holds for any person who with the help of binoculars or other devices unauthorized observes such persons'.

As noted, the ban is directed only at *unauthorized* photographing etc. of the individual who finds himself in a not freely accessible place, e.g., in a private garden. The prohibitions do not make any explicit exceptions for the police but, according to the *travaux préparatoires,* if the aim is a proper enforcement of the law, this might make the method lawful.

In the police headquarters in some countries so-called transparent mirrors are used in some rooms (or cells), i.e., mirrors that from the inside look like a common mirror and from the outside constitute a window. Thus, from the outside everything happening in, e.g., a prison cell or an examination room can be observed without the knowledge of the individual concerned.

I have been informed by leading police authorities that transparent mirrors are not utilized in Norway, except in the case of police line-ups where the witness in question can observe the persons paraded (among whom the suspect is placed) through such a mirror. This form of usage ought to be accepted out of consideration for the witnesses involved. But otherwise this method is hardly permissible, e.g., for observing a suspect who believes himself to be out of view in his cell. Such a utilization must be regarded as a violation against his person.

It is clearly impossible to stop technical progress, and a comparatively new level in the process of development is the television camera. As everyone knows, this device is used to an increasing extent in connection with surveillance at railway stations, subways, and other crime-exposed areas. As long as it is done in such a way that persons using the area clearly know about the surveillance, it can be accepted, at least if one restricts the use to areas where it is otherwise difficult to keep order and prevent crimes.

The use of television surveillance is much more questionable when it is done secretly, and particularly when it occurs in areas where one can reasonably demand to be by oneself, e.g., in one's private residence.

The Danish penal code's § 264, which deals with unauthorized photographing, is also assumed to cover unauthorized use of the television camera.

A Swedish report on photographing (SOU 1974:85) contains a proposal for a special law on TV-surveillance. This proposal was separately handled, and the law was adopted in 1977. As a condition for legitimate TV-surveillance, the law states that those visiting the area must be informed about the surveillance through notices or in other ways. It is further stipulated, that the surveillance camera shall be used in such a way that 'due considerations are taken with respect to the individual's personal integrity.'

As a condition for using the surveillance camera in public places, permission must according to the law be obtained from the county government. Such permission is also needed for the TV-surveillance of traffic.

In Norway the use of TV-surveillance is not regulated by law, but there are reasons for introducing legislation along the same lines as the Swedish enactment.

In most countries secret surveillance is used by the police in one particular area, i.e. concealed traffic surveillance through the use of radar and similar technical aids. In these instances primarily the *motor vehicle,* not the particular individual, is observed, a circumstance which, from the point of view of protecting personal integrity, makes the surveillance only insignificantly objectionable. The most decisive reason supporting the acceptance of secret radar surveillance is its importance in traffic safety, including the possibility of preventing traffic accidents.

VII. APPREHENSION AND PRE-TRIAL DETENTION OF SUSPECTS

The police in the Nordic countries have often been criticized for apprehending suspects to a much larger extent than the law allows. There is scarcely any other area in which police practice in the Nordic countries has been under such constant criticism for a long time. Several investigations have been carried out which show the discrepancy between law and practice in this area.

The objections can be summarized in the following main points:

1. The law's requirement that normally an arrest can only take place after the court's ruling has been obtained is not followed in practice. For a very long time the Norwegian police have carried out arrests without first having obtained the court's consent. On several occasions this practice has warranted complaint. For example, the Supreme Court of Norway took sharp exception to the practice in the following case (*Rt*. 1936, p. 566). The Oslo police had arrested a lawyer who was under suspicion without in advance getting the court's decision, which there was ample opportunity to obtain. The charge crumbled, and the lawyer demanded compensation for unwarranted deprivation of liberty, according to § 469 of the criminal procedure act. He was awarded a large sum of money, and simultaneously the court strongly repudiated the argument by the chief of police, which, among other things, stated that the police had only followed well-established practice. However, mainly this criticism became an empty gesture. By and large practice continued as before, except for the fact that the police became more careful in arresting, without the court's decision, lawyers and others who could easily involve the state in a large compensatory liability if the charge did not hold up.

Subsequently judicial practice has continued along the same track. The law committee on criminal procedure notes with a sigh that 'such a discordance between law and practice is in principle not satisfactory' (p. 241). The committee points out considerations for and against changing the law to conform with practice, and arrives at the conclusion that the reasons for eliminating the requirement of the court's consent before an arrest can take place are the most acceptable.

The proposal seems to have many advantages. A main favourable argument, mentioned by the committee, is the difficulty the court faces at a very early stage of the investigation in taking a balanced view regarding the need for arrest. Thus the court's ruling will easily be characterized as superficial.

Furthermore, at the next stage, when the court has to decide on the question of remanding in custody, it might feel bound by its first decision on arrest. And it is in no instance desirable to have legal rules that are plainly neglected in practice.

In Denmark, too, where the rule is not followed in practice either, many seem to favour a similar legal revision (see, e.g., Mogens Koktvedgaard, in *Juristen,* 1969, p. 375).

2. To some extent arrests occur in instances where the law's material conditions are not fulfilled. This was especially the case before a legal revision in 1963. In that year the power to apprehend was extended in many areas, since a discrepancy had developed between law and common practice. This legal revision only aimed at implementing the most necessary reforms. The necessity of a further extension of the power to make apprehensions, in order to create a better conformity between law and practice, was pointed out.

This was effected by an Act of 1971. The chief purpose was 'to legally authorize the police's practice with regard to arrests concerning so-called checking and the like'. (The report by the law committee on criminal procedure, p. 247.) In such cases deprivation of liberty is limited to 4 hours.

The committee was not willing to legalize common practice in all respects. It is noted that the law proposal hardly covers 'all the instances in which the police in following the existing arrangement have carried out unauthorized arrests – but the committee presumes that the new provision will cover all significant needs and that it is incorrect to go any further' (p. 248).

3. To some extent arrests occur in order to promote aims not allowed by the law, e.g., to punish a suspect or to weaken him whereby he confesses, and so on. In another context I have further examined the significance of these non-recognized purposes of an arrest (*Pågripelse og varetektsfengsel* (Apprehension and Pre-Trial Detention), with a summary in English and German, Oslo 1957; see also my article in the *University of Pennsylvania Law Review,* Vol. 108, 1960, pp. 343–347).

There are reasons to believe that also the *court,* when it decides to place a person charged in custody during the investigation, to some degree contributes to the promotion of these non-recognized purposes. This occurs when the court in many instances fairly routinely approves the police's demand for custody instead of independently and critically considering their request. Such a practice is facilitated by the fact that the court seldom gives a real justification for the admission to custody. As a rule the court is content with referring to one or several of the grounds for custody mentioned in the law, e.g., danger of escape or danger of destruction of evidence, without further examining why the reason for custody is present in the specific case.

Danish and Swedish practices have also been subjected to criticism similar to that directed against Norwegian practice with regard to arrest and pre-trial detention.

VIII. DISCUSSION AND CONCLUSION

Above an account has been given of the fact that the police to some extent act somewhat freely in regard to the rules limiting their competence – contrary to the principle of legality according to Norwegian (and Nordic) law. This applies in particular to rules regarding the power to arrest a suspect in the course of an investigation. In this area a well-established tradition prevails to stretch the rules of competence in many instances.

How is this practice to be judged? Undoubtedly, the situation must be characterized as disquieting when the police, whose main task is to administer law and justice, do not follow the rules that govern the conduct of their authority. The neglect of the *material* principle of legality is particularly precarious, e.g., deprivation of liberty without legal authorization and con-trary to the requirement of § 99 of the constitution. The violation of the formal rules regarding arrest also infringes § 99, even though the objections against such a practice are not as fundamental as in the case of a breach of the material rules.

The police's habit of taking liberties with the rules of competence is not confined to Norway. As long as there has existed an organized police and prosecuting authority, in most countries more or less frequent criticism from legal scientific and other quarters has been directed at the circumstance that the rules are often not followed in practice. That became evident during the large international seminar on police law in Chicago in 1960, where the conditions in this area were described in detail and evaluated by a succession of experts from Western Europe, Canada, Japan, and USA. These trans-actions are presented in the book *Police Power and Individual Freedom* (edited by C. R. Sowle, Chicago, 1962).

The tendency was the same everywhere, but in a few countries the neglect of the rules occurred more frequently and more severely than in other countries. In general the police in the Nordic countries seem to stand high in such a comparison, in so far as their breaches are of a less serious character. For example, there is not much police brutality or use of other illegal investigation methods (e.g., illegal eavesdropping on the phone, and the like), which are so extensively used in some countries.

Nevertheless, there might be grounds for anxiety when the police in some areas clearly go beyond the rules of competence, and in this connection two questions present themselves: What causes the breaches of the rules of competence? What can be done to have the rules respected?

The norm transgressions must be seen in relation to the widespread inclination to break legal rules when good subjective reasons are assumed to prevail, and simultaneously the risk of negative sanctions is small or totally absent.

In the evaluation of the police's norm transgressions, one especially has to take into consideration the often respectable motives behind the breaches: the wish to prevent crimes and clear up criminal acts. The rules that are broken are commonly viewed as more or less unreasonable obstacles to an effective practice by the appropriate authority, and thus often go against the police's sense of justice, at least in those instances where an effective criminal pursuit is considered particularly important. In regard to practice, the discretionary character of the broken rules probably also plays a part, since one can in some cases believe that one is working within, or partially within, a defensible evaluation. But when the practice is seen in a proper context (e.g., the almost consistent omission to obtain the court's ruling on arrest), the prevalence of a manifest neglect of the law's clear words becomes evident.

Furthermore, the circumstance that most of the policemen who are involved in the immediate maintenance of the law lack legal education, and thus have insufficient qualifications to fully understand the norm-violating character of the approach, can contribute to the explanation of existing practice. Those high in office who have the controlling function generally realize the poor conformity between law and practice, but they easily submit to the established pattern. Additionally, once a specific practice has continued for some time – the establishment can occur almost imperceptibly – the approach followed will be felt to be as binding as the law. When good colleagues can act in this manner and supervisors do not complain, the practice *must* be all right. In some ways the same psychological situation develops as when legal customs are established.

Midboe, who himself worked in the police force for many years, has given a lively description of the strong influential impact an irregular practice can have: 'Even a clearly formulated legal rule will in the course of time prove itself to be totally powerless vis-à-vis professional tradition. The order saying this is the way to act rebounds from the parole 'this is the way we do it in practice' (*Bøtestraff og subsidiær fengselsstraff* (Fines and subsidiary imprisonment), 1960, p. 222).

In such instances when the practice is already established, the criticism is commonly rejected as detached from life or unreasonable, since the practice is conceived of as the real thing. But even if the criticism does lead to a certain modification in practice, old ways are soon returned to, since so many weighty reasons support the established approach, and since in spite of all it has been followed for a long time. In that case, after some time the traditional way will easily be experienced as even more correct than before, because one somehow feels that the objections have now been combated for good. That was evidently the situation at the end of the 1930s regarding the practice of arresting without the court's decision. When the lower courts after the 1936 ruling by the Supreme Court did not follow up the Court's hint by reacting against the condemned practice, there appeared to be a silent sanctioning of the traditional approach by the courts.

A similar thing happened in regard to the practice of making arrests to a wider extent than the law entitled. Neither in this case did the courts or other significant authorities react strongly. To be sure, in the 1960s a certain amount of criticism was periodically directed against the police practice, among other things, through questions in Parliament. The result was a slightly greater caution than before in arresting without legal authorization. But after a while the criticism took the opposite course: the police were reproached for their *passivity*, e.g., they did not effectively clear up Karl Johan, the main street in Oslo, with regard to certain gangs who disturbed those passing by and others. This gave the police authority the incentive to start with large tidying-up actions, which lacked authorization in the law on criminal procedure. This action was greeted with satisfaction by the public and in the press, and nobody found reasons for introducing the question of legal warranty.

And here we address an important cause of the liberties frequently taken by the police vis-à-vis the law's requirements. They know that in many instances they have public opinion behind them in their non-legal practice. Most people, including the legislature, are more interested in an effective crime control than in adherence to the rules.

Thus in this situation, so to speak, both public opinion and the legislators desire a strict principle of legality coupled with a flexible application of the principle. Thereby one manages to maintain high ideals while simultaneously having a practice that ensures a rather effective maintenance of the law. The advantages of this arrangement are obvious, but so are the scruples, too. Hereby in reality a public double standard is established, and it is hardly easier to defend this in principle than other forms of dual morality. The arrangement is particularly serious because of its socially discriminatory nature: primarily a low status clientele is affected. In the case of socially higher status clients, it would probably not have been possible to establish a practice in such clear opposition to the law's rules. Thus, symptomatically, the rule requiring the court's authorization of an arrest is often followed in apprehending more prominent persons.

Moreover, it can be maintained that the double morality can have harmful effects in the form of increased bitterness and feelings of suffering from injustice among those who are affected by the practice – to the extent that they pay attention to the fact that the law's rules are not followed. This situation might make resocialization difficult and be instrumental in strengthening the view that the law is the vehicle of the strong against the weak. What can be done to move away from this untenable situation?

Some help seems to be close at hand. Firstly, in legal regulations it is important to give the most realistic possible rules regarding the competence of the police; rules that reasonably incorporate the considerations of effectiveness. So far the legislation has not always been characterized by enough realism.

If it is shown that the rules do not correspond to practical needs, they should be revised as soon as possible instead of choosing the least troublesome way and overlooking the discrepancies. (The proposal for legislation extending the powers of arrest comes at least 30 years too late.)

In those instances in which one can expect that practice will exercise a strong pressure on the rules protecting individual legal rights, it is important already at the stage of preparing the law to deliberate thoroughly what can be done to prevent discrepancies in practice. Experience has fully shown that it is not always sufficient to have legal *rules* to protect individual rights; simultaneously through special guarantees or control arrangements one also has to institute systems ensuring that the rules are followed in practice. For instance, it may be necessary to choose solutions that leave little discretion to the authority concerned, although it might have been thought best to leave a great deal of discretion in administrative hands, if only one could count on loyal compliance.

In the formulation of the rules that aim at attaining an effective compliance, the legislative authorities have shown a careless optimism, in so far as they have been inclined to consider the sacred object well protected by the sole aid of the rules of competence.

Violent Criminality and Social Control during Stockholm's Industrialization

BBY *Sven Sperlings*

During the latter decades of the nineteenth century, a rapid industrialization and a large population increase took place in Stockholm – processes that affected all aspects of society. The level and character of criminality also changed during this period. This paper will analyse the changes in criminal violence and the mechanisms in society which influenced these changes.

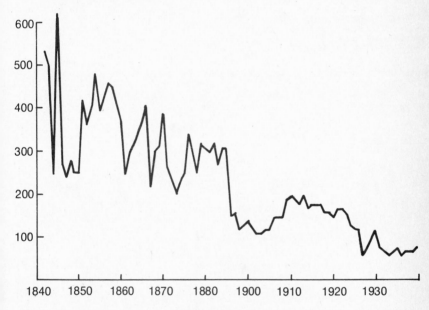

Fig. 1. Stockholm: Persons sentenced for assault and breach of the peace per 100,000 population, 1842–1930.

As is shown in Fig. 1, the annual number of criminals sentenced for violent crimes in Stockholm varied greatly until about 1880. After that date the level remains relatively consistent until the sharp decrease during the years 1885–86. The new level was considerably lower than before 1885. The number of persons sentenced increased again at the turn of the century and again around 1910. The subsequent low level was maintained until the beginning of the 1950s, after which a sharp increase occurred.

This pattern, reflecting a high level of criminal violence in pre-industrial society and during the initial phase of industrialism followed by a decrease, recurs in several western societies and cities (Christie, 1975; Gurr, 1976). Schematically the development of criminal violence during the last 100 years can be seen as an U-curve.

The decrease in criminal violence during the establishment of an industrial system of production in Stockholm was followed by an increase of striking proportions. This paper focuses on the most analytically interesting movement on the U-curve, i.e. this decrease. To what factor is it due? Were fewer crimes committed or were fewer crimes registered? Any decline in actual criminality would have been the result of changes in social relationships; thus, the level of criminal violence must reveal something about the level of conflict in society.

In an industrial society, labour is the principal determinant of human relationships for both individuals and groups. In order to explain human relations and conflict, it is necessary to understand how production has been ordered during different periods. The mode of production constitutes the basic control mechanism in a society. It underlies several other forms of control, both primary or informal and secondary or formal controls. The organization of labour influences housing, leisure time, family structure, the pattern of alcohol consumption, political and trade union organization, national and local administration, police organization, legislation, and the formation of institutions for care and punishment. During the period in which the number of crimes of violence dropped in Stockholm, changes occurred in all these control mechanisms.

The majority of people living in Stockholm at that time belonged to the working-class – a class consisting of recruits from the agricultural population, from craftsmen, and from the old urban lower class. Most persons who were sentenced for crimes of violence came from this class, and therefore it is important to study the possible connection between changes in criminal violence and the formation of and changes within the working class. Using Eric Hobsbawm's scheme of the establishment of the English industrial working class as a model, Jane Cederqvist (1972) has divided this development in Stockholm into four periods: (1) the partially pre-industrial period until about 1870; (2) the formation stage until the late 1890s, with the emergence of an industrial workers' class and its particular life-style and life-view; (3) the intermediate stage from the late 1890s until World War II, which was characterized by the separatism and class-consciousness of the working class; and, (4) the period of disintegration, when the most important material needs of the industrial workers had been satisfied or at least made less oppressive, and when the national economy had become further dependent on the purchasing power of the workers.

The number of violent crimes was on a markedly low level during only one of these periods, the third stage, i.e. the period when a genuine working class was actualized. Unlike earlier ones, this working class was characterized by a high degree of class-consciousness. As shown in Fig. 1, the decline had already begun during the formation stage. However, these temporal divisions do not apply similarly to all segments of the working class, as some categories of workers reached the period of separatism later than others, and some remained entirely outside this process.

It is important to stress the fact here, that there was a differentiation within the working class even during these early periods. It is commonly believed today that such differences, indicated by the number of different occupations, is a new phenomenon, peculiar to contemporary society and especially to the modern city. Industrialization led to greater specialization and increased education for only a part of the working class. The former aristocratic workers' groups were replaced by new ones. For the most part, however, industrialization had a levelling effect and reduced the differentiation within the working class. It is hypothesized here, for that reason, that conflicts in the form of criminal violence occurred mainly between members of a stratified working class. When this differentiation was weakened towards the end of the nineteenth century, the bases for many conflicts disappeared. Aggressions were instead directed against representatives of authority or against members of other classes.

Modern victim surveys have shown that the majority of violent crimes occur within primary groups. During the intermediate stage described above, most Stockholmers did not live in isolated primary groups. Despite big changes in the organization of labour and housing patterns, collective activities continued to be prevalent throughout the period. Contacts between neighbours were especially significant. The concept of near-group relationships better characterizes this life-style than does the concept of primary groups. Consequently, this study suggests that most crimes of violence during this period were committed within the near-groups, i.e. between people living and working within a relatively limited area of Stockholm.

The political and trade-unionist labour movement which was organized at the end of the nineteenth century was to a large extent based on the changes within the working class and primarily on the changes in the mode of production. In order to clarify the potential implications of the hypothesis that assumes a connection between the level of violent crimes and the appearance or formation of the working class, it is necessary first to describe the changes within labour and the consequent changes in the remaining areas of control.

LABOUR

There were several labour markets in Stockholm during this third, intermediary, stage of our model. Public consumption demanded an enlargement of the water-supply and sewage systems, and improved paving and lighting. Thus, a great number of unskilled workers were needed. This work was often seasonal. The construction industry expanded with the rising population, and likewise needed unskilled labour. Towards the end of the century, the manufacturing industry also altered its demands on the workers. Increasing mechanization reduced the need within this industry, however, for unskilled workers. Around the turn of the century, further specialization within and between companies took place. Craftwork lost its importance not only as an independent phenomenon, but also as an organizational form for industrial work.

According to the social historian Uno Gustafsson (1976), the industrial development in Stockholm can be divided into two phases. The factory system took hold during the period before the 1890s. Steam engines gave a technological advantage to the factories over craftwork, but they created a demand for bigger entities to make operations profitable. After this period, the steam engine was replaced by electricity, and the rate of increase in personnel within the companies dropped below the level of that before the 1890s. Instead, the productive capacity of each worker increased. The extent of seasonal work was reduced, because the machines needed permanent personnel. The demand for industrial workers was especially high during the first phase of factory development, and these workers were recruited from the craftsmen and from the migrants. Primarily, however, it was the section of the labour market that had the most need for unskilled or untrained workers that recruited workers who had migrated from the countryside. The construction industry, for example, employed a large number of such workers as excavators, transporters, and bricklayers.

A rapid shift towards large companies took place during the period between 1860–1910. In 1860, 60 per cent of the industrial workers were employed in enterprises with less than 25 employees. The corresponding figure in 1910 was 20 per cent. While medium-size companies moderately expanded their staffs, the largest increases occurred in bigger companies. In 1910, 34 per cent of workers were employed in enterprises with more than 250 employees; in 1860, this figure was 5 per cent.

The growth of industry was sporadic, but paralleled the fluctuations of the business cycle, which in turn strongly affected the number of migrants arriving in Stockholm. The first half of the 1870s was characterized by high business activity, but a shortage of workers. This shortage was due in part to the lack of housing, which discouraged newcomers to Stockholm. Industry reduced its demand for manpower at the end of the 1870s, but construction rose sharply, peaking in the first half of the 1880s. In the period 1880–85 there was a surplus of migrants, considerably exceeding the national average for the latter decades of the nineteenth century. The collapse of the construction industry, however, had an immediate impact on migration so that this surplus was soon reduced to one-quarter of its size during the early 1880s. After a slight increase at the end of the 1880s, the demand for workers was low again in the early 1890s, and the surplus of migrants was again reduced. A business boom, which lasted from 1893 to 1899, revived the construction as well as the manufacturing industry. The surplus of migrants rose again, only to drop during the crisis years of 1900–01 (Gustafsson, 1976).

Despite periodically intense building activity, the rapidly increasing population (from 170,000 to 300,000) suffered a severe over-crowding problem between 1880–1900, and a widespread lodging system was developed as partial compensation.

HOUSING

Increases in the population and the expansion of industry strongly influenced housing patterns. So long as production was largely done manually and small companies were numerous, members of different classes lived together in the same areas and even in the same structures. Thus, no distinct housing segregation existed in pre-industrial Stockholm. August Strindberg presents the following picture in his autobiographical novel, *Tjänstekvinnans son* (The servant woman's son), 1962, p. 7:

> Society still rests on the classes, rather natural groups, according to professions and occupations, which keep each other in check. This system maintains a certain apparent democracy, at least in the upper classes. They have not yet discovered their interests in common, which unite the upper segments, and the new battle-formations, specially separated into upper and lower classes, do not yet exist. That is why no separated city blocks yet exist, where the upper-class occupies the entire house, segregated by their high rents, elegant entrances, and strict doorkeepers. That is why the house close to the Klara cemetery, despite its favourable location and high assessment, is still in these first years of the '50s a rather democratic family circle. The building forms a square, with an inner courtyard. In the front of the house, on the ground floor lives the baron, on the second floor the general, on the third floor the Justice of the Supreme Court, who is the landlord, on the fourth floor the grocer, on the fifth lives the retired chief cook of the late Carl Johan. In the west wing lives the carpenter, the house's care-taker, who is a pauper. In the second wing live the leather craftsman and two widows; in the third wing lives the procuress with her girls.

At this time pure slum areas already existed on the outskirts of the town. The housing picture was fundamentally altered by the building boom during the 1880s. Tenements were built for the working class, and it became more and more impossible for everyone to live near their working places. This housing segregation continued, so that by the end of the 1890s, Stockholm comprised isolated upper class as well as working class districts.

FAMILY CREATION PATTERN

Despite a continuous migration during the latter part of the nineteenth century, the intensity of this movement decreased at the end of the 1880s and during the 1890s. Gustafson (1976) asserts that the parallel industrialization led to a societal stabilization. The new economic structures brought an increased regularity to workers' lives. Traditional craftsmen could no longer work in a free and unstructured fashion, always able to fall back on their specialized skills. The demand for much unskilled labour disappeared with increased industrial mechanization, which resulted in workers remaining in jobs despite bad working conditions.

Reduction in mortality rates also added to the stability of people's lives. Child mortality rates, in particular, dropped in the beginning of the 20th century to a level of one-third of what they had been during the 1860s. Adult life expectancy rose, too, especially for men of working age. The mortality of men between the ages of 20–39 years fell 60 per cent in the period 1860–1910.

Increased regularity in people's life styles and reduced mortality rates brought new possibilities for entirely different forms of future planning. Because of this, the average age for marrying sank at the end of the nineteenth century, and the nuclear family grew in importance. Gustafson says (1976, p. 50):

> The family remained an entity during a longer period of the life cycle than earlier, as the children lived longer and more often reached mature ages, and the husband lived longer and did not leave his wife a widow and sole supporter of the family as early as before.

Instalment of running water in the tenements and improved cooking conditions encouraged people to begin spending a larger portion of their leisure time at home.

THE ALCOHOL CONSUMPTION PATTERN

The work, housing, and family structures during the period under discussion had obvious effects on the patterns of alcohol consumption. The consumption of hard liquor had long been quite high in Stockholm and the number of public houses was considerable. For many people liquor then had a completely different meaning than to people today. Abuse, of course, existed, but hard liquor was widely regarded as a healthy and beneficial beverage, giving the extra strength needed for hard outdoors work. Wages were often distributed in the pubs, and daily drinking was a part of life. This pattern of consumption, however, became unacceptable when the work demands were changed so that workers were expected to work the same regular hours every day, and when technological developments created demands for new skills and persis-

Table 1. Number of public houses and retail-sale shops in Stockholm 1877/78–1912

Year	Retail-sale shops	Public houses (Sales on the premises)
1877/78	76	176
1878/79	73	176
1879/80	64	173
1880/81	67	172
1881/82	71	166
1882/83	72	157
1883/84	76	154
1884/85	77	149
1885/86	77	151
1886/87	78	150
1887/88	78	153
1888/89	78	150
1889/90	78	151
1890/91	78	148
1891/92	78	143
1892/93	78	141
1893/94	78	143
1894/95	78	144
1895/96	78	140
1896/97	78	139
1897/98	79	142
1898/99	78	140
1899/00	78	138
1900/01	79	139
1901/02	79	131
1902/03	79	127
1903/04	79	121
1904/05	79	119
1905/06	79	121
1906/07	78	116
1907/08	77	96
1909	77	96
1910	76	96
1911	74	95
1912	74	94

The table includes licences operated by the Company for Sales-on-the-Premises as well as licences that have been transferred.
Source: The Statistical Yearbook of Stockholm.

tence on the job. Complaints from the industrial employers as early as 1864 about the heavy drinking among workers caused a total reorganization of the retail sale of alcohol and the practices of serving alcohol by the end of the 1870s. The local authorities of Stockholm decided to sell the rights for both

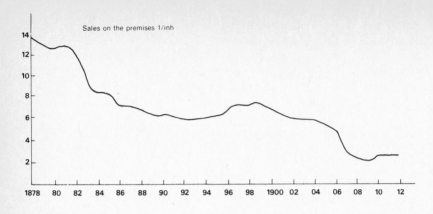

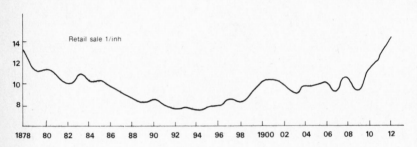

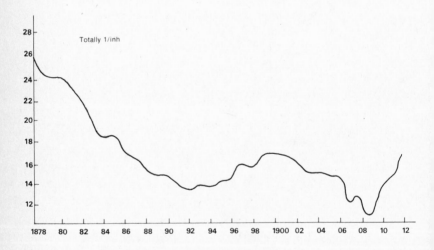

Fig. 2. *Sales on the premises and retail sales in Stockholm 1878–1912.*
Source: The sales figures of the Company for Sales-on-the-Premises,
published in the Statistical Yearbook of Stockholm.

the selling and serving of alcohol to one company in order to limit the number of pubs and to better regulate the serving of alcohol on these premises.

In 1877, during its first year in existence, *Stockholms stads utskänknings-bolag* (The Stockholm Company for Sales-On-the-Premises) established 98 public houses and 28 hard liquor shops. In comparison, there were 400 pubs in Stockholm in 1860.

The old-style consumption thrived largely because there were pubs located throughout the whole city, which enabled people to drink during working as well as leisure hours. After 1877, new rules were introduced restricting the business hours of the pubs and adding the obligation to consume food whenever one bought liquor in the pubs. The motivation behind these rule adjustments, however, was to reduce the number of pubs and to transfer most of the sale of alcohol to retail sales. The number of pubs decreased gradually towards the end of the nineteenth century. Table 1 shows the distribution of the number of pubs and of retail shops for the period 1877/78–1912.

The new policy for the sale of alcohol contributed to a substantial reduction of the overall consumption. As is shown in Fig. 2, the Company's sales diminished markedly during the 1880s and the 1890s, but it is also obvious that the largest reduction was in the serving of alcohol in pubs. It is not total consumption that these curves reflect. The information on the number of litres sold per inhabitant was obtained from the sales figures of the Company. Although no figures on the total sales are available, according to the Statistical Yearbook of Stockholm, sales by those enterprises whose licences were transferred over from the Company were as high as those by the Company itself. The number of transferred licences was relatively constant during this period, but those for pubs dropped slightly during the 1910s. The figures on the consumption in litres per inhabitant are misleading, because both women and children are included in the population. Of course some women consumed liquor during this period, but men were responsible for most of the consumption. It has been estimated that about 25 per cent of the inhabitants in Stockholm between the years 1860–1910 were below 15 years of age. In addition, there were, on an average, 120–125 women per 100 men, creating a surplus of women. Thus, a rough estimation of the consumption in litres per adult male reveals an extremely heavy alcohol consumption rate. According to such estimation, each adult male consumed almost 60 litres in 1880, 36 litres in 1890, and 41 litres in 1900.

Consumers who lived outside Stockholm accounted for at least part of the recorded sales of alcohol, the amount of which was probably balanced by the number of Stockholmers travelling outside the city boundaries to buy their liquor. Home-brewing also took place. The number of offences against the home-brewing prohibitions rose during the second half of the nineteenth century, peaking twice. The most striking peak was reached in the middle of the 1850s as a consequence of the 1855 legislation which outlawed distilling for household use. These offences increased again during the beginning of the 1870s, but this occurred before the establishment of the Company for Sales-on-the-Premises. Offences against the regulations of sales-on-the-premises are included in the statistics citing distillation crimes, so that they do not directly reflect the extent of home-brewing. The estimates, however, are likely to be too low.

The controlling of the consumption practices was not the only factor affecting changes in alcohol consumption. The extent of consumption was reduced during periods of economic depressions, as is shown in Fig. 2. The decrease at the end of the 1880s and the beginning of the 1890s coincided with the general business slowdown of that time. Propaganda from both the labour and the temperance movements certainly affected the level of consumption. In addition, the growing significance of the nuclear family encouraged lower consumption, as did the rising political and trade-union activity.

THE POLICE

As stated, general consumption of public services increased during the advent of industrialism in Stockholm, leading to the development of city services such as lighting, paving, garbage collection, city-planning, the transportation system, and the municipal administration. The organization of the police force developed during roughly the same period. By 1850 Stockholm had a police system based on districts, but this system underwent no important changes until the 1870s. The direction that these changes finally took was towards specialization. In 1850 almost all of the personnel were assigned to patrol duty, but in 1924, a year before the new Swedish national police legislation, 24 per cent of the policemen had specialized assignments and duties (Gurr, 1976).

When four constables were appointed in 1853 to specially supervise persons sentenced for serious crimes and other suspects, a modest foundation was laid for the police detective units of modern times. In 1864, this department was enlarged and renamed the Department of Detectives.

Traditionally, the administrative police authority in Stockholm performed judicial functions and adjudicated the so-called police cases, with the governor-general of the city as the judge. These duties were later transferred to the police commissioner. All the criminal cases were handled by the administrative authority. The more serious criminal cases were remitted to the magistrates court, while minor cases were adjudged by the police authority. In 1864 the police commissioner declared that the remitting procedure could be speeded up considerably if his responsibilities for the minor criminal cases were delegated to another body. Thus, in 1869 a special police court was created to hear the breach of regulations cases, alcohol offences, and minor violent crimes. The administrative police authority retained the vagrancy cases.

The newly formed district police force had serious internal discipline problems. Most of the constables were on part-time duty and had other occupations as well. Little training was given. Drunkenness on duty and departure from the patrolling routes were recurring complaints. Consequently, the police commissioner requested an appropriation in 1855 in order to create a position of instructor. Although this request was approved, the position was hard to fill. The salary offered was too low for any suitable candidate to seek the job and the demands were high. The instructor was expected to have knowledge about police systems in other capital cities, and to be capable of training the policemen, supervising the patrollers, assisting with the inquiry in criminal cases, and serving as a substitute for the police commissioner if necessary.

Other deficiencies were evident in the police force besides the lack of training and bad discipline. The low number of policemen was criticized, and newspaper stories frequently cited the difficulty in finding a policeman on the streets when the need arose. The police commissioner explained that the extra demands for policemen in such places as the central railroad station, market places, theatres and other entertainment places drained personnel from the ordinary patrolling routes.

Drawing on a model used in Copenhagen, a central police department was established in 1876 in order to correct the training deficiencies and the lack of patrolling constables. The personnel in this department were not assigned to any special district. It assumed the special guarding duties and the training of extra policemen. The number of these extra policemen was definite and fixed, and these officers were forbidden to serve in other professions. They became police recruits, but their training remained very limited. They participated in theoretical studies of police statutes, which were followed by practical training in the form of joint patrols with the regular constables from the central department.

The ratio of police in relation to the population (see Fig. 3) dropped sharply during the 1880s as migration into Stockholm increased. The police reacted to this phenomenon by reducing the training time of new policemen to a minimum, and new recruits were often given patrolling duties only hours after their instruction began.

Offences committed by policemen were curtailed somewhat by the establishment of the central department. Still, every year during the 1880s one-tenth of the constables were guilty of misdemeanours committed while on duty. In 1892 the central department appointed inspecting constables who helped further lower the offence rate. Internal discipline was raised by a new recruiting policy, too. This new policy enacted radical changes within the department, primarily with the hope of widening the distance between the police and the working class. As late as the 1880s most of the police in Stockholm had been recruited from the working and craftsmen classes, but in 1900 at least 76 per cent of the policemen were former professional soldiers.

The lowered police misdemeanour rate is also partially accounted for by the fact that the general changes in the patterns of alcohol consumption resulted in a changed overall outlook towards alcohol consumption. The central department created a mounted police division in 1884 and a riot squad in 1887.

A special dispatch department was set up by the Stockholm police in 1885 with instructions to 'take those steps necessary in order to supply assistance, care or other help to persons, who have the right to receive the benefits of such aid through the police'. Thus, the department became a connecting link between different aspects of the increased control machinery then operating in society. The personnel of the department was expanded to keep pace with the enlarged control duties and specialization required of the police. In the first year, the staff of this department consisted of one superintendent and six constables, but in the year before the new police legislation, it amounted to 39 men.

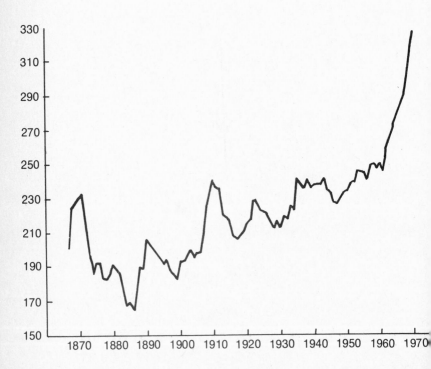

Fig. 3. Stockholm: Police manpower levels per 100,000 population, 1867–1970.

Owing to the changes in the organization of labour, the housing structure, and the political and trade-union activity of the working class, it was no longer possible for the police to continue their individually based control model, a system built on personal relations between the police and the public. The focus became instead a group-oriented control mechanism. Some tangible manifestations of this shift were the bureaucratization of the department, the police barracks, production of police statistics, and a more limited area of operation for the individual policeman.

DRUNKENNESS

The governmental efforts to control the consumption of alcohol and to establish the central police department directly influenced the number of interventions by the police in drunkenness offences.

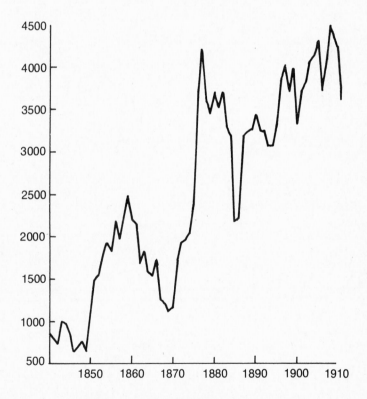

Fig. 4. Stockholm: Persons sentenced for drunkenness per 100,000 population, 1850–1910.

As seen in Fig. 4, the number of persons sentenced for these offences per 100,000 population increased markedly towards the end of the 1870s. Henceforth, the police adopted a more systematic intervention policy. The low number of voluntary court appearances by the offenders probably explains the decrease in the number of persons sentenced in the years 1882 to 1885. Only those offenders without employment or permanent addresses were taken into custody and detained. Non-appearances also rose, owing to the increase in migration and the construction industry's expansion. These two factors created a potentially mobile population, and thus, many prosecutions were dropped after the offenders had moved to other regions of Sweden, etc.

The decrease in the number of persons sentenced for drunkenness offences during the late 1880s and the early 1890s must partially be due to reduced consumption. The considerable drop in cases in the years 1885–1886, however, is also due to the then increasingly common practice of the police escorting drunks home, instead of arresting them. During this period of great expansion in Stockholm, 1880–1885, the police were operating under heavier work loads than previously.

A rise in consumption during the end of the 1890s and the first decade of the twentieth century again only partially explains the increase in the number of persons sentenced for these offences. The major influencing factor was increased activity by the police against drunkenness. In 1888 a new report form was introduced for use in drunkenness cases, a form requiring the recording of much personal data about the offenders. This new reporting system was created by the police and the Company for Sales-on-the-Premises, and extensive statistics on drunkenness were produced by the Company on the basis of these personal data. Obviously then, the rise in the curve at the end of the 1870s is increasingly a function of the changes in police organization and operating procedures.

Partly as a result of the heightened intolerance of drunkenness, the number of offences against public authorities increased, especially in the form of resisting arrest, as one can see in Fig. 5. Drunkenness and forcible resistance occurred together at an increasing rate towards the end of the nineteenth century. The correlation between them may also be manifested by the fact that during 1886, one of the years when the police escorted the drunkards home, this combination of offences occurred in only a small percentage of the registered cases.

CRIMES OF VIOLENCE

The correlation between violence against the person and drunkenness does not appear to be as evident as that between forcible resistance and drunkenness. Thus, the first-mentioned category of crime was probably not to the same degree a function of police intervention in drunkenness offences. There

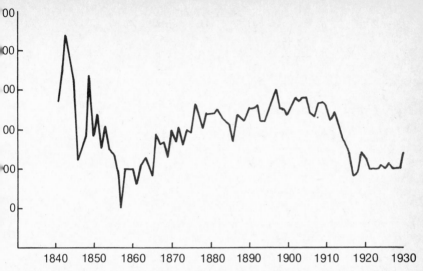

Fig. 5. Stockholm: Persons sentenced for violence or threats against officials, forcible resistance to officials, and other offences against public authorities per 100,000 population, 1841–1930.

is, however, a correlation between the number of persons sentenced for crimes of violence and the alcohol consumption rate, as reflected in the Company's statistics mentioned above. For the period 1878–1912, r^{xy} is 0.87. This correlation could indicate some real changes in criminal violence towards the end of the nineteenth century, but can hardly serve as a total explanation. Something more than aggregated statistics is needed for a proper investigation. Studies of the police reports themselves are necessary in order to discover who committed the crime, who was the victim, where did they live, and what were the likely changes in the reporting routines by the police during this period.

For the purpose of this study data have been collected for each fifth year concerning all cases of violence against the person which were handled at the police court. The first year studied is 1876 and the last year is 1901.

Table 2. Number of crimes of violence adjudicated in the Police Court

Year	Number
1876	582
1881	1 084
1886	855
1891	494
1896	693
1901	1 026

It is clear from these reports that the police reporting methods and skills became more efficient. This improvement can be shown by examining to what extent certain information is found in the reports.

Information on the offender's birthplace was rarely noted in the reports from the early study years, but appeared in almost every report during the later years.

Table 3. Number of cases without information about birthplace

Year	Number	Per cent
1876	500	86.0
1881	617	57.1
1886	564	66.7
1891	67	14.0
1896	131	19.2
1901	102	10.6

There is a sharp distinction between the reporting done in 1886 and that done in 1891, owing to the changed reporting procedures that were introduced in 1888. Another factor of interest in the reports is the number of persons without housing at the time they were apprehended. Again, the increase in the number of homeless as entered in the police reports may reflect real changes in the housing situation, but more likely it is evidence of changes in the police procedures. The occurrence of this item also noticeably rose between 1886 and 1891. These figures can be compared to the number of reports lacking address information entirely.

Table 4. Number of reports noting lack of housing and without address information

Year	Lack of Housing %	Without Address Information %
1876	4.8	14.2
1881	6.9	11.1
1886	6.9	6.7
1891	14.0	4.8
1896	15.8	1.7
1901	16.0	2.8

The entry 'incorrect information' also rose in frequency. Obviously the police began checking the addresses given to them. This enhanced efficiency was not limited to the police's interest in the defendants. They also began noting the victims' addresses on a regular basis, which practice may have had a negative effect on the willingness to report crimes.

The police reports rarely state how the crime came to their attention. Because most of the crimes were violent street crimes, it is possible that police intervention was done on their own initiative, but it is hard to draw any conclusions about the willingness to report crimes from these reports. If the widened separation between the police and the working class and the more systematical method of reporting did, in fact, discourage victims from reporting crimes, the observed reduction of violent crimes may be an illusion. Indications can be found that certain groups were less willing to report crimes. The number of cases of violent crimes summonsed to the municipal court decreased strikingly during this period. In 1876 more than 21 per cent of all crimes of violence against the person were summonsed to court. These cases concerned violence committed on private property and very seldom in public places, i.e. violence that would not be the subject of a public prosecution when of a petty nature. By 1901 this number had been reduced to 1.5 per cent. This development parallels that of defamation cases, a type of crime that steadily decreased towards the end of the nineteenth century. The reduced number of cases that are summonsed to court indicates not only a reduced willingness to report certain types of crime but also a general resistance to having contact with the authorities.

The information found in the police reports concerning the relationship between the victim and the offender does not confirm the above-stated hypothesis about near-group violence. But this view is changed when one compares the distances between the addresses of the persons involved (see Table 5). Near-group distance has been defined as when the victim and the offender live within an ecological distance of 180 metres. Today such information would indicate little about contacts between persons living within such an area. During the nineteenth century, however, large networks of contacts were established despite the large migration into town and the periodically heavy migrations within the town's borders. The measurement of ecological distances is, of course, a very crude indication of the intensity of relationships.

Table 5. Number of relationships mentioned and the number of persons living within 180 metres of each other

Year	Relationships mentioned		Persons living within 180 metres	
	Number	Per cent	Number	Per cent
1876	104	17.9	297	51
1881	81	7.5	375	35
1886	76	8.9	265	31
1891	28	5.7	330	67
1896	39	5.6	426	61
1901	85	8.3	513	50

One reasonable assumption is that during periods of low levels of violence there is generally a higher percentage of near-group violence, and a high level of crime indicates a lower percentage. This hypothesis is confirmed for two of the years studied, 1891 and 1896, which are located at the bottom of the graph showing persons sentenced. The year 1886, however, has the lowest percentage of near-group violence, and is also the year with the lowest value on the graph. If one instead proceeds from cases registered at court, the picture changes specifically for 1886. That year more than a third of all cases were withdrawn due to non-appearances, i.e. the defendant did not appear in court and could not be found by the police. If cases withdrawn are included, the number for 1886 will be higher than that of 1901, and the hypothesis can be considered confirmed for that year too.

While the overall level of violence decreased after the rapid population increases of the 1880s, the percentage of near-group violence increased. The general increase near the turn of the century is accompanied by a reduced percentage of near-group violence. This indicates a relation (or correlation) between criminal violence and migration (into town). The high-risk groups became the male migrants who were employed as unskilled workers. If a computation is done on the cases registered at court and the percentage of male migrants in the population, the correlation is high (r^{xy} 0.85) for the period 1876–1910. The distribution of occupations also apparently confirms this hypothesis. The predominant number of crimes were committed by working class people. The number of craftsmen committing crimes dropped somewhat. Manufacturing workers constituted the largest group of workers throughout all the study years. A majority of this group consisted of workers doing outside jobs for the building and construction industry and others without specified vocations. The second largest group consisted of handymen and unskilled workers.

The numbers of skilled workers in the engineering workshops and printing shops were always quite low, although the number increased somewhat as the industry expanded its personnel generally.

For enlisted soldiers in the army the changes were in the opposite direction. Although they appeared in great numbers in police reports at the beginning of the period, their representation in the reports dropped as the number of soldiers in Stockholm was reduced.

The fact that many of the violent criminals were members of the unskilled labour force may be evidence that the decrease in crimes of violence was an actual decrease. As the participation of this group in Swedish production industries diminished because of the introduction of new technology and new demands for skilled labour, the level of criminal violence sank. Despite great changes in Swedish society at the time, this risk group still faced the obstacles of high mobility and few opportunities for a regular stable life-style or for future planning, and it may have been common not to report crimes when committed by people from the working class as well as when committed by people from the upper and middle classes. But there is still reason to believe that the described development of criminality, as seen from the police reports, indicates real change. This is because for those people who settled in towns, with professional training and relatively good opportunities for obtaining employment, the reasons for conflicts were to a high degree removed.

Other information, however, stresses the importance of the unwillingness to report crimes rather than real changes in the crime rate. The scene of the crime is one such factor. In 1876 about 20 per cent of the crimes were committed inside homes and other private properties. In 1901 this figure was 7 per cent. As the number of pubs fell, so did the role of pubs as scenes of crimes. Towards the end of the period, almost 90 per cent of the crimes were street crimes, which implies that the police were to a greater extent intervening on their own initiative, and that the crimes probably being committed within the homes were not being reported. It can also be seen here that the bases of the conflicts had been altered. Not only had the housing structures changed, but also the general living milieu. Most of the shanty settlements on the outskirts of the town had been removed, the overcrowding was eased, and the lodging system was reduced.

Those members or groups of society with small chance of integrating themselves into the new living patterns were particularly vulnerable to the formal control mechanisms in society. Outlooks on drunkenness and violence shifted. Modern society demanded law and order. People who retained the old cultural model in their life-styles, those who did not adapt to the new industries and remained without occupations, and those without permanent dwellings were then regarded as deviant, and thus became the group that society's custodial apparatus incarcerated. In 1891 Sweden opened its first institution for the treatment of alcoholics, the Sans Souci treatment home outside Uppsala, and so-called delirium wards were established at many regular and mental hospitals. In 1913 legislation for the compulsory commitment of alcoholics was passed, and in the official committee report encouraging such legislation, the investigators called attention to,

> the exposed position in society of these degenerated chronic alcoholics, whose careless and unrestrained behaviour in society is continuously harming order and decency and causing considerable danger to the public security.

Institutions for the care of children with behaviour problems, mentally ill persons, alcoholics and criminals sprang up throughout the country. In the committee report cited, the value of increased institutional care for scientific research was emphasized. The researchers then had access to 'valuable material'. Positivism influenced research in Sweden at this time and a great number of publications by leading continental criminologists were translated into Swedish. At this point, it is interesting to note that even the Social Democrats approved the given motives for the government's selection of forms for the institutions. Hjalmar Branting (1900), the leader of the party, wrote an article criticizing the administration of justice for not being individualized. He also advocated the use of indeterminate sentences, and implied his sympathy with the criminological-psychological theory of 'born criminals'.

In spite of the significant reduction in the conviction rate for crimes of violence, the authorities reacted strongly when these rates slightly increased around the turn of the century. Concern about the increase of violence, as well as about the increased seriousness of violence, entered into the discussions of laws on the treatment of children with behavioural problems, and on conditional sentences and conditional releases which were being proposed in 1906. It is possible that more serious violent crimes were being committed towards the end of the period, and that the dark number for instances of violence within primary groups was high. The changes in housing patterns that promoted or improved the conditions for family life and the reduction in the number of pubs may have caused such a development. Furthermore, there is evidence that the willingness to report crimes was decreasing.

This disputable development did not, however, prompt the discussions about criminal violence that were being conducted at this time. It was the violence that disturbed the public peace on the streets that was considered alarming. Examples were given in the parliamentary debate *(Riksdagsdebatten)* of cases where persons had been assaulted by strangers in the street. A definite reduction in near-group violence has been confirmed during 1901 in relation to 1891 and 1896, but a reasonable assumption is that this reduction above all reflected a fear of being subjected to the overall increasing violence. Changes in the organization of labour, the segregation of housing into class districts, and the efforts of the political and trade-union organizers created a threatening picture of the working class for the upper and middle classes. These fears were not only caused by the violence in the streets. The increased number of crimes against public authorities must have added to the general sense of alarm.

Table 6. Percentage of upper and middle class victims

Year	Percentage
1876	11.7
1881	16.8
1886	14.9
1891	15.8
1896	14.2
1901	29.6

In their coverage of strikes and demonstrations, the bourgeois newspapers equated demonstrators with vandals. During the last study year, 1901, there were relatively more members of the upper and middle classes among the victims of crimes of violence. Information given in the police reports about victims' professions was the basis for this class distribution. Such classification is, however, troublesome and must be cautiously interpreted.

But more victims did, in fact, belong to the upper levels of society towards the end of the period studied. Police practices in the reporting of incidents could have influenced these statistical results. The investigator is here compelled to accept the policemen's assignment of the roles of victim and offender, and the potential for discrimination against the working class is present here also. Even with these limitations in mind, it is obvious that members of the upper and middle classes were more often reported as parties in conflicts. The figures in the table may even reflect too low an involvement of these classes. A large number of persons prosecuted for crimes of violence in 1901 were found not guilty because the police reports listed the victims as unknown. These offenders were instead convicted for disorderly conduct. The requests of many victims not to be named as such must have led to this common police practice. It is to be suspected that these 'unknowns' belonged to the upper and middle classes.

The fear of being exposed to violence may depend on several factors: the actual risk, the distance from the feared person/s, and the apprehension of the risk. This subjective apprehension is not based upon the relative criminality. It may be based on wrong information, law-and-order campaigns in the mass media, etc. During the period under study, both the influence of the mass media and people's own experience of violence on the streets of Stockholm probably influenced the level of fear of violence. The city's population had increased heavily, and mainly in the same areas. The relatively lower number of crimes of violence at the end of the nineteenth century could be expected to have been experienced as a heavy increase.

Nils Christie (1973) has maintained that it is impossible to study the development of criminality in a historical perspective. Criminal statistics must instead be viewed as expressions of the interest in criminality that authorities have taken during the different periods. With this approach, it is easier to explain or explain away an increase than a decrease. This seems to be particularly true for the period in question, since it is hard to state that the police and other authorities had a low interest in law-and-order considerations at the exact time when, according to Tove Stang Dahl (1974), 'state interventions were necessary both to make the progress of capitalism possible, and to neutralize its harmful effects'. In this paper, on the contrary, it has been stated that the police department was reorganized and their reporting practices improved precisely when the conviction rates were obviously less.

The implication of this need not be that the reductions were actual. The willingness to report crimes apparently decreased, and the reorganization of the police may have had a general preventive effect.

To explain the development of criminality, it is a mistake to approach it from the role of the police only. The reasons for many conflicts were removed through changes in the organization of labour and in housing patterns towards the end of the nineteenth century, and thus it must be stated that the simultaneous reduction in violent crimes was a real reduction. The police system was only one of many instruments used to maintain and develop the new power structure in the industrialized society. An enhanced power on the part of the state was necessary in all spheres for this system with its larger units and increased specialization to function. The police was one of the most visible parts of the new control machinery, but held no dominant position. Stedman Jones' (1974) description of London applies to Stockholm as well:

> The policemen and the workhouse were not sufficient. The respectable and the well-to-do had to win the 'hearts and minds' of the masses to the new moral order and to assert their right to act as its priesthood.

REFERENCES

BRANTING, H.: in *Socialdemokraten 29 May 1900*.

CEDERQVIST, J., GUSTAFSON, U & SPERLINGS, S.: Industriarbetarklassens uppkomst: Stockholms arbetare 1850–1914. *Historisk Tidsskrift. 1972.*

CHRISTIE, N.: The Delinquent Stereotype and Stigmatization *General Introduction, Section L, 7th Int. Congress on Criminology*, Beograd 1973.

CHRISTIE, N.: *Hvor tett et samfunn?* Copenhagen–Oslo 1975.

Fattigvårdslagstiftningskomitténs betänkande I: *Motiv till förslag till lag om behandling av alkoholister* – Stockholm 1911.

GURR, T.: *Rogues, Rebels and Reformers – A Political History of Urban Crime and Conflict* Beverly Hills – London 1976.

GUSTAFSON, U.: *Industrialismens storstad – studier rörande Stockholms sociala, ekonomiska och demografiska struktur 1860–1910.* (Stockholm 1976) passim.

SALMOSE, K.: *Stockholmspolisen och arbetarklassen.* Stockholms Universitet Historiska institutionen, 1977. Opubl. uppsats.

STANG DAHL, T.: State Intervention and Social Control in Nineteenth-Century Europe. *Paper prepared for the Second Conference of the European Group for the Study of Deviance and Social Control,* Essex 1974.

STEDMAN JONES, G.: Working-Class Culture and Working-Class Politics in London 1870–1900. *Journal of Social History.* Vol. 7, 1974.

STOCKHOLMS POLICE: *Instruktion för ordonnansavdelingningen. 23. februari 1885 § 7.*

STRINDBERG, A.: *Tjänestekvinnans son. Del I.* Stockholm 1962, s. 7f.

Finnish Gypsies and the Police

BY *Martti Grönfors*

A. PREAMBLE

Visible ethnic minorities form a special case in the exercise of social control by judicial personnel. Ethnic groups may be differentiated from others by such criteria as physical differences, style of clothing, conduct, language or dialect. Often all of these are involved. This special visibility can make some ethnic groups vulnerable for selection as targets of control. Often ethnic minorities are despised by the members of the majority for a variety of reasons. As the majority is frequently ignorant of the nature of the social organization and culture of minorities, stereotypical notions govern the majority's assessments. The minority is imputed certain characteristics, and the behaviour of the majority towards the minority members is in line with these stereotypical notions.

The police force is the prime agent in judicial control. Police officers are usually drawn primarily from the majority, or at least from sections of the community which support the existing status quo. A survey conducted among officers of the London Metropolitan Police established the police as people who were conservative, afraid of change, suspicious of differences, and suspicious of foreigners and coloured people.[1]

Conformist tendencies tend to become further emphasized during the officers' working lives. Workfellows share similar views, and much of the policemen's free time is also spent with other policemen. This means that they are somewhat cut off from the realities of life, and so are unable to follow the changes that take place in society.[2] It is natural that when the police spend their free time as well as their working lives with fellow officers:

> . . . group solidarity increases in direct proportion to their isolation from the rest of society. Similarly as it is strengthened, so are commonly held values and ethical beliefs . . . this aspect of group behaviour is particularly interesting, for the evidence is that this police loyalty and solidarity is often sufficiently strong to make them tolerant of their own crime; that is of police action beyond the limits of the law.[3]

The particular nature of this quasi-military, undemocratic institution,[4] where individual officers cannot hold widely differing ideologies of policing, means that

> the task, structure and internal life of police forces together with the work environment of the policeman both call for and stimulate certain attitudes to authority, to the state, to violence, to politics and to life itself.[5]

This attitude puts a high premium on law and order in society, this order being easily upset by a variety of deviations from the policeman's conception of 'normality'.[6] Society is seen largely in terms of the clear-cut 'normal' and 'abnormal'. The 'normal' individual, for example, carries out his responsibilities to society as a tax-payer, is a non-bludger, who is married and raising a family, and is non-protesting and compliant.

In Finland gypsies form the most clearly distinguishable visible ethnic minority. Their dark appearance and traditional dress sets them apart wherever they are. Little is really known generally of gypsies, of their social organization and culture. Having been persecuted for centuries, gypsies find security in remaining as closed a group as possible. Any close association with non-gypsies is avoided, and knowledge of gypsy social life and culture is guarded zealously.[7] As a consequence, others have to rely on occasional observations and hearsay for their 'knowledge' of gypsies. It is not surprising that under these circumstances stereotypes are formed.

Unstructured interviews with 55 police officers in Helsinki and Tampere carried out in 1977 showed that the police in Finland shared these stereotypical notions about gypsies. However, they tended to focus on the issues that were considered important from the point of view of their own work. It was characteristic that no policeman interviewed was willing to say that he was not familiar with the gypsies or their culture. They all saw themselves as experts. This partly at least is because gypsies are thought of *in toto* as something that the police ought to know about, something they should have control over, i.e., the gypsies are one section of the Finnish population to be managed by the police. On the whole the police viewed gypsies in a very unfavourable light, gypsies being seen to violate most or all of the norms that were highly valued by the police officers.

B. POLICE VIEWS OF GYPSIES: EMPIRICAL ILLUSTRATION

Portrayal of the police as a conservative and conformist occupational group can be elaborated at the empirical level, when the police-stated views on gypsies are analysed. Below, I shall utilize Jock Young's elaboration of Matza and Sykes'[8] concept of subterranean values, extended here to act as a conceptual device in dealing with the opinions of the police about gypsies.

> The major content of this model is geared to a neo-Keynesian image of the economy, a nuclear family image of sexuality, and a mundane concept of religious experience. Economically, the ideal citizen is one who works hard and acquires an increasing consumption power as a result. The consensus consists of a twin system of values which are brought into play at normatively appropriate times . . . The formal values are related to the structure of modern industry. They are functional for the maintenance of diligent, consistent work and the realization of long-term productive goals . . . You work hard in order to earn money, which is spent in pursuit of leisure; it is in his free time that man really develops his sense of identity and purpose.[9]

The police operate within a conformist system of values and have a consensual framework, wherein activities that are in opposition to the system are against the established order, and are therefore deviant.

Formal work values (police values)	*Subterranean values* (values attributed to gypsies by the police)
1. Deferred gratification	Short-term hedonism
2. Planning future action; acceptance of external constraints	Spontaneity; freedom from external constraints
3. Conformity to bureaucratic rules	Self-expressiveness
4. Routine, predictability	New experience, excitement
5. Instrumental attitudes to work, hard productive work seen as a virtue	Disdain for work, activities performed as an end in themselves
6. Support of status quo in manners, speech and possessions appropriate to one's social position	Flouting appropriate signs of social class position

As maintained by Matza and Sykes, and accepted by Young, everybody holds these subterranean values. However, under normal circumstances such values are expected to be kept firmly under control and their expression reserved only for specific situations, places or times.[10] Such occasions could be leisure hours, sports events, holidays, etc. To express these subterranean values outside the appropriate occasions is condemned, and is therefore viewed as deviant. Looked at in this light, the entire social organization and culture of gypsies was seen by the police as *the expression of subterranean values outside their proper place, and therefore the gypsy way of life is deviant in toto.*[11]

1. Short-term hedonism

Gypsy sexual lives were seen very much in hedonistic terms, especially in the case of the men. The 'virtue' of gypsy women was acknowledged, but as this would be a contradiction of the police idea of gypsy society being hedonistic in nature the explanation for such virtue was sought not in the women themselves, but in other factors surrounding their lives. Or, when the police lacked evidence of the sexually licentious behaviour of gypsy females, it was implied that they make themselves available only to gypsy men.

Incest is common among them. The whole kin lives together, and breeds together.

> They marry so near, or don't get married at all, and then one doesn't know in whose name to register the child. A half-brother might marry his half-sister. That possibly may be the reason for their poor state of health. That's why they've managed to stay racially rather pure in Finland.

> The gypsy women actually lust after white men, but if they get mixed up with them then they get a hiding and are thrown out of the tribe. The gypsy men also lust after white women, but they are allowed to use them.

Gypsy hedonistic tendencies were also evidenced in their wanting to evade taxes, payment of which is seen by other people as insurance against ill-fortune, illness, unemployment and old age. Gypsies were described by the police as willing to exploit and undermine this system for their immediate benefit:

> Taxation is getting stiffer all the time, because we spend so much on social welfare benefits. A greater and greater rift comes between us and the gypsies – between people who pay their taxes and those who spend them.

Getting a living through illegal activities was another form of hedonism in which the gypsies as a whole were thought by the police to engage. The gypsies were considered to be unprepared to put into the system the amount of work that would entitle them to a living from it. They were prepared to shortcut the system by minimizing the input and maximizing the output by resorting to illegal pursuits.[12]

> They are unable to accept working for somebody else, and they must get their income from somewhere. So they steal, mainly shoplifting or robbing.

2. Spontaneity: freedom from external constraints

Spontaneity as a subterranean value is a characteristic in people who plunge into things without considering the long-term effects of their actions. It is a quality which, if practised by everybody, is seen as creating chaos in society. There are groups of people, for instance artists, who are given some licence for spontaneity, but as artists are anyway seen as not fitting into the main fabric of society, their behaviour is not considered threatening. It must be kept in mind, too, that the way of life even of artists is not uniformly accepted in our society. In addition, artists, in spite of being allowed some leeway in their expression of spontaneity, are not expected to become bludgers either. The price of their freedom for spontaneity is often thought to be poverty!

Freedom of movement is central to the gypsy way of life. For the police in Finland, the gypsy expression of this aspect of their culture, however, was very clearly seen as an untimely expression of subterranean values, or as a characteristic typical of children:

I think it is their nature which makes them into children of the moment. Sort of wandering blood.

Any curtailment of the freedom to wander was expected to bring about a violent reaction from gypsies. Instant violence as an answer to a dilemma can be seen as another subterranean feature connected with spontaneity. 'Ordinary' people are expected to control these tendencies, or to exhibit them only on appropriate occasions, such as in sports and wars:

> They are very emotional people, very quick tempered. When they are confronted, they resort to violence.

3. *Self-expressiveness*

Conformity to bureaucratic rules is seen as functional for order and continuity in society.[13] Its opposite, self-expressiveness, is seen as an obstacle to order, and hence it should be curtailed, or at least confined to situations where it does not hinder the orderly, bureaucratic running of affairs. The more one tends towards the selfish expression of emotions, values and culture, the less one is thought to be able to contribute to order in society. If the values that stem from the ego and its environment and those which stem from the wider society are in conflict, then for the person to be a 'good citizen' the former values must give way. To persist in expressing these 'private' values is then an untimely expression of subterranean values and therefore deviant.

The gypsies' sense of obligation to their family and kin was acknowledged by the police, and even admired by some. However, at the same time such gypsy feelings hindered the work of the authorities, and thus became inappropriate expressions of subterranean values:

> They are very united in tribal love. The feeling of belonging is strong among gypsies, as are the family bonds. If one family rents a flat, the place is soon filled with gypsies. They lie side by side on the floors, packed like sardines. When we have to ask after them at their homes, they are always 'visiting relatives'.

> Even in court there is always the entire kin screaming. Family love is really strong. They are all the time bringing money and cigarettes. No white will do that. Whites might telephone us sometimes, but they don't come here making a nuisance of themselves.

The gypsy preference for their indigenous culture, to the exclusion of the Finnish culture, was also seen by the police as unacceptable and deviant:

> If only they could stop wearing their national costume, and come half-way to meet us that way. They must adjust. These days, as there are so many mixed marriages,

they should think of the future generations and shouldn't try to draw too much attention to themselves. They are a whining small group of people for whom too much has already been done – patted on the head, they've been.

In addition to their *preferred* differences, the biological features of gypsies were not thought by the police to conform to the usual, accepted patterns either. That aspect was also seen as making life a bit harder for the authorities:

Not even the devil can tell them apart. They're all like brown-eyed carbon copies of each other. For instance, if one in a family gets a driver's licence, then everybody else in the family uses it.

They're a bit like the Chinese, in that they all look the same to us. So our photographic aids for identification are not all that much use.

4. New experience – excitement

To seek experiences and excitement as ends in themselves is not compatible with the consensus view of society. Routine is a necessary prerequisite for predictability, and anything that differs from the routine is seen as aiding the unpredictability of events. Police work depends a great deal on predicting the likely course of events, and suspicion is aroused by the unusual. It is acceptable to become excited if there is a clear reason for the excitement, because then the excitement can be dealt with. Any excited behaviour for which there is no clearly observable reason, and thus no clear course to follow, is inappropriate and suspicious:

The gypsies want some excitement in their lives. As far as stealing goes . . . they're not poor any longer, so they don't have to resort to stealing for that reason. It's a sort of sport for them.

The gypsies were also thought by the police to show unacceptable tendencies in their expression of fear.

They have a quite clear tendency to claustrophobia. They are afraid of dogs, too.

They're afraid of the dark. Also they have a sort of fear of enclosed places. They can't stand much pain either.

5. Disdain for work: activities performed as an end in themselves

Consistent with the ideology of the police is an attitude which views work as a means towards an end. Work is seen as a sacrifice of pleasure, not as something one does in order to obtain gratification from the act itself. Work-like activities which in themselves produce pleasure, and are seen as an end in themselves, are undesirable expressions of subterranean values, mixing work and pleasure. Gypsies, if they pursue their traditional occupations, are seen by the police as 'not really working', as they do not suffer the constraints of regular working hours nor do they separate work from family and social life. A 'responsible' attitude towards work is, more than anything else, the required characteristic of a 'good citizen'. To shun these responsibilities is seen to strike at the very roots of ordered society. This 'responsible' attitude does not mean the same as 'liking' work, but concerns doing work in spite of disliking it. The gypsies, as seen by the police, deviate so much in their attitudes to work that the police were quite unanimous in their condemnation of them on the grounds of their presumed preference for not working:

> It's very rare to find a gypsy employed in a lawful occupation. Avoiding work is in their blood . . . There are even jokes to prove it. Jokes always have some truth in them: 'Ho ho', said the gypsy lady, 'must watch out, or work might become a habit!'

6. Flouting the appropriate signs of social class position

Knowing one's place in the social scale, and sticking to it, is a conservative and conformist idea. With each step in the social ladder there are some appropriate signs which point to one's place. Some of these signs are highly ritualized, such as executive washrooms, company cars with chauffeurs, residence in certain areas, and so on. Not to observe the conventions appropriate to one's position creates hostility and suspicion. The gypsies were associated by the Finnish police with the poverty and squalor appropriate to the social position they hold. To exhibit signs and symbols which did not tally with this was suspicious, and so condemned:

> They have magnificent cars, and leather jackets. Sometimes one wonders how they get the money. In many sporting events they even sit in the front rows.

> Some of them have even got good cars, Mercedes and the like, and 30 or 40 thousand marks in their bank accounts.

C. WHAT TO DO WITH THEM?

As shown above, gypsies and their culture were seen in their entirety as untimely expressions of subterranean values. They did not meet the requirements of good citizenship. The police were asked to make suggestions as to what they thought should be done in order to make gypsies into 'responsible citizens'.

First of all, Finland's liberal social welfare policies were heavily criticized by the police, as was any special help directed by the State towards the gypsies, such as housing aid:

> I do not accept our social policies. By giving these people social welfare benefits, their impetus for work is removed. On the one hand they are given rights, but on the other hand there are no demands made upon them to take responsibilities. They don't have to attend school, which is a pity. They're handled with kid gloves and are all the time 'understood'. It is not necessary any more to talk about racial discrimination. Gypsies get favourable treatment, for instance in housing. In the police force they are considered difficult as a group, and some officers have occasionally blown their fuses. It can happen very easily.

Without exception, all officers thought that the situation needed something done. Most were reasonably moderate in their suggestions. A significant proportion, however, were hardliners:

> I've often wondered whether tougher penalties might be the answer, although that probably wouldn't help either. Force them to work! Of course that's no solution, but it might be worth trying to utilize the sorts of labour camps we had during the war.

> We have a saying here in the police force that we don't hate anything as much as racial discrimination and gypsies!

> Isolate them from society – although I don't suppose that would help either. Perhaps a kind of camp could be established for gypsies only. That way they at least wouldn't hurt other people. Not quite into cages, but perhaps their own suburb so that they are not spread over every bloody place.

No attempt was made to disguise contempt and real hatred in some cases, and two policemen suggested extermination as a 'solution'.

D. CONCLUSION

All in all, the police see gypsies as being against everything that the police value, and in their descriptions of the characteristics of gypsy society and culture there seems to be more or less complete opposition between the values of the police and those perceived by the police to be the values of the gypsies. Expressions of gypsy culture and expressions of criminal culture are seen as one and the same by the police. The gypsies are a group that 'has to be managed', and a body of ideas has evolved in police practice as to how this can be achieved. The ideas that the police have about gypsies, often erroneous in the extreme, govern the way in which they observe, detain, and deal with gypsy cases.

The gypsies, on the other hand, perceive the police as a section of the Finnish community with whom contact must be avoided altogether. Gypsies seldom put themselves into a position where they are cut off from the support that the gypsy society can give its members. Contact with the police means an inevitable break with the gypsy community. This means that the gypsies attempt to limit their contact with the police, even in cases of arrest, to a minimum achievable time. The police know that the gypsies are desperate to leave the police station, and the officers translate this desire into quasi-psychological terms, such as claustrophobia, fear of the dark, fear of being left alone, and so on. They can therefore resort to tactics to produce a desired result, such as an admission of guilt. Since contact with the police, or with any other Finnish authorities, is not stigmatic to gypsies *per se,* the gypsies are likely to agree with whatever the police allege, just to get out of a disagreeable situation. Both parties to this transaction are reasonably satisfied with the outcome. The gypsy gets his freedom, even though it may be only to await a court case, and the police get a 'confession' and another entry is made in the statistics. This, I would claim, is a good example of the sort of process involved in the labelling of deviants, defined by Becker as

> the process by which deviance is imputed by some people to other people and the contingencies that govern whether those imputations succeed or fail.[14]

In the case of Finnish gypsies, it appears that the police have been successful to the degree that at least the police themselves are satisfied that their initial assumption of gypsies as a criminal group is a correct one.

NOTES

[1] BELSON, WILLIAM A.: *The Public and the Police.* London, Harper & Row, 1975, pp. 39ff., 53ff. See also ROCK, PAUL, *Deviant Behaviour,* London, Hutchinson, 1973, pp. 186ff.
[2] See e.g. SOLNICK, J. H. *Justice without Trial: Law Enforcement in Democratic Society.* N.Y., Wiley, 1966. GRÖNFORS, MARTTI: *Ethnic Minorities and Deviance: The Relationship between Finnish Gypsies and the Police.* University of Helsinki. Sociology of Law Series No 1, 1979.
[3] BOWDEN, TOM: *Beyond the Limits of the Law: A Comparative Study of the Police in Crisis Politics.* Harmondsworth, Penguin, 1978, p. 30.
[4] See e.g. BOWDEN, TOM. *op.cit.,* p. 31.
[5] BOWDEN, TOM: *op. cit.,* p. 23.
[6] GRÖNFORS, MARTTI, 1979, *op.cit.*
[7] See GRÖNFORS, MARTTI, *Blood Feuding among Finnish Gypsies,* University of Helsinki, Department of Sociology. Research Reports No. 213, 1977.
[8] MATZA, DAVID and SYKES, GRESHAM M.: 'Juvenile delinquency and subterranean values.' *American Sociological Review,* 26 (5), 1961 pp. 712–719.
[9] YOUNG, JOCK: 'Mass media, drugs, and deviance', pp. 233–234 in Rock, P. & McIntosh, M. (eds.) *Deviance and Social Control.* London, Tavistock, 1974.
[10] YOUNG, JOCK. *op.cit.,* p. 235

[11] Cf. HALL, STUART, et al: *Policing the Crisis: Mugging, the State, and Law and Order.* London, Macmillan, 1978, pp. 140ff.

[12] Cf. HALL, STUART, et. al., *op.cit.,* p. 142, where they say that 'Crime in the proper sense, when involving robbery or rackets for gain, is set off *against* work in the public mind, precisely because it is an attempt to acquire by speed, stealth, fraudulent or shorthand methods what the great majority of law-abiding citizens can only come by through arduous toil, routine, expenditure of time, and the postponement of pleasure.'

[13] Cf. HALL, STUART, et al., *op. cit.* pp. 142–144.

[14] Becker in foreword to SELBY, HENRY A.: *Zapotec Deviance: The Convergence of Folk and Modern Sociology.* Austin, University of Texas Press, 1974, p. ix.

Work Adjustment of Swedish Policemen

BY *Jan Forslin*

INTRODUCTION

When starting in a new occupation an individual will have to adjust to a number of more or less new requirements and unknown limitations. For some, this adjustment is difficult. Studies of labour turnover show that a considerable proportion of the newly employed leave again after a very short time (Hedberg 1967).

The decision to leave one's employment can be interpreted as a result of unrealistic expectations when taking on that position – possibly also lack of insight into one's own needs and qualifications. Little is known about the psychological changes that occur during the first period in a form of employment that in some cases ends with a separation, in others with a transition to a more stable and permanent position with the employer. The purpose of this study is to illuminate what takes place during this first critical period by using a longitudinal approach in comparing the expectations of police recruits with their actual perception of their work after some years.

The occupational position of the police force in society makes it deserve more attention in terms of its internal conditions, work, and relation to the public and other authorities. Presumably, the welfare of the individual policeman in his work situation and the social climate he is moulded by in the police force will have a decisive influence on his performance of his duties and the functioning of the police in society.

This paper is based on a follow-up of a prior study of policemen that had as its main objective to empirically test a model of work adjustment and a new application of psychological scaling (Forslin 1971, Forslin 1978, Forslin & Mägiste 1978).[1]

The group under investigation was first studied while doing original training as police recruits in 1968, and the follow-up study was done in 1974, when the group had acquired six years of experience in their occupation. The intermediate years should have given this group quite enough experience to make it comparable to the group of senior policemen who had participated in the first study and had an average seniority of 14 years. After the first couple of years, the policeman probably encounters few new experiences, and the adjustment to his occupation that has taken place also results in such later experiences having less effect.

Because of the unusual employment stability of policemen, this project benefited from very favourable conditions for a follow-up study. In spite of the six years that had passed, few of the participants in the original sample had left the police force. Of the initial 150 recruits, 114 were selected for the follow-up. Replies could not be obtained from 26 per cent of them owing to incomplete addresses and a few refusals. The data collection was carried out by means of a mailed survey with a standardized questionnaire identical to the one that had been used six years earlier. The questions entailed rating factors in ten areas of the work situation. The rating reflected different cognitive aspects related to expectations and perceptions. A presentation of the investigated areas and the cognitive aspects will be given in connection with the findings.

The following data are thus derived from three different groups, which are all included in the comparative analysis:

Group	Age	Tenure
I Police recruits, interviewed 1968 ...	19–25 years Md 22 years	> 1 year
II Same as I, interviewed 1974	25–31 years Md 28 years	≈ 6 years
III Senior Policemen, interviewed 1968	32–55 years Md 40 years	10–33 years Md 14 years

All three groups contain only non-promoted personnel. This means that group II includes persons who will be promoted in the future, while in group III promotions to a large extent have already taken place and thus these non-promoted policemen are subject to some selectivity.

POINT OF DEPARTURE – WORKING CONDITIONS 1968

When the original investigation took place, the recruits were undergoing their first training, lasting for ten months. At that time they did not have any practical experience of police work. Their image of the occupation was based on hearsay, on what had been communicated during training and recruitment. Their perception of police work therefore to a large extent had the character of expectations with a small experiential basis. These expectations had made them apply for the present job, and they expected to fulfil them. The older policemen, who were also interviewed during training, had a long experience of their job, and their expectations were based on a rich experiential background.

By comparing the data obtained from the recruits and from the senior policemen, some conclusions could be drawn concerning the degree of realism in the recruits' expectations. The situation in 1968 can be summarized as follows. Recruits and senior policemen alike had an unsatisfactory work situation, since their assessment of their present work situation in all investigated areas – apart from relationship to comrades – was lower than their lowest demands, i.e., below the level of acceptance (Figs. 1 and 2). This deficiency was larger for the recruits, as their assessments generally were lower than those of the senior policemen, with a few exceptions: opportunities for personal development, working conditions, and meaningfulness of work.

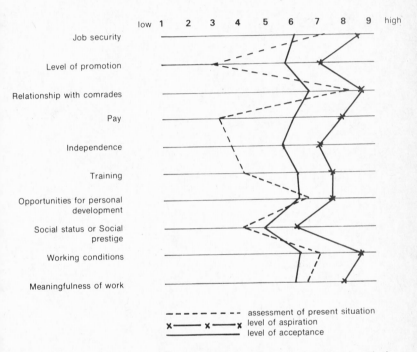

Fig. 1. The recruits' assessment of their present work situation in relation to their demands.

In spite of the fact that they perceived their present situation as less rewarding, the recruits were more satisfied – or less dissatisfied – than the senior policemen (Fig. 9). This paradoxical observation was attributed to the circumstance that the recruits had greater expectations for the near future (Fig. 3). In almost all areas the recruits had expectations that were higher than the level of acceptance. There was thus a big discrepancy between the perception of the present situation and even the short-term expectations. Corresponding ratings by the senior policemen, however, showed that the recruits' expectations were probably unrealistic.

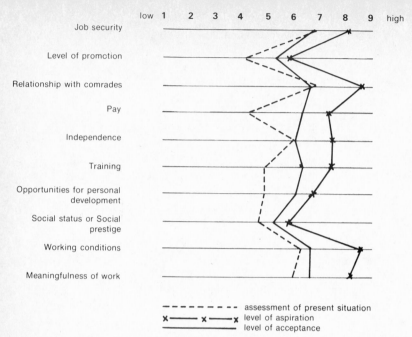

Fig. 2. The senior policemen's assessment of their present work situation in relation to their demands.

Other observations also indicated a greater optimism on the part of the recruits. They regarded the possibilities of influencing their situation and the chances of achieving their aspirations as better than did the senior policemen. In these cases too the experiences of the senior policemen make one expect that the recruits would become disappointed.

Around the turn of the year 1969–70, a number of wild-cat strikes hit the police, and longlasting wage negotiations took place in a rather animated atmosphere. Thereafter the industrial relations have reassumed a more relaxed and stable state. Interviews with the Swedish Police Association *(Svenska polisförbundet)* suggest that no thoroughgoing changes occurred between the times of the two studies. However, the relation between police and the public was pointed out as a factor that had become more critical for the satisfaction with police work.

Some organizational changes have also taken place during the follow-up period: changes towards:
– *further specification* – tasks that do not require police training have to some extent been transferred to other staff;
– *increased technical proficiency* – improved radio communication has been introduced;

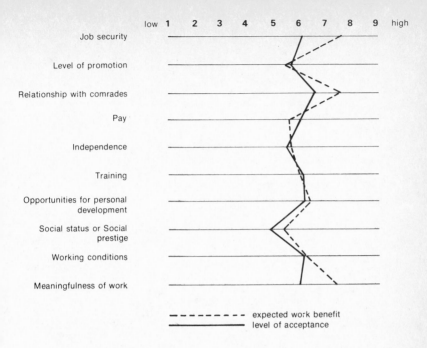

Fig. 3. Work benefits expected within one year by the 1968 recruits in relation to their lowest demands.

– *further centralization* – some working groups and small districts have been merged;
– *a higher structure* – changes in the district organization have, among other things, resulted in a greater number of higher positions;
– *a higher risk of forced transfers* – the state takeover of the responsibility for the police force from the municipalities (which took place before 1968) has made it possible to temporarily transfer personnel between districts, according to demands.

With the exception of increased opportunity for promotion, these changes do not seem to have improved working conditions. In the view of the author, the actions have rather generated a more bureaucratic organization.

How is the situation perceived six years later?

Figure 4 shows that in many areas the assessment of their present situation is higher than in 1968. The individual has reached a higher position – though not yet been promoted; the wage is higher; the work is more independent; one has received more training; and the social status has increased. On the other hand, in some areas the situation is regarded as less rewarding: the relationship with comrades was better in school than later on; opportunities for personal development are now seen as substantially lower; and the same applies to the meaningfulness of work. Furthermore, the working conditions have become less favourable. Lastly, job security is viewed the same way as before, and this area is the only one in which – quite reasonably – the rating has not changed over the past years. A state employee is almost undismissible in Sweden.

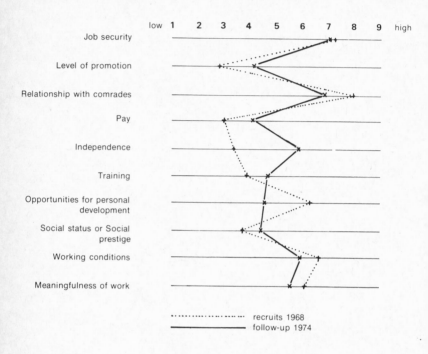

Fig. 4. Assessment of the present work situation by the recruits in 1968 and by the follow-up group in 1974.

Even if the assessment has improved in some areas, the general outlook has hardly changed (Fig. 5). Even if the absolute level has increased, they still regard their situation as too low to be satisfactory in relation to their lowest demands. Further, many of the recruits' expectations have not been met. In some cases the conditions have changed from being acceptable to being less acceptable, i.e. as regards opportunities for personal development, meaningfulness of work, and working conditions.

In relation to their expectations in 1968 (Fig. 6), in all areas but relationship with comrades and independence they have not in 1974 reached the level of expectations. The ratings made in 1968 concerned one year ahead; after six years these expectations are still far from being complied with.

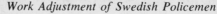

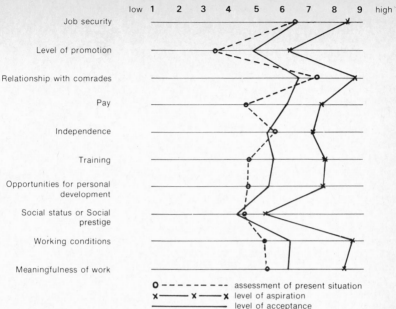

Fig. 5. Assessment of the present work situation by the follow-up group in relation to their demands.

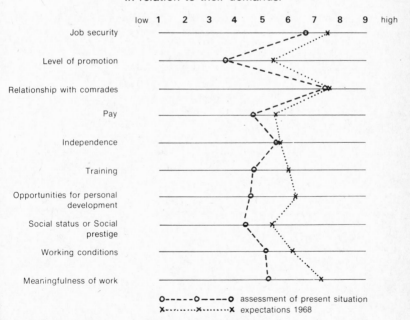

Fig. 6. Perceived work benefit by the 1974 follow-up group in relation to their expectations in 1968.

So far there is strong agreement between the picture that emerges from the follow-up study in 1974 and the description by the senior policemen in 1968. Based on the notion of unrealistic expectations, one interpretation would be that estimates of the future always tend to be too optimistic. Figure 7, however, shows that the estimated picture of the future which the follow-up group made in 1974, in no essential respect deviates from their assessment of the present situation. Thus today (1974) the policeman does not expect any decisive improvements in his work – at least not within a short time perspective. In this respect too the recruits have become similar to their older colleagues from 1968.

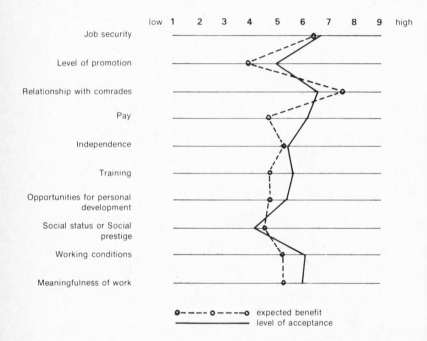

Fig. 7. Expected work benefit by the 1974 follow-up group in relation to lowest demands.

A comparison between the perception of the situation by the recruits in 1974 and that of the senior policemen in 1968 demonstrates that their respective work situations are scarcely different (Fig. 8). On the other hand, the assessment is very different for the recruits in 1968 and in 1974, as has already been shown (Fig. 4). Accordingly, data indicate that, firstly, work has not changed since 1968 and, secondly, the ratings have a high degree of accuracy.

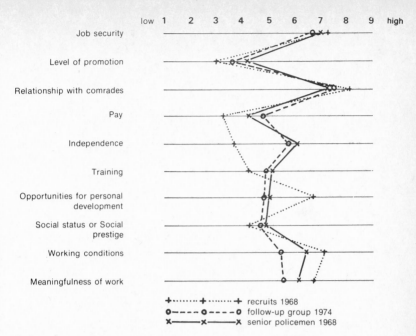

Fig. 8. Comparison between the assessments of their present work situation by recruits in 1968, the follow-up group in 1974, and the senior policemen in 1968.

As shown previously, since 1968 the recruits have achieved improvements in some areas. In others deterioration has taken place, and in some of these cases they perceive their situation in 1974 as lower than it was assessed by the senior group in 1968. In general there is a slight tendency towards a higher assessment of the present situation by the senior policemen.

A cautious interpretation would be that with increasing length of service there is some improvement. Alternatively, this observation can be interpreted as due to the circumstance that the situation has – especially in some respects – become less favourable since 1968.

In the original study in 1968 it could be demonstrated that satisfaction with work was not directly related to the assessment of the present situation. In spite of considerably lower benefits than the senior policemen, the recruits were still more satisfied. This observation was seen in the light of the recruits' expectations as regards satisfactory benefits in the future. The differences in satisfaction are shown in Figure 9. Simultaneously we can also see that the recruits of 1968 are less satisfied at the time of the follow-up study. Despite increased benefits in several areas six years later, they thus get much less satisfaction out of their work, and their lower satisfaction is almost identical with that of the senior policemen in 1968.

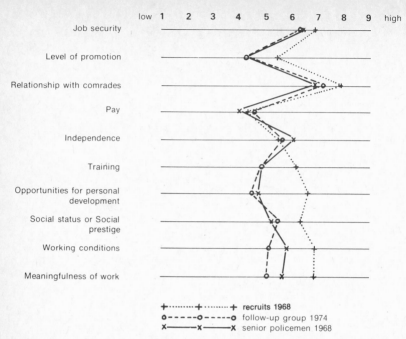

Fig. 9. Comparison of satisfaction between the recruits in 1968, the follow-up group in 1974, and the senior policemen in 1968.

The development of the work situation can briefly be summarized:

The job expectations as a policeman which the respondent held as a recruit have not been met. Although he now perceives the present work situation as more positive in many areas, this increased level still does not correspond to the expectation he had as a recruit. Neither does the present situation meet even the lowest demand in the majority of work areas, with the result that work satisfaction has dropped. The satisfaction during the initial period was related to the expectations, which later turn out not to correspond with the actual work situation. Neither does the respondent expect any improvements in the near future; he is drastically less optimistic concerning possibilities of achieving his aspirations than at the time of being a recruit.

In 1968 there were big differences in the perception of the possibilities in police work between the recruits and the senior policemen. These differences almost entirely disappeared. The follow-up group makes assessments that are identical with those of the senior policemen six years earlier. Johansson & Flint (1973) were able to demonstrate an increasing similarity in occupational interests and values between police recruits and senior policemen during the first year of service. Such a socialization process during the initial period in a new occupation probably contributes to the adjustment to the work situation, and maybe to the acceptance of what 'normally' would have been considered an unsatisfactory job.

The six years that passed between the studies evidently did not bring about any major changes in the work situation in many important respects. For the recruits these years have meant an increased insight into the limited opportunities in police work – a picture that strongly deviated from their expectations. The lack of expected future improvements would, according to the perspective used here, lead to a process of resignation. From the observations made so far, we thus expect that the follow-up group have adjusted to work by a process of resignation.

HOW HAS THE RECRUIT BECOME ADJUSTED?

Resignation is a reaction to an unsatisfactory situation which the individual feels it is impossible to change. Resignation means, among other things, that one gives up personal ambitions and lowers one's demands. From Figure 10 it can be seen that since 1968 the recruits' perception of what constitutes an acceptable situation has decreased somewhat. The difference is not big, and not big enough to make the present situation acceptable. In spite of higher

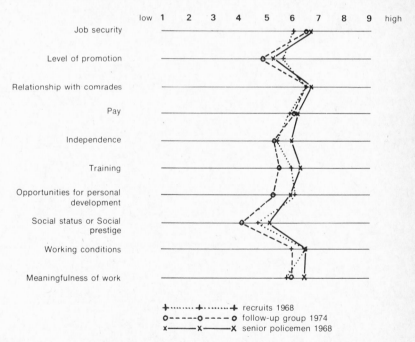

Fig. 10. Comparison of level of acceptance between the recruits in 1968, the follow-up group in 1974, and the senior policemen in 1968.

assessment of the present situation, the general lowered level of acceptance thus indicates a process of resignation on the part of the recruits.

Somewhat unexpectedly, the senior policemen had higher demands than the recruits had on either of the two occasions. However, the assessments by the senior policemen indicate that one does not lower one's aspirations further with increasing age. The senior group has the lowest aspirations in two significant areas: level of promotion and opportunities for personal development. As they belong to a non-promoted group of relatively high age, this observation supports the hypothesis of lowered aspirations in the light of opportunities.

Another form of passive adjustment could be to lower the importance attributed to areas where the perception of the present situation is low and expected to remain so. The ratings of importance, as depicted in Figure 11, show only small and non-systematic differences between the groups. One interpretation could be that this aspect is so strongly influenced by social norms that more situational factors do not have any noticeable effect. In two important respects, however, the recruits have made a re-evaluation. Promotion and training have become less important. In the case of promotion their evaluation now coincides with that of their elders. Training is now

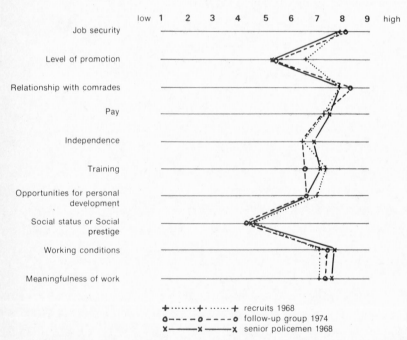

Fig. 11. Comparison of importance of each area between the recruits in 1968, the follow-up group in 1974, and the senior policemen in 1968.

attributed even less importance by the recruits than by their elders, while earlier there was almost complete agreement. These two areas then to some extent indicate declining professional ambitions, which would be in line with the lowered demands for promotions. One can further notice that meaningfulness of work and working conditions become more important with increasing age and experience.

So far one can thus speak of a process of resignation among the recruits. They have lowered their demands and attribute less importance to a career. Nevertheless, the lowered demands have not led to their demands being met. For most areas there are still discrepancies between the present situation and the level of acceptance, as previously shown.

An active way to react against an unsatisfactory situation – the opposite of resignation – is to try to change it for the better. In work this can be done, e.g., by acquiring new skills, further training, applying for promotion or transfer. In some organizations there are better prospects for this kind of improvement than in others; variations depending on e.g. size, policies, organizational structure, and age structure of employees. Figure 12 shows how the policemen perceived their possibilities of improving the situation.

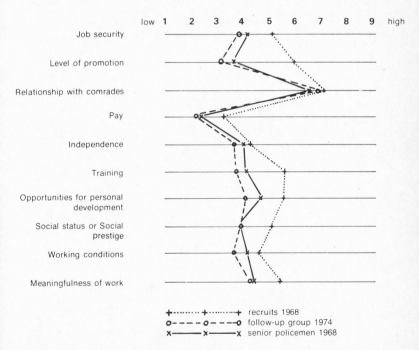

Fig. 12. Comparison of possibilities of improving one's situation between the recruits in 1968, the follow-up group in 1974, and the senior policemen in 1968.

Since the period as a recruit, the belief in possibilities of improving one's situation has decreased drastically in all areas. The opinion after six years coincides almost entirely with that of the seniors six years earlier. In most cases the follow-up group is even slightly more pessimistic, which can be due to the factual organizational changes that have taken place during the follow-up period. Typically, the agreement is strongest in the area of relationships with comrades, which also receives a very high assessment.

In particular, the belief in the opportunities of influencing the level of promotion has decreased. This tendency again supports the earlier observations on resignation in this area. The possibilities of improving the situation are regarded as lowest in the pay area, which supposedly reflects the position of the individual employee in relation to a centralized wage bargaining system without local negotiations or allowance for individual adjustments.

In a similar study from industry almost identically low values were obtained for middle-aged workers, and the assessments of the opportunities are made on such a low level that it seems well-founded to speak of powerlessness. Van Maanen (1975) found in a study of police recruits that work motivation declined strongly over time. This drop in motivation was linked to lowered expectations of achieving personal success by one's own effort. Also, the adjustment to reality from the period as a recruit meant lessened belief in one's opportunities. Van Maanen ascribes these effects to the bureaucratic and hierarchical organization of the police and a reward system that encourages passivity: 'lie low, relax, and don't expect too much'.

PROMOTION – THE ONLY OPENING FOR PERSONAL DEVELOPMENT?

The results here support the impression that during the six years covered by the study little seems to have changed in police work – at least not for the better. After six years' service the recruits view the situation in the same way as the older policemen did six years earlier. The work is also regarded as much less favourable than was expected as a recruit. In the original study the opportunities for promotion and personal development together with pay level were seen as the most critical areas:

> Against this background of seemingly very small opportunities for further training and little encouragement towards personal improvement, the differences between the groups in the area of opportunities for personal development should be viewed. This area is one of the three that the older group perceives to be far below their demands, while the young find it well level with theirs. The young also have high expectations for the future and their demands are higher. Regarding opportunities for personal development, the difference in satisfaction is the largest; the old being much less satisfied. The perceptions by the two groups in this area are in most respects so different, that one would expect a rough adjustment to reality on behalf of the recruits after the completion of training.

This follow-up shows that after six years the picture drawn by the senior policemen is still valid, and that the prediction has been verified. With the present organization of the police, promotion still seems to be the critical factor with regard to wage level, as well as opportunities for training and personal development. The strong interest in promotion finds its expression in a recent survey on Swedish policemen by Wahlund & Nerell (1976), and this area in particular has lately been subjected to experiments in increased employee participation with so-called Appointment Councils.

The promotion area is the most unfavourably evaluated in almost all respects. There is a big gap between the lowest demands and the assessment of the present situation. Expectations are far from being reached, and promotion is seen as difficult to influence – particularly in comparison with what one thought as a recruit. An investigation in the Kristianstad region in Sweden also showed that the majority of the policemen (75 per cent) – for policemen of lowest rank 90 per cent – were dissatisfied with the opportunities for promotion (Liedberg & Rasmusson 1971).

Since 1968 the composition of positions of different rank has been changed and thereby also the opportunities for promotion. In 1968 the chances of achieving a position as *'polis assistent'* or higher were one in three. In 1974 there was a 50 per cent chance of acquiring a position above the first step – a considerable improvement as it seems. In the follow-up group some 30 per cent had still not reached higher than the first stage after training *(extra poliskonstapel)*. The other two-thirds are on the next level *(e.o. polisman)*, which is not a promoted rank. One person seems to have become police inspector, but it is safe to say that almost no one in this group has yet received any promotion after six years of service.

The development for Swedish policemen is – apart from the results from central negotiations – directly and entirely connected with rank and seniority. Progress within the profession, however, can also be achieved through further training and thereby not necessarily in connection with a promotion. Apart from the basic training during the recruit period, there is a higher police course, available at present after about six years of service. The follow-up group had at the time of this study not yet participated in this second training step. It turned out that in the following year this age group was given the training. The perception of training opportunities shall thus be viewed against the background that the recruits had not yet received any general further training but only short courses on an individual basis. Sixty per cent of them had participated in this kind of shorter training. There is a rather big and varied supply of short courses, but they do not seem to meet the demand for further training. A strong wish for more training is expressed in the interviews.

It should then be stressed that owing to the strong connection between the opportunities for development and promotion, the police organization seems

172   JAN FORSLIN

at present to have insufficient resources as regards utilizing the interest among
the employees for personal improvement. Such a development depends on
training and progress to more qualified duties. Both these means depend on
promotion, which is something that takes time and is not achievable for many.

INCREASED EMPLOYEE PARTICIPATION?

One of the major political issues during the 1970s has been democratization
of work, and one objective has been to increase the influence of the individual
on his own work. The follow-up study shows that particularly in this respect,
there is a big difference between the expectations and the small opportunities.
Looked at as a whole, the possibilities of influencing the situation for the
better seem to be very small. In 1974 recruits assessed their later opportunities less favourably than the senior policemen did in 1968. If one judges from
these observations, the development in police work in Sweden seems to have
moved in a direction opposite to the value change in society at large and to
factual changes that have taken place in work towards increased democracy.

In the interviews this issue was treated with some additional open questions. The answers support the earlier observation as to insufficent influence
by the individual policeman. Almost all of the interviewees thought it to be
important to have influence on all levels in the police organization and more
room for individual initiatives. Some discontent was expressed towards their
own union with regard to its ignorance about the views of the members. In
the survey by Wahlund & Nerell (1976), the police personnel was the group
among all public employees that made the lowest assessment of their
possibilities of influencing decisions concerning their work situation. Increased bureaucracy, too big units, and centralization are also reported by
Cedermark & Klette (1973) as serious obstacles to a satisfactory work
situation in the police organization.

Opinions that reflect the presence of strict boundaries and large distances
between different groups of personnel and between departments were found
in the follow-up study. Such factors make communication and interaction
difficult, and the consequence is lack of understanding between different
groups in the organization. As expressed by one interviewee: 'Management
should act with more concern for their personnel and stop being morbidly
suspicious'. All those interviewed wanted increased support from above and
co-determination in important matters, so that vital questions were not carried
out against the opinion of the personnel. Those concerned should participate
in the decision-making. The development towards bigger units is experienced
as sacrificing democratic values in favour of efficiency. What is gained by
rationalization of work is lost by decreased interest in work. The individual
policeman is getting fewer and fewer possibilities of influencing the situation,
and his freedom is reduced. Suggestions from lower ranks are not considered.

Changes are designed at the office desk with insufficient knowledge about the practical reality out in the field.

An attitude survey by the police union and the employer has presented a similar picture. It disclosed a strong dissatisfaction with the management. One thought that there was a lack of training for personnel in supervisory positions. In another study on recruits and senior policemen by Andreasson (1969), managment and supervision were also found as critical areas. Much criticism was also formulated against individual lack of influence.

Even considering that by questions of this kind an overcritical attitude is easily evoked, the conclusion must still be that the conditions for police personnel are unsatisfactory and undemocratic. Especially remarkable is the decrease in the possibilities of influencing and improving the work situation – a decrease appears to have taken place during the six years that have passed between the two studies. It seems that in order to implement the programme for personnel policy accepted by TCO-S *(Tjänstemännens central organisation)* – the umbrella organization for the police union in 1976 – vast changes would be necessary in the organization of police work and in personnel policy.

QUITTING POLICE WORK?

If the policeman regards the benefits from his work as not satisfactory and sees no possibility of improving the situation in the future either, one possible course of action is to quit – to leave the present employer and try to find another position. It is therefore of interest to know how the policemen regard their prospects of finding a better alternative to police work – Figure 13.

In 1968 the senior policemen made a very pessimistic estimate of their possibilities of finding alternative and more rewarding employment. Their rating was at the same low level as that of industrial workers of the same age. This low faith in the labour market thus constituted an explanation why the senior policemen remained in police work in spite of the fact that they regarded it as unsatisfactory. The recruits made a much more optimistic evaluation of their chances in the labour market. Nonetheless, they assumed that they would remain with the police, since they expected that an acceptable situation would materialize after training. After they have stayed in their jobs for six years, got the same experience as their seniors, and shared the unfavourable working conditions with them, how do they then look upon opportunities for other jobs? In 1974 the follow-up group is even more optimistic than in 1968 and has in this respect *not* approached the opinion of their older colleagues.

Going back to our starting point, one would expect that a number of the young policemen would leave their work. The work situation in many important areas does not meet even their lowest demands. Neither do they expect decisive improvements or see opportunities to better the situation by

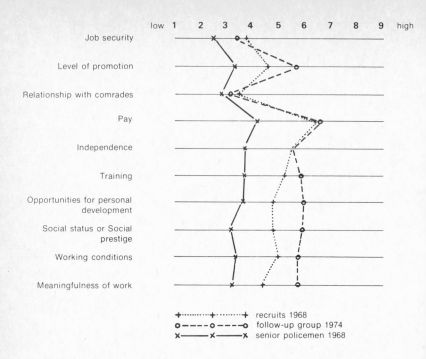

Fig. 13. Comparison of prospects of getting a better job between the recruits in 1968, the follow-up group in 1974, and the senior policemen in 1968.

their own initiatives. At the same time the opportunities for better employment are regarded as relatively good. Sixty per cent thought they would have good opportunities of finding a better occupation – which in the case of a policeman means a change of occupation.

The follow-up group must now make the decision either to remain in a work situation where they know the limitations and assess them in the same way as their many years older colleagues, or on the basis of their optimism regarding the labour market decide to abandon the police job. After another ten years in police work they will also have given up their ambitions regarding a better occupation.

From the personnel statistics, however, we know that the overwhelming majority will remain policemen till they retire. Seventy per cent of the former recruits were in 1974 certain that they would remain with the police in the next ten years. The other 30 per cent thought it to be the likely outcome. The same distribution was obtained from middle-aged industrial workers with low mobility. In comparison only 25 per cent of the highly mobile youngest group expected to remain in the occupation. The results from the follow-up group thus defy the most important assumption of the model used here: namely that one leaves an unsatisfactory work situation if one sees any better alternative. This is also the basic question in the study of work adjustment. Why does a person choose to adjust to an unsatisfactory work situation instead of looking for a better one? Here there should be introduced one more aspect of change in jobs. To leave a job and take on another is in most cases connected with economic and other costs for the individual – mobility barriers and vested interests. To be with the police for some years entails considerable sacrifices in terms of a long recruitment period with low pay, exclusion of alternative educations, and several years in the lowest wage category. At the same time the individual participates in a regulated promotion system with at least a theoretical opportunity of success and a high degree of security. Still the answer is lacking to the question: why does a policeman remain in the police force – in the same way as to the question why does a thief remain thievish?

NOTE

[1] I am highly indebted to Mrs Edith Mägiste for her assistance in this follow-up study. *Svenska Polisförbundet* (The Swedish Association of Policemen) has kindly given access to address files of its members and its representatives have participated in discussions of preliminary findings. *Rikspolisstyrelsen* (the governing body of the police) in Sweden has made lecture time available at *Polisskolan* (the Police Training Center) in Solna for data collection and discussions of results. Fil.mag. Gunilla Cedermark – teacher in psychology for policemen – has given invaluable support and assistance.

REFERENCES:

ANDREASSON, B. (1969): *Vikt- och nöjdhetsupplevelse av vissa arbetsområden. En jämförelse mellan olika åldersgrupper.* Stockholm: PA rådet. (mimeo).
CEDERMARK, G. & KLETTE, H. (1973): *Polis, myndighet – människa.* Lund: Studentlitteratur.
FORSLIN, J. (1971): *Förväntat och upplevt utbyte i arbetet. En jämförelse mellan en grupp polisaspiranter och en grupp äldre polismän.* Stockholm: PA rådet. Rapport nr. 32.
FORSLIN, J. (1978): Arbetsanpassning. *Utvärdering av en psykologisk modell mot bakgrund av två empiriska studier.* Stockholm: PA rådet. Meddelande nr. 71.
FORSLIN, J. & MÄGISTE, E. (1978): *Arbetsanpassning – en uppföljning av polisaspiranter.* Stockholm: PA rådet. Rapport nr. 121.
HEDBERG, M. (1976): *The process of labour turnover.* Stockholm: PA rådet. Meddelande nr. 52.
JOHANSSON, C. B. & FLINT, R.T. (1973): Vocational Preferences of Policemen. *Vocational Guidance Quarterly 22*, 40–42.
LIEDBERG & RASMUSSON (1971): *Arbetsförhållanden inom poliskåren. En undersökning av arbetsanpassning och trivsel i Kristianstads och Simrishamns polisdistrikt.* Lund: Pedagogiska institutionen vid Lunds universitet (mimeo).

MAANEN VAN, J. (1975): Police socialization. A longitudinal examination of job attitudes in an urban police department. *Administrative Science Quarterly, 20* 207–228.

Medbestämmande i praktiken. (1973) Stockholm: Delegationen för förvaltningsdemokrati. DEFF-rapport nr. 5.

WAHLUND, I. & NERELL, G. (1976): *Tjänestemännens arbetsmiljöer.* Stockholm: TCO. Arbete-hälsa-välbefinnande. Rapport nr. 1.

Policing Labour Conflicts

BY *Jørgen Jepsen*

I. INTRODUCTION

This paper comments upon the changing situation of the police in a so-called welfare state. It is based upon a series of incidents occurring in Denmark during the years 1973–1978 in which the 'public peace and order' were challenged. In these incidents the police and the legal system were used to maintain order and to contain social problems in a manner that involved a serious challenge to police self-perceptions as 'neutral' and to the legal ideology of 'equality before the law'.

This paper is not confined to dealing with labour conflicts in a narrow sense, in as much as conflicts involving workers and employers only make up one section of the analysis – although the predominant one. But the handling of these conflicts is also contrasted with the handling of parallel conflicts between farmers and the state, and between fishermen and the state.

The common feature of these conflicts is that they were carried out by an occupational group or class in order to further the economic interest of that particular group or class. The means applied by the demonstrators in each case have allegedly involved violations of ordinances protecting 'public order', traffic law (the farmers' demonstrations), or ordinances of the local port authorities (the fishermen's demonstrations).

In all three types of cases the grounds for action were major social problems, to which the law and the legal system had no adequate response, i.e. questions to which the 'legitimate answer' was basically unacceptable to the actors.

In all of them the police and the legal system as a whole have been called into action, because of the 'breach of the peace' which these actions have involved. From the standpoint of the duty to maintain law and order, the role of the police has been at issue.

In all three types of cases the actual behaviour of the police – activity or passivity – has been an important public issue. All three sets of cases have formed the basis for discussion and political disagreement on the proper role of the police and the legal system both in and outside parliament. Furthermore, lawyers and legal scholars have disputed over the relative merits of the modes of police behaviour, and a series of publications, legal as well as popular, has been issued, dealing with these incidents and their interpretation.

But it is the important differences in the response of the legal system in general and in the behaviour of the police in particular in relation to the different cases that form the basis for the following analysis. There are variations of a geographical nature, variations in the time-dimension, and variations related to the type of conflict. It is these variations that arouse interest from the perspectives of criminal policy, police science, sociology of law – and from a class perspective.

II. SOME BASIC FEATURES OF THE DANISH POLICE AND PROSECUTION SYSTEMS

In connection with the use of the term 'prosecution' it is necessary to draw attention to the structure of the Danish police and its discretion in relation to the investigation and prosecution of offences and the maintenance of order.

Denmark is divided into a total of 54 police districts, each headed by a *politimester* ('police master' or 'chief of police') (in Copenhagen *politidirektør*). This head of the local police is a lawyer by training and has a double function: as head of the police force, and as local chief prosecutor.

The police force, again, is divided into two sections: *kriminalpolitiet,* the investigative police (plain clothes), and a (uniformed) force to maintain order, including traffic, *ordenspolitiet* ('order police'). The great bulk of these two sections of the police force are not lawyers by training. *The investigative police* primarily investigates criminal law violations, while *the 'order police'* regulates public behaviour by patrols and by responses to calls, as well as through traffic regulation, but they also investigate certain minor offences, primarily those termed 'police offences' in the Code of Criminal Procedure. The latter include violations of the local police ordinances, which regulate behaviour in public places such as streets, railway stations, etc. The local police ordinances are modelled on a *Standard Police Ordinance,* promulgated by the Ministry of Justice and amended only occasionally.

In addition to being the head of the police proper, the local chief of police is also the head of a local staff of *'police prosecutors'* (all trained in law), who decide on and carry out prosecutions in minor cases, and who make recommendations to the regional prosecutor, the *District Attorney,* on the question of prosecution – or waivers of prosecution – in major cases ('DA-cases').

There is a total of 9 such regional prosecutors *(statsadvokater* – District Attorneys' 'DAs'), each with his own legal staff. The 'DAs' carry out prosecutions in major cases and supervise the local police prosecutors.

Finally, the *Attorney General (Rigsadvokaten, RA)* supervises the District Attorneys, receives certain important types of cases for review and/or prosecution-decision, and issues general instructions to the lower prosecutors. In addition, he carries out prosecution before the Supreme Court, either personally or through a special DA located in his office. The Attorney General is the top person within the hierarchy of appointed officials.

However, the *Minister of Justice* (assisted by his Ministry of public servants) is formally the supreme head of the prosecution. He may – also on political grounds, but naturally under parliamentary responsibility – either stop a prosecution started or recommended by a lower prosecutor, or he may order a lower prosecutor to prosecute a case which the latter might be inclined to drop. In recent years, this power has been used very little by ministers of justice, an unmistakable decline in relation to the practices of former times.

The local chief of police has little room for discretion in relation to prosecution/non-prosecution, as he is here 'the low man on a rather tall totem-pole' of hierarchical organs. Nevertheless, the official concept of prosecution in Denmark is not the legality principle, but the 'opportunity principle', which affords the local chief of police a certain, but not uncontrolled, field for discretion. It is, however, the control of the lower strata exercised by the DAs and the RA which in reality regulates the discretion of the police prosecutors, and not the decisions of the Minister of Justice.

In relation to *the maintenance of public order, and the prevention of crime* – i.e. the traditional police functions – the local chief of police has a much wider discretion. In principle, the local chief of police has the supreme decision on what measures to take against incipient crime and disorder, and he can not fall back upon the prosecution hierarchy in this sphere. In relation to the police functions, there does exist a hierarchy on the national level, involving a *National Chief of Police (Rigspolitichefen)*, but he has only administrative responsibilities and powers (personnel, budget, etc.) and controls a few special-service branches, including a 'flying squad' for major complex cases. He has no formal line of command of the local police forces. Until recently, local chiefs of police have thus had considerable powers and discretion in relation to 'maintaining order'.

In recent years, however, inroads have been made on these powers. Firstly, regional forces have been created, which may be used in the case of major disturbance, because, inter alia, they have greater resources – dogs, arms, etc. Secondly, in disturbances involving several police districts, the line of command changes, so that the National Chief of Police *may* take command and coordinate the actions of the local districts involved.

According to an Ordinance of 26 June 1968, '. . . if simultaneously in several police districts there should occur violent, suddenly arisen riots which require assistance from outside . . . the National Chief of Police himself will – when possible after negotiation with the local chiefs of police involved – take the initiative to coordinate the actions of the police.'

In one of the labour conflicts described below (the 'Bækkelund case') the local chief of police publicly declared that he would have liked to have a 'hot line' to the Ministry of Justice. But he did *not* have such a hot line; the

Minister of Justice himself (Orla Møller) declared that the maintenance of order was the responsibility of the local chief of police, and that he himself could not – and would not – interfere with or try to advise on such decisions.

From this description of the situation of the local chiefs of police it should be clear that it is an important issue *how the local chief of police defines the situation: If* he judges that a crime has been committed, he is obliged to follow the practice and the line in the prosecution section, *but if* he defines the situation as one of maintaining order, he is free to decide on his own.

This *Definitionsmacht der Polizei*[1] (definitional power of the police) is normally initially exercised by the local policeman on the beat, and his decision to handle the matter himself – informally – or to refer the matter 'upwards' is a touchstone for the way the powers of the police are perceived by the public and crucial for the actual effects of the definitional power. It gives room for abuse – as well as for 'reasonable' handling of situations, based upon the knowledge and evaluation of local conditions by local policemen. An informal handling of the situation is more likely, the closer the policeman is to the local community. To the extent that 'foreign power' and control is introduced, the situation will become more complex and a formal, legalistic response more likely.[2]

Thus the exercise of the power to 'define the situation' may result in reporting, prosecution, and other actions defining the situation as a crime, *or* in the definition of the situation as a matter for informal handling as a matter of maintaining order.

III. TYPES OF POLICE ACTION

To denote two ideal-types of response I shall use two key-terms: *confrontation* and *absorption,* to describe the behaviours of the police and the legal system as a whole.

The term *'confrontation', indicating open and acknowledged conflict,* is used in a double sense. On the part of the police this includes *firstly* the most extreme form of police behaviour: the exercise of force, of physical violence. But *secondly* – and more importantly – it indicates the use of stronger, more severe measures where a milder measure *might* have been used, e.g. dispersion of a crowd instead of regulation, reporting instead of oral warnings, the taking of names of individuals instead of general regulation, prosecution instead of dismissal. In general, then, the term confrontation indicates a *choice of stricter measures* in situations where the police do have a discretion. It thus indicates *a tendency in the selection* of means of action, rather than the specific actions in and of themselves.

Absorption, on the other hand, may be seen as the use of *milder* courses of action in a situation where the police has a choice, where there is room for discretion. Most importantly, it may occur when a situation is defined as a problem of public order, rather than as a violation. *If* a law violation is assumed, absorption may also occur, e.g. in relation to: 1) the legal subsumption – which violation is deemed to have occurred, 2) the way the violation is handled: with a warning on the spot, or through reporting, 3) the evaluation of whether the case can 'carry' a prosecution – an evaluation involving the severity of the offence and the quality of the proof, 4) the amount of effort invested in clearing up the case, 5) the number and types of persons to whom the offence is attributed, and finally, 6) the sanctions demanded, once the prosecution has been decided upon: fine or imprisonment, etc.

On each of these points of decision, the police has some room for discretion. But also in the very early stages, one might find room for choice of action: the policeman on the beat may ignore certain indications of disturbances or illegalities – he may 'look the other way', physically or mentally, and the policeman at the station may ignore a call, *or* he may define the situation as not requiring further investigation or intervention. Finally, he may point to reasons for not intervening, e.g. lack of resources, or to official policies. Such a choice of a 'milder' response, either in the form of passivity *or* in the form of the choice of less severe forms of intervention, again, will be termed 'absorption' as opposed to the more formalistic-legalistic type of response.

As long as the policeman's exercise of this discretion stays within 'reasonable limits', his decision is 'correct'. In most situations the police are probably likely to avoid criticism by choosing an absorptive rather than a confronting approach.

The handling of a situation involving violations of public peace and order may be criticized from an administrative perspective, mostly: were the means adequate? But it is hard to nail the police in its exercise of this discretion. It is more difficult to avoid criticism when it is a question of the handling of a crime: here passivity may more easily be criticized as a breach of the principle of 'equality before the law', provided the facts are reasonably well-known. But the most difficult and controversial issue is really the definition of the situation.

IV. OPEN SOCIAL CONFLICT IN DENMARK – AND THE POLICE

In the following accounts of a series of incidents, an evaluation will be given of the actions of the police (and of the legal system as a whole) on the basis of official accounts, including, where possible, court material and public reports. In relation to one of the incidents – the 'Hope-Computer case' – the report is also based upon a special study, involving observation of the court proceedings in the lower and superior courts and upon interviews with the 'actors' in the case: the local chief of police, the District Attorney, the lower court judge, the Counsel for the Defence and most of the accused themselves, as well as interviews with journalists and eyewitnesses.

1. 1871–1972

The history of the governing Social Democratic Party in Denmark contains cherished elements of confrontation between the early socialist movement, which ultimately resulted in the establishment of the Social Democratic Party, and representatives of the oppressive bourgeoisie, confrontations in which the police were used against the workers – such as the imprisonment of the early socialist pioneers Pio, Brix and Geleff on temerary charges, the corruption of Pio by the Copenhagen Chief of Police, and the maltreatment of these pioneers in prison.

The official social democratic historians also tell of the role of the police in fighting the workers' movement with physical violence, e.g. in the battles in Fælledparken, Copenhagen (1871), Grønttorvet (1918), Esbjerg (1923), Randers (1924) and Nakskov (1931). Even when the King violated the parliamentary constitution and almost brought on a revolutionary situation in the Easter Crisis of 1920, the police were battling demonstrators, backed up by the knowledge that military forces were held discreetly in reserve should the police force prove insufficient or 'unreliable'.

But with the advent and growth of the Social Democratic hegemony during the 1930s and 1940s, these battles came to be considered a thing of the past. The police were accepted as part of the state apparatus taken over by the workers' legitimate governments. An ideology of legality and neutrality gradually prevailed and glossed over the skirmishes.

The '40s (post war), the '50s, and the '60s saw no major conflicts between the police and the working population. On some occasions, the workers in labour conflicts might use physical blockades in their struggle with the management and in their attempts to increase workers' organization.

The post-war years also saw the occasional use of physical (and organizational) blockades of employers' premises, and of moderate physical violence against workers who behaved in a fashion perceived as unsolidary by colleagues. But the police would use absorptive responses in such incidents: stay away, or arrive too late, demand a formal notification, react only with mild reproaches, etc., all under the guise of an 'ideology of neutrality'. There were no organizational or political protests against this mode of reaction, nor did any of the incidents become so serious as to evoke major attention.

Danish fishermen have occasionally staged demonstrations that entailed a potential 'show of force'. Thus major parts of the fishing fleet on some occasions sailed to Copenhagen to draw attention to their cause (as e.g. to demand the creation of a fishing port in North-West Jutland (Hanstholm)). But no major confrontation resulted between the police and the fishermen.[3]

The predominant theme, however, was relative peace and an image of police legality and neutrality. The absorptive response of the police neutralized potential conflicts. But on the other hand it also gave the workers the impression that the legal system tolerated some physical means as part of the 'well-acquired rights' of the working class in Denmark.

In the 1960s, however, the police came into more direct confrontation with other population groups in connection with a growing number of demonstrations, e.g. popular marches against the stationing of nuclear devices on Danish soil, anti-Vietnam-war demonstrations, demonstrations outside foreign embassies, the 'World-Bank demonstrations' etc. Several of these demonstrations went peacefully, while others resulted in scuffles between police and demonstrators. Mutual antagonism resulted, the demonstrators protesting against police harassment, violence, and undue interference, while the police maintained that 'professional troublemakers' and 'communist (or just leftist) infiltrators' tried to excite riots. These altercations evidenced unsystematic variation between techniques of absorption and the use of confrontation, some of it rather drastic in nature.

In these incidents, the police acted as upholders of 'public security, peace and order' on behalf of the state. To some extent they legitimized excesses by asserting the need for the state to protect the physical integrity of foreign representatives, regardless of political background. The groups with which the police clashed comprised more or less spontaneous groupings with no specific economic or occupational interest behind them. They were 'leftist' or 'rightist' political dissenters, not classes. They were moved by ideological and political protests, rather than by occupational interests.

On one occasion (the anti-USA-Vietnam demonstrations) an open legal conflict ensued when demonstrators were brought to court to be fined for violence against officials and obstruction of traffic. They hired a well-known leftist defence counsel, who turned the court hearing into a 'process against the police', in which films and other evidence were used to demonstrate excessive use of force by the police. It had no effect upon the outcome of the case, but led to heated public debate, which undoubtedly nourished police hostility against 'leftist troublemakers' – and vice versa.

2. 1973–78

This period is economically and politically distinguished from the preceding years: economically by the termination of the 1960s 'boom' and the advent of the economic crisis; politically by the growth of the Glistrup tax-protesters' party, the end of the Social Democratic hegemony, and the shift of political power from left to right, followed by a swing of the Social Democratic Party in the same direction. The occupational groups were differently affected by the development. Thus *the farmers* experienced some years of adjustment of Danish agriculture to large-scale production in connection with Danish entry into the EEC, with consequent problems of employment in agriculture. Furthermore, the development-concentration of industry and capital, so-called structural rationalization, resulted in bankruptcies and economic difficulties for sections of the petty bourgeoisie. This led to frustration and diffuse protests from small producers and businessmen.

Danish *fisheries* had experienced a major boom in catches during the 1950s and '60s – primarily in fishing for industrial production (fish-meal and fish-oil made from consumption and non-consumption fisheries combined). But the unhampered growth – aided by tax-subsidies – of the fishing industry and the fishing fleet contributed to the quick exhaustion of the resources of the North Sea. The Danish 'greediness' in using edible fish for oil and fish-meal aroused hostile reactions against Danish fishermen among their colleagues around the North Sea. Quota negotiations in the NEAFC, and the difficulties in agreeing upon an EEC fishing policy further led to restrictions on the incomes of Danish fishermen, and ultimately to economic crises and bankruptcies. Whether due to fishing politics or to exhaustion of resources, the situation created desperation and frustration among Danish fishermen.

The economic and political changes led to negative consequences in other sectors as well. The liberalist parties that made inroads on the social democrats and split off traditional SD electorates into new parties (Glistrup's 'Progress Party' and the 'Center Democrats') and the creation of a right-wing 'Christian People's Party', splitting off to the right from the Agrarian Party, made their influence felt in parliament. This gave rise to new dissatisfaction in other groups, e.g. through reduction in support for students and welfare clients, the dismissal of staff in kindergartens and other institutions, and the opening up of the housing market and dealing in land for speculation and quick profits, to the detriment of the poorest part of the population.

This development put students and the poor in a similarly frustrated situation. A growing political consciousness among students as a result of the 1968 students' rebellion manifested itself in growing alliances between young intellectuals and 'the people', and in the growth of organized protest.

The 'legal system' had no outlet or means of resolution for these conflicts. There was no quick and legitimate solution to the insecurity of the farmers (only time gave the solution in the form of huge profits to those farmers who 'thought big' soon enough); the negotiations on EEC fishing policies in the North Sea could not replenish the exhausted resources; political solutions to the situation of the students and the tenants were blocked by the groupings of the political parties. Finally, the situation of the workers deteriorated as part of the general crisis of the Western world, and furthermore the entrance into the EEC gave grounds for fearing that Danish wages and Danish employment would be threatened by the European partners. Growing unemployment further weakened solidarity within the workers' class and their organizations, and employers were quick to grasp the opportunity to fix wages and conditions of work and to act to control dissidents among the working class by various methods of discipline – including the use of unorganized workers, where possible.

It is not surprising that these rising economic and political tensions demanded an outlet. In spite of Danish traditions of 'reasonableness' and non-violent solutions, the tensions increasingly manifested themselves in open social conflict. On the political level, the battle was fought first between the Social Democrats and the parties to its right – most prominently the 'Progress Party' and the 'Center Democrats' (seconded by the Conservatives and the Christian Party), later between these parties *and* the Social Democrats on the one side, and the parties to the left on the other.

The political system was not able to channel off these frustrations and aggressions, since all solutions were blocked by the political stalemate. Therefore, the conflicts increasingly came out into the open.

This 'openness' of conflict manifested itself as challenges to 'public peace and order', which escalated during the years following 1 January 1973 – the day when Denmark entered the Common Market. These conflicts necessarily involved the police as responsible for the maintenance of order. However, the police were no longer allowed to define the situation as one of 'maintaining order' only. The conflicts escalated to such an extent that it became a question of the power of the state apparatus to contain radical dissent and to preserve the legitimacy of the state. But a dislocation occurred, so that instead of being defined as a problem of conflict resolution, it became a question of maintaining order, i.e. police action.

Caught in this conflict between political and economic interests, between the majority and the minority, the police tried to maintain an image of 'neutrality', mainly by using the techniques of absorption. But the opportunities for using such techniques were drastically reduced by increased public and political attention to the conflicts.

This attention was mediated and to some extent steered by the mass media. The involvement of newspapers and – predominantly – TV made the daily operations of the police an instant political issue and thereby reduced the opportunities for the police to define the situations as 'problems of order', i.e. for informal handling, rather than as issues of law violations.

The behaviour of the police during this period followed an unsteady course, as the political influences made themselves felt in the daily operations. The discretion and balance exercised by the police could not therefore rest on the premises for police behaviour in general, but instead made the political function of the police more visible – and therefore more vulnerable.

This unsteady course of events showed *geographical* variations, variations *over time*, and variations related to *types of conflict*. In giving a brief survey of the events, I shall organize them in relation to *the* criterion that most distinguishes the differences in response: the criterion of the objects against whom the intervention was directed, i.e. occupational group or class.

V. OPEN CONFLICTS 1973–78: CLASS BEHAVIOUR – POLICE BEHAVIOUR

A. The farmers

Farmers blocking the Lillebælt bridge (28 March 1973)

On 28 March 1973, several groups of farmers in various places in Jutland blocked roads and road-crossings with their tractors and harvesters to protest against an ongoing major conflict in the labour market, which prevented the supply of ammonia for fertilizing. The aim of the demonstrations was to make the government interfere and dictate a solution to the conflicting parties (labour and management).

This was a clear act of desperation and did not have the desired effect (the conflict was solved through normal negotiations a few days later). The blocking itself involved a clear breach of the traffic law – a violation which the farmers readily admitted. Except for one police district, the police used absorption as a response: either by staying away, or regulating traffic, or – at the most – taking the names of the demonstrators. Only in one district was prosecution of several farmers undertaken. They were fined a symbolic amount (100 Dkr. each) – a sentence which was upheld upon appeal.

Although the incident was a serious challenge to public order and peace (it resulted in a serious accident on the Lillebælt bridge), it had no long-term perspective as a challenge to the basic political order. The appeal of the farmers to be acquitted as a measure of 'equality before the law' was not accepted by the court, and the Attorney General refused to withdraw charges, allegedly saying: 'We are not administering millimetre justice.'

B. The fishermen

Fishermen blocking the port of Halsskov (5 May 1978)

On three different occasions – in 1973, 1975 and 1978 – Danish fishermen seriously challenged 'public peace and order' by blocking the sailing or landing of ships, with measures of escalating severity.

1. In the *summer of 1973* several fishing boats blocked for almost one month the sailing of a ship, 'Grindal', from Esbjerg – the largest fishing port on the West coast of Jutland. The ship had been chartered to dump chemical waste near the breeding grounds of the fish in the North Sea. Government attempts to promote negotiations failed, and the attempts to 'outstay' the fishermen did not succeed. After one month, the dumping company gave in, hired another ship – and dumped into the Atlantic instead.

Here too, police action was predominantly absorptive – with no physical interference during the whole month. The only official action of control was a single policeman noting down the numbers and names of the blocking fishing boats. Although the action was in clear violation of the Port Ordinance, the authorities chose to ignore the violation, and not even to define it as a matter

13. Policing Scandinavia

of maintaining order. There may have been acceptance from above (by the regional DA's office and probably even from the government) of non-interference.

2. In *November 1975* a quota-crisis led to a blocking of several Jutland fishing-ports for several days in an attempt to put pressure on the Minister for Fishing to raise the limitation on fishing. The pressure had no immediate effect, and no real solution was – or could be – achieved. The action was rather dramatic; it involved violations of the Port Ordinances (not to mention threats of physical violence against fishermen and workers about to break the blockade). The incident led to a question in Parliament on why *this* incident was handled by absorption, when the blocking by workers of the Hope-Computer factory (see p. 189–190) had been met with confrontation. The question was evaded by the responsible minister, in part through a juridical construction (negotiations were going on, and no violation had been observed), in part by pointing to the drastic measures that would have to be taken to break the blockade. Several months later, however, several of the blockading fishermen were fined, albeit leniently.[4]

3. In *the spring of 1978* the quota problem broke out again. This time the fishing fleet from Bornholm blocked the harbour of Copenhagen for most of a day (May 5th) while other fishing boats blocked harbours in various other Danish ports, including the traffic ports connecting Copenhagen with the rest of the country. After several days of hesitation in the face of the threats, the Prime Minister finally stated that no negotiations would be undertaken to help the fishermen, as long as the illegal blocking was taking place. Furthermore, the government indicated that it was considering using the navy to break any further blockade. The fishermen gave up their blockade, and a few months later had legislation passed giving them (symbolic) economic support.

At this point, the use of absorption on the level of prosecution quickly reached its limit, undoubtedly influenced by the serious questioning in parliament of the legitimacy of non-intervention against the fishermen. The result was a swift order from the Attorney General to the local police chiefs to prosecute owners of the blocking fishing-boats. No charges were brought, however, against members of the 'Progress Party' who directly or indirectly encouraged the fishermen to break the law.

C. The workers

While it is notable that no physical confrontation occurred between the farmers or the fishermen and the police, the workers' actions were met with increasingly confrontative responses, both on the police order maintenance level *and* in the form of prosecution of several of the participants in the workers' actions. Viewed over a longer period, the response changed clearly over time in the direction *from* (attempted) absorption – the mode of

Workers demonstrating outside the Appellate Court in Ålborg in connection with the Hope-Computer case (3 February 1974).

adaptation preferred up until the early 1970s – to clear confrontation, characterized by the preference of more severe measures and the growing use of physical violence.

1. The first incident of this kind was the 'siege' of the *Hope-Computer* factory in Hadsund, Jutland, where angry workers demonstrated around the company plant during the evening and night of 8–9 January 1973, with the result that the (unorganized) workers, the staff, and several foreign visitors felt prevented from leaving the factory until 4.30 a.m. the next morning, when a major police force with dogs 'liberated' them. During part of the evening, TV was present. An incident that seemingly showed people being pushed back into the factory by angry demonstrators was broadcast in the late newscast.

The handling of this incident showed a shifting course between confrontation and absorption, varying over time, and varying in relation to the forum for decision.

The local chief of police tried to maintain an absortive response as long as possible, by traditional techniques: by staying away (he could not be located for several hours, but was finally found in the local Rotary Club), by not defining the calls of the director as the 'reporting of an offence', by passive observation of the events, etc. Not until it was clear that no negotiatory settlement would be reached, did he order intervention – by a 'riot squad' with dogs from the regional command – and only at such a late point that there was no risk of physical conflict – the 'detainees' could freely leave the factory.

The police chief continued this line of absorption when he stated to the press next morning that although he felt that a law violation had been committed, he would not prosecute anyone, as he felt the police should be cautious not to be seen as 'the extended arm of the employer'. This statement, however, released a confrontative response from the regional District Attorney, who had seen the incident on TV and ordered an investigation. Ultimately – supported by a question in parliament – the DA brought charges for illegal deprivation of liberty under the penal code against a total of 7 union leaders and two 'rank and file' demonstrators, accused of violence. The Minister of Justice refused to accept the suggestion of the unions to recall the charges.

The case brought out thousands of demonstrating workers in front of the court house in Hadsund on the first day of the hearings. The local court acquitted all but the one local union leader (the closest to an absorptive response the court felt it could go). Nevertheless, the sentence was immediately appealed by the defence, and the whole labour movement reacted heavily to the conviction, with strikes in several parts of the country.

On the first day of the hearing before the Appellate Court, 15,000 demonstrators with red (social democratic) banners went in procession through the streets of Ålborg as an indication of the workers' insistence that the case was in violation of 'well-acquired rights'.

The result was absorption: acquittal of all. The judgement of the court, a masterpiece in ambiguity and diplomacy, *in part* justified the acquittal with reference to police passivity, thus indirectly laying the way open for stricter action in the case of future blockades.

There can be little doubt that the vehement protest of the official labour movement and the crisis of legitimacy for the whole legal system produced by this case was operative in furthering the acquittal.

After the Hope case, the scene was quiet for some time, although the aftermath of the parliamentary and public debate of the Hope, the farmers' and the Grindal cases lasted for many months. However, in *January 1975*, a group of workers resumed the physical tactics in a situation where they felt their occupational situation seriously threatened by the crisis.

2. The workers of '*UNIPRINT*' occupied the plant of the firm in a protest against the owner's plan to move the work to Sweden to obtain higher profits. For several days police used an absorptive response, leaving the workers alone and waiting for negotiations between owner's and workers' representatives. Finally, however, the owner requested the police to remove the workers, and they were hauled out, mobilizing only passive resistance. After

a fresh occupation due to unsuccessful negotiations, they were removed anew in *March 1975*, this time with more use of force and with protestations of undue police violence. Charges for trespassing were dropped as a last measure of absorption. Ultimately, the owner carried out his plan and moved the production to Sweden.

3. The next confrontation came in the *summer of 1975* when *Copenhagen bus-drivers (the 'HT conflict')* tried to block the driveways as part of a strike for better wages, but were hauled away by policemen. Although their colleagues then refused to drive under police protection, the strike soon broke down for lack of union support.

4. In *September 1975* a situation arose bearing closer resemblance to the Hope-Computer case, but with more drastic results. Several union members tried to block the access of unorganized workers to the *Bækkelund Paper Works* in a small village in an unemployment area of Jutland. An 'extended demonstration' went on for several days, but was rather inefficient. Owing to lack of demonstrators, the unorganized workers managed to slip through. The whole action was closely supervised by the police. The local police chief – taking a lesson from the Hope case – initially tried to give his absorptive action a veil of legitimacy by regulating the picketing so as to keep it outside the company grounds, while leaving the company van free to come and go. On the other hand, the police chief accepted the 'right' of the workers to stop unorganized workers from entering the plant by means of physical blocking, not involving violence (the locking together of arms). The police chief furthermore regulated a counter-demonstration by farmers and others taking the side of the factory against 'organizational harassment'. The event was heavily attended by mass media – press and TV – and by national politicians, who publicly criticized the local police for passivity. The workers, on the other hand, accepted the restrictions imposed upon them as 'fair', even to the point of entering into 'agreements' with the police on the extent of the picket-line.

The demonstration was dissolved when the workers finally reacted to a breach of the agreements by the management (who were not intercepted by the police when they entered the plant through what had been agreed to be treated as 'no man's land'), by blocking the exit of the company van. The police went in and removed the workers, who made only passive resistance.

5. Only a few weeks later (October 1975), a similar situation arose in Copenhagen (Frederiksberg), when workers blocked the entrance to the graphical firm *'INFO'* in an attempt to get a 'closed shop' agreement with the firm to employ only organized workers. Here too the union was involved, and the picket-line was more efficient in preventing access by unorganized labour and others. Thus, on several occasions, workers and visitors were physically prevented from entering the plant.

Here, too, the local chief of police first tried a technique of absorption by allowing the 'demonstration' for several days, although heavily supervised by police – and by mass media and politicians. The demonstration was finally dissolved with force on a night when the owner and his attorney were prevented from re-entering the factory, and several demonstrators were arrested, their leader being charged with public drunkenness. Behind the breaking of the blockade was *firstly* the heavy political attention to the incident (which gave rise to criticism of both police and government in parliament), *secondly* the fact that top union officials finally indicated that they were no longer behind the demonstrators. The use of the physical blockade was now threatening the position of the social democrats in the government and union stability.

This was the last instance when police (and the legal system) formally acknowledged the use of absorptive techniques as a legal measure for the police.

The 'INFO case' gave rise to a parliamentary debate over the legality of the use of physical blockades, which was finally resolved in *early June 1976*, when parliament (with the Social Democratic votes, but under pressure from the Center Democrats) passed a resolution ordering the Minister of Justice either to amend the wording of the standard police ordinance to clearly indicate the illegality of physical blockades, *or* to issue a 'clarifying interpretation' that the existing wording should be understood as prohibiting such blocking of the free passing in and out of persons (and/or goods, as the Minister of Justice added). This resolution was followed up on *30 June 1976*, with a circular letter from the Minister of Justice 'interpreting' the standard police ordinance and instructing the police to intervene to break up such blockings in the future.

In the interval between the Bækkelund case (September 1975) and the INFO case (October 1975) and the parliamentary resolutions in June 1976, there was a heated *debate in parliament* over the status of the physical blockade. The right-wing parties tried to have legislation passed to clearly outlaw such actions, but the Social Democrats, aided by the smaller parties to the left and in the middle, warded off these and other attempts to interfere with labour conflicts and unions by legislation.

As one of the means to take the pressure off the government, the Penal Law Commission was asked to make a report on the legal situation. The report diplomatically weighed the various legal provisions, warning against the use of the penal code (as had been tried in the Hope case and was also demanded in the Bækkelund case). Instead the Commission advised using the local police ordinance (in itself a measure of absorption) and proposed in practice a wording of 'clarification', which was ultimately adopted by the Minister of Justice in the circular letter of 30 June 1976.

6. In *April 1976* – shortly after the publication of the report of the Penal Law Commission – a physical blockade was made of the plant of a Copen-

hagen wine company *(the 'Skjold Burne case')*. Here, too, the workers attempted to play a legalistic game by observing rules so as to obstruct only the traffic of goods and persons to and from the company plant.

These demonstrators were removed without more ado, and an attempt by the left-wing parties in parliament to establish a right of non-violent, but effectively blocking, picketing by sticking to the 13-point programme of this group, were swept aside by the Minister of Justice. There was no longer any doubt. The police had to go in and remove such 'demonstrators' – and they did so with considerable vigour. No charges were brought against the demonstrators, however.

7. The first physical blockade *after* the issuance of the new 'circular of clarification' of *30 June 1976*, came in early *November 1976* when a group of pickets tried to block the *Hertz Rent-a-car* office at the Copenhagen airport in protest against the use of underpaid and unorganized clerks. They were quietly informed by the local police that their picketing was prohibited by the standard police ordinance, as interpreted by the Ministry of Justice circular of 30 June. They quietly gave up their physical blockade without any protest.

Since then, the police have been employed on a series of occasions against demonstrators blocking access to plants involved in labour conflict, regardless of the occasion for the blocking.

8. It happened in the case of *the 'BT conflict'*, where a large-scale conflict involving the major national conservative newspaper, *Berlingske Tidende*, and its tabloid 'BT', resulted in physical blockade of the driveway in *April 1977*. Here, too, the physical blocking resulted in discussion in parliament. A dramatic debate resulted in charges being brought against two union leaders, who allegedly had threatened strike-breaking clerical staff with the publication of their names and pictures. Although the Prime Minister himself had ordered the police and prosecution 'to look into the illegalities taking place at the BT plant', the two union leaders were acquitted (absorption).

9. In *August 1978*, a group of demonstrators were removed from the Copenhagen Carriers' Terminal *(Fragtmandshallen)* in Glostrup, with considerable use of physical violence. This case, in which several demonstrators were fined under the police ordinance, also became a 'process against the police' with solid documentation of excessive police violence.

D. *Other instances of open conflict*

While the incidents discussed so far have had rather clear class-perspectives, there have been several other incidents in which the police have intervened, which were less clear, but where the same provisions have been at issue. One of them involved attempts of local residents and sympathizers to prevent the moving away of a mobile children's institution from an underprivileged neighbourhood – *'the Todesgade case'* (August 1977) – in protest against

Police using the 'blockade-grip' at the blockade of Fragtmandshallen *(August 1978)*
(Medical doctors have termed this grip potentially lethal. It was prohibited by the
Minister of Justice in May 1979).

municipal institutional policies. The institution was finally removed while a
major police force kept demonstrators away. One of the arrested was charged
with violently resisting arrest, but was acquitted. Several other demonstrators, however, were fined under the police ordinance (as interpreted by the
Minister of Justice). The massive show of force by the police, and the fac
that the action was being eagerly filmed by police officials were taken as an
indication that the police were now escalating confrontation.

During *1977–78* the police were on several other occasions involved in
removing demonstrators against the new housing policies, which gave (legally
doubtful) permission for property owners to divide up apartment buildings
into separately owned flats by so-called 'modernizations', triggered by a
complex legislation. In some instances the demonstrators managed to prevent
illegal speculations; in others they were removed by the police before
achieving their result. In all cases, the demonstrations had the effect of calling
public attention to the doubtful – and possibly illegal – practices and to the
basic immorality of the law, but with little or no political effect. On the other
hand, demonstrators were able to point to the laxness of the police and other
authorities in enforcing housing provisions that made demands on the
property owners.

The manifest 'inequality before the law' was now becoming evident, but although it shattered the legitimacy of the police actions against demonstrators, it did not prevent ultimate action to remove demonstrators from the occupied buildings. Thus the police also in this respect came to appear as an integral part of an apparatus of class justice.

In one of the first such cases in which demonstrators were brought to court, charged with violation of the police ordinance, *the Godsbanegade case,* (July 1977), they were convicted, but exempted from punishment with explicit reference to the vagueness of the legal standard laid down in the circular of 30 June. This was the last case of absorption.

VI. VARIATIONS IN SYSTEM RESPONSE – AND THEIR DETERMINANTS

Without going into the details of the many incidents in which the police were involved during the period 1973–78, it can be stated in summary that police behaviour has undergone a development in the direction *away from* absorption and increasingly *towards* confrontation. This development involved not only the use of 'tough' techniques – i.e. confrontation in a narrow sense, increasing amounts of physical violence – but also the tendency to select tougher responses in situations where milder responses could have been used.

This development involves, of course, increased risk of physical injury to the individual policemen (not to speak of their clients). But, more importantly, it involves a change in the perceived role of the police among large segments of the population.

1. Prosecution

The development is least obvious in relation to prosecution, i.e. the sector of Danish police responsibility which is least 'police-like' in nature. Thus, although the heads of seven local unions *were* prosecuted in the Hope-Computer case, it was the DA, and not the local chief of police, who pressed the charges. Furthermore, although considerable leniency was shown towards the road-blocking *farmers,* some of them *were* actually prosecuted and sentenced. In the case of the 1973 fishermen's blockade, both the police proper and the prosecution showed maximum absorption against the fishermen, this representing the clearest case of 'inequality before the law' as compared to the Hope-Computer action. But in 1975, at least some of the fishermen who blocked the harbour of Frederikshavn were fined, and immediately at the end of the 1978 port blockade the Attorney General ordered investigation and prosecution against *fishermen,* both for the Copenhagen and for the provincial port-blockades.

After the Hope case, there were no notable prosecutory actions against the *workers,* until the case of the *'BT conflict'* in 1977, when the Social Democratic Prime Minister himself from the rostrum of parliament directed the Attorney General to 'investigate the illegalities being committed at the BT plant' – an order that was supported by a majority in Parliament. The result, however, was an acquittal in court.

The latest actions against workers' blockades happened around the blocking of the Copenhagen Carriers' Terminal *(Fragtmandshallen, August 1978),* where several demonstrators had been charged with violation of the police ordinance, some also with the violent resistance of arrest. Here too, however, only rather mild sentences resulted.

Finally, in the case of other disturbances – housing-actions, university-occupations, and even when the front office of the Ministry of Defence was briefly occupied by demonstrating communists – either no prosecution or only very 'mild' charges were brought. Only in one case did the police prosecutor bring penal-code charges against a demonstrator-activist, namely against the presumed 'chief instigator' at the *Todesgade* action (against the removal of a mobile children's institution), but here the presumed instigator was acquitted by the court.

2. The courts

The seeming 'mildness' of the reactions on the lawyers' side was largely shaped by the decisions of the courts. Thus, it was the courts who represented the ultimate line of absorption in the Hope-Computer case, by first sentencing only one union leader mildly (the lower court) and later acquitting him, too, (the appellate court). It was the courts that rejected several attempts on the part of the prosecution to use penal-code provisions against the most active demonstrators in the *Todesgade* and *Fragtmandshal* cases. And it was the court that refused to mete out any punishment, in spite of a verdict of guilty, to the housing-occupants in the *Godsbanegade* case. So, in general, the courts have been clearly more absorption-minded than the prosecutors. In two cases, the courts even uttered cautious, and indirect, but significant criticism of parliament in connection with decisions, namely in the *BT* acquittal and in the decision in the *Godsbanegade* case. Furthermore, the courts in the Hope-Computer case in circumscribed terms indicated considerable criticism of the action (or rather passivity) of the police.

3. The lawyers' consciousness

There seems to be little doubt that the element of legal training represented by *judges, the police prosecutors* (the local chiefs of police), and, finally, by the reasoning of the *Permanent Penal Law Commission* in its recommendation to use the local police ordinance, rather than the penal code, for reaction against open social conflict, may account for this considerable 'mildness' – or absorption – in the response of the legal system to open social conflict. Whether this preference for absorption is an indication of a greater amount of respect for the protestors and their legal rights, *or* is a preference for a less challenging way of channelling the conflict is another question, however. The absorptive response may, in the long run, be more efficient in containing social dissatisfaction than the confrontative response.

Nevertheless, the legal situation as interpreted also by the courts now, is that physical blockades, be it by farmers, fishermen, workers or housing activists, are illegal and punishable. This also means that in future there is a definite legal basis for the police to break up attempted, incipient, or full-blown physical blockades in pursuance of their duty to prevent an offence from being committed or to bring it to an end.

In relation to the police proper, both the 'soft' decisions by the courts *and* the (slightly) less soft actions of the prosecution thus may have had their most important effects as legitimation for more confrontative police action by the other sector of police: the 'order police'.

Behind the order police, there is 'the connecting link' of *the local chief of police*. Whether the chief of police is absorption-oriented or confrontation-oriented, one would expect it to be reflected not only in his prosecution decisions, but also in decisions concerning the maintenance of order. *Some* of the variations in police behaviour seem partly explicable by such personal variations in orientation or attitudes on the confrontation-absorption scale. Indeed, such variations seem to have occurred. It may explain the differences in relation to actions against the farmer-demonstrators (rather wide local variation, with prosecution in only one district), but hardly in relation to the fishermen's actions.

The police chief in the Hope-Computer case was clearly the most absorption-oriented of all those involved – and was criticized for being so, both in parliament and in the court decision. Nevertheless, he persevered in later cases where 'public order' and 'law and order attitudes' were also notable. The police chief in the Bækkelund case (formerly chairman of the National Council on Crime Prevention) followed the same line very far, but finally 'had' to intervene against the workers after considerable legalistic hide-and-seek with the demonstrators, the employer, and politicians. The police chief in the INFO case started out on much the same line as his colleagues, but ended up with rather strict confrontative responses, which resulted in charges from workers of police brutality and undue interference with a legal demonstration. He later continued this more confrontative response in other cases within his district. Finally, the chief of police in Glostrup (the *Fragtmandshal* case) on several occasions assailed demonstrators with quick terminations of demonstrations, rough techniques of dispersal, and eager prosecution of demonstrators.

In relation to the behaviour of the police chiefs in these cases, the more strictly 'legalistic' part of their role – the prosecutory function – seems to be less critical than the more discretionary role in *the maintenance of order*.

4. Influences on police decisions to maintain order

Here there are formally greater opportunities for selection of the mode of action by the police, owing to the official lack of control and instruction from 'above' (the DA, the Attorney General and the Ministry of Justice). According to the official ideology, the local chief of police is 'free' to decide on the correct course of action.

Undoubtedly, the police chief has some element of personal choice in the selection of the correct mode of response. Nevertheless, this 'room for selection of action' was clearly narrowed down during the period in question. The increasing use of confrontation instead of absorption is hardly *only* a matter of personality, attitudes or 'consciousness' of the acting chiefs of police. These actions were under cross-pressures from other significant sources.

The actions of the local chief of police – or of his subordinates – in maintaining order are not, of course, 'free' in any broad sense of that term.

The most important influences here seem to be politicians, 'the public', higher echelons in the hierarchy of justice, the *lower* level police, *and* the historical situation of the class struggle.

(1) *The public and the (national) politicians* have had major influence on police behaviour in the instances of open social conflict discussed here. This influence has to a significant extent been shaped by the mass-media and their selection of events for reporting, as well as by *their* definition of the situation. In the Hope-Computer case, the TV-filming of the nocturnal incident triggered legalistic demands in parliament and in the public debate, as well as evoking professional comment by a judge and a professor of law. It did not influence the maintenance of order in the Hope case, but it laid the basis for action in later cases.

This 'high visibility' also hampered the opportunities for absorptive responses in the Bækkelund and INFO cases. Owing to this visibility, the public in general and the politicians in particular became involved in discussions of law-and-order issues and in questions concerning the role of the police in society, to a much greater extent than is normally the case. The most intimate details of police behaviour – normally protected from public scrutiny – became daily public issues.

The tenuous political balance in the electorate and in Parliament between left and right brought about an approximate stalemate in relation to legislation: the Social Democrats for a long time managed to ward off attempts at legislative action, but were finally induced to issue the circular of 30 June

1976 as the 'path of least resistance.' This circular, nevertheless, in spite of its low formal status, had very important effects in reality. But until the moment of 'clarification', the public and political debate raged between left and right. One of the results of this insecurity was the concomitant insecurity in police behaviour, the unsteady course between confrontation and absorption.

(2) *The higher echelons in the legal system* formally remained in the background, pushing the local chief of police into the foreground as *the* person responsible for decisions. But there is little doubt that the local police chiefs have had discreet consultations with superior levels: the regional District Attorney, the Attorney General, and the Ministry of Justice, either directly (as in the Grindal case) or indirectly (as in the INFO case). In the Hope-Computer case there were clear differences in viewpoints between the local and the central level, in the Grindal case there was harmony, in the Bækkelund case there was probably very little upward contact, and in the INFO case and later cases there are likely to have been very discreet consultations with very high levels in the system of justice as well as in the political system.

Once the parliamentary situation became clear – by the issuance of the 1976 circular – there was little variation in police action. In the first case after the 'clarification' – Hertz rent-a-car – the action was very 'soft', but effective, but in the later cases of Skjold Burne and *Fragtmandshallen,* police action was swift and at times brutal. Absorptive tactics were used only initially, and when they proved ineffective, the necessary physical force was used. Although it was maintained that the circular of 1976 did not change anything, but only 'clarified' the legal situation, there is no doubt that this 'clarification' meant a shift from absorption to confrontation. It is ironical that it was a social democratic Minister of Justice who carried the measure that led to this drastic limitation in the weaponry of the Danish working class. His actions in the field of physical social conflicts (blockades) – along with later serious incidents in the 'law-and-order-sphere' (the Defence Intelligence scandal of 1977 and the extradition of a Mexican citizen in 1977) – probably contributed to his resignation as Minister of Justice in 1978.

(3) Although the local chief of police is formally in charge of decisions, he must naturally rely heavily on his *subordinate uniformed police* in relation to the maintenance of order. He must rely not only on their 'savoir faire' – their good sense in handling difficult situations – but he is also dependent upon their attitudes and self-perceptions.

We know nothing of the discussions and relations between the local chiefs of police and their forces. Available information indicates, however, that the local police forces in the Hope-Computer case and the Bækkelund case supported the absorptive behaviour for which their chiefs were responsible – actually workers' representatives have complimented the uniformed policemen in these cases on their 'neutral' behaviour. Whether the excesses of police action in the INFO case and in later cases (most notably the *Fragtmandshallen* case) were due to attitudes only of the rank-and-file uniformed police, *or* really were inspired by the chiefs themselves is not known. To what extent a chief of police is the captive of aggressive feelings and attitudes among his subordinates can only be guessed. In Denmark there are grounds for suspicion that actually the top echelons of police are very sensitive to pressure from below, as evidenced e.g. by their routine denial of the problem of police violence.

However, the attitudes and social conscience of lower level order policemen are not necessarily monolithic either. On repeated occasions representatives of 'the rank-and-file' have expressed pro-labour sympathies and warned against over-reaction to physical conflicts, pointing to the risk of the police becoming identified with the management-side.

(4) *Police class consciousness.* Without going into this complex question at any length, there are indications that police definitions of the class background of their opponents in physical blockades influence their behaviour. The use of violent confrontation has been most manifest in those altercations where the demonstrators have been identified as students, leftists, or 'professional troublemakers' (in most police statements these are invectives on the same level). On the other hand, where the activists have been most clearly recognizable as belonging to the working class, police behaviour has tended more in the direction of absorption than towards confrontation, to the point of entering into peaceful agreements or even co-operation with the demonstrators. This is not to say that policemen conceive of themselves as workers, only that they perceive themselves to be in opposition to students and 'leftists'. Thus, in legitimizing the harshness of police behaviour in the *Fragtmandshallen* case (the Carriers' Terminal), police spokesmen alleged that only one of 49 persons prosecuted in this case were striking workers themselves.[5]

5. Police behaviour in a class perspective

Even when looking ahistorically at the incidents reported on here, it is evident that the factor that most strongly differentiated between various police (and legal system) responses to the problem of public order – absorption or confrontation – is the factor of class.

It is thus clear that the predominant use of absorption as a response to *the farmers' violations* is related to the fact that these actions were clearly a solitary act of desperation from a class squeezed in a conflict between opponent workers and employers. The road blockings did not contain any element of class opposition and had no long-range political perspective.

The use of absorption towards *the fishermen* was in no way related to a 'mildness' in their actions – on the contrary, the demonstrations of the fishermen were by far the most flagrant violations of public order. But, of course, the level of action was *so* serious that the amount of physical force needed would be too high to be politically feasible. Furthermore, the fishermen are a class in motion, representing a mixture of small-producers with a small-capitalist mentality and wage-earners accepting the same outlook in spite of an objectively different position.

The fishermen's actions were also acts of desperation, which did not threaten any other (opponent) class, but were only aimed at mobilizing state support in the international competition with *other* petty producers in competing EEC fisheries (notably England). Furthermore, during the time of the fishermen's actions, all parties on the political scene were trying to capture the votes of this group in attempts to break the political stalemate. The combination of toughness, bordering on ruthlessness, a romantic aura around the profession, and the political key position of the fishermen dictated an absorptive response towards their illegalities. Only when the 'Progress Party' threatened to capture the votes of the fishermen by encouraging their action in 1978 did the Prime Minister find the courage to threaten to act confrontatively. The public romantic image of the fishermen was also wearing thin when they blocked the important harbours of Denmark and even prevented the Royal Yacht from sailing from Copenhagen.

In the case of the *housing-actions,* police responses were also relatively mild – if not absorptive in a narrow sense, then at least occasionally marked by sympathies with the lot of the victims of housing speculations. Again, student and leftist demonstrators were 'fair game' for confrontative action.

But the use of confrontation was, of course, increasingly clear in the case of *workers' actions.* In spite of initial attempts at using absorptive techniques, confrontation was ultimately resorted to in practically all the situations where the maintenance of order was at issue. Thus, in the Hope-Computer case, the regional squad with dogs *was* finally called in. In Bækkelund, the police reacted forcibly against the workers who blocked the exit in protest against the violation of the 'agreement' with the police by the other side – a violation against which the police had not intervened. In the INFO case the period of absorption was even briefer and the final confrontative action more relentless. And after the 1976 circular, there was little or no hesitation before confrontative order maintenance was used.

Thus, a mere comparison between reactions, regardless of the time-factor shows a clear class-bias in the order maintenance action of Danish police.

But when we introduce the time-perspective, the class-determinants of police action become even clearer:

In the beginning of the period 1973–78, absorption was still a possibility, as evidenced by the police passivity in the *Hope-Computer* case (January 1973). But confrontation was an acceptable alternative, as evidenced by the prosecution of the union leaders. Only when the unions mobilized thousands of workers in demonstrations with red flags outside the courthouse and threatened to call wide-spread strikes on the following days did the legal system absorb the conflict with an acquittal.

In *Bækkelund* (September 1975) the absorptive tactics were used successfully for several days. However, the actions and mobilization of the workers were not forceful enough to win the battle, and confrontation was the end-result – the union had over-estimated its own potential. Just about one month later the union – and shortly thereafter the Prime Minister himself – indicated that they no longer found the physical blockade acceptable – and from then, starting with the dissolution of the *INFO* blockade, the way was open for the use of still clearer confrontation, with the Carriers' Terminal intervention as the most drastic action against a physical blockade.

VII. CONCLUSION: THE STATE OF THE POLICE IN A CLASS SOCIETY

The development sketched above indicates that economic and political crisis in a welfare society like Denmark removes possible uncertainties as regards the class character of the police. In conditions of relative peace, absorptive police behaviour may for some time be functional in neutralizing and veiling social conflict. To a large extent, workers go along with and accept legality and legitimacy in the organized class struggle. But as the crisis increasingly makes inroads on the vested interests of labour, and demands harder exploitation of the working force, the conflict can no longer be swept under the rug.

The legal system has no acceptable solution to this conflict: the 'correct' legal answer is simply insufficient. Social conflict comes out into the open; the class struggle is returning to the streets. The police may for some time try absorptive techniques, but the increasing visibility of police action and the tightening of political control of police behaviour reduces the scope for compromises and 'local' solutions.

Policemen with a distinct ideology of neutrality or even with a working-class consciousness may for some time succeed in hiding their action and bending the law, or using the existing ambiguities in the law for making 'deals' and adjustments. But in spite of the wide discretion available for maintaining order, there is indeed a limit to such discretion, given a basic political conflict.

Confrontation is the ultimate result of the role of the police as part of the repressive state apparatus. When ideological control, under the guise of legality and illusions of harmony of interest, is insufficient, the true situation of the police vis-à-vis social classes is revealed, and outright repression is the result.

It is notable that police action tended to be absorptive as long as official union policy and action backed up the physical blockade. This was clearly the case in the Hope-Computer situation, where the national union top brass participated in the demonstration outside the courthouses. In the Bækkelund case too the union officials backed up the blockade, but the rank and file members did not show up in sufficient numbers to make the blockade effective. The years from 1945 until the Hope blockade of 1973 saw action in unison between unions and workers, a phenomenon with two sides: support for workers from their unions – and control of the workers actions by the unions.

The Hope case may have been the first indication that the control of union members from above was diminishing as the crisis made it difficult for the union to guarantee acceptable conditions for their members – the threat from the EEC was becoming too great. So the unions had the somewhat lesser effect of avoiding open conflict by 'persuading' the legal system to adopt an absorptive response – both on the police level and on the court level.

But, starting with the INFO case, official union policy was directed *against* the physical blockades: the unions would no longer restrain police and other legal system action for fear that the physical blockade-movement would in reality weaken union influence and strengthen other influences of a more radical persuasion – expressed as a fear of 'Chinese' influence (a phrase alluding to certain groups on the far left, not so much of Maoist persuasion as of a more radical communist affiliation). In reality, then, union policy now sided with the police to control the workers in their fight against capital.

In these attempts to contain dissatisfaction within the traditional system, two questions became critical: How well could the unions safeguard workers' interests with such traditional means? and, on the other hand: Would the system in fact be successful in containing physical blockades in a manner perceived as legitimate?

The latest developments around the deadline for the present article highlight this 'crisis of legitimacy'.

In summer 1979 a series of cases were brought in several harbour-towns in Denmark against fishermen who had participated in the great port blockade of 1978. The prosecutors started out toughly by demanding prison sentences for the most active fishermen, but the results were only relatively mild fines (below 1,000 Dkr.) imposed on a large number of fishermen. Once again, the courts have shown an absorptive response, accepting the apologies from fishermen that the demonstrations had been justified by their fear for the future of their trade. In this way the court diplomacy combined a formal 'equality before the law' with a mild response acceptable to the fishermen, thus saving the face of legitimacy for the system.

As for the workers' physical blockades, however, the development was more critical: As the economic and occupational crisis was felt to be increasingly serious in relation to the national collective bargaining situation in the spring of 1979, large numbers of people from several occupational groups went on strike, some of them utilizing physical blockades as a means of protest. Thus, on one day in May large numbers of public employees – including the police – staged a stoppage of work for three hours in the morning, an action that drew vociferous criticism from the right wing in parliament against the government and led to demands for heavy sanctions. Students who had their canteen prices raised because of the EEC-VAT struck against supermarkets, where they helped themselves to food and paid only a symbolic 1 Dkr., which was what they allegedly could afford. Copenhagen busdrivers (who had experiences from the HT conflict in 1975) stopped public transportation in the capital and its suburbs for several days with a combination of strikes and physical blockades. On 6 June 1979, angry taxi- and transportdrivers blocked several throughfares in and around Copenhagen for hours in protest against alleged police brutality in connection with police intervention against a physical blockade by cement-truckers the day before. In June 1979, a ship's crew from a Danish shipping company sold to a German firm and now registered under a Cypriotic flag tried to block the sailing of the Rømø-Sild ferry, but were finally removed by the police, who have maintained a constant guard at the ferry for months.

These actions indicate that the official labour movement is *not* able, by the use of the traditional methods, to find an acceptable solution to the crisis for their constituents – and there is every reason to expect that this failing will become increasingly clear in the years to come. It is therefore to be expected that groups preferring more radical modes of action will have increasing attraction for workers. The legitimacy of the labour unions and of their control of workers is thus becoming attenuated.

Furthermore, the legitimacy of police methods in reacting to militant workers' actions, is becoming increasingly doubtful. On the one hand, the right wing in parliament has demanded swifter and more 'efficient' police intervention against blockades and even legal measures against strikes. The Social Democrats try to ward off the demands for legal action and increased police intervention. The left wing in general and the militant workers in particular, on the other hand, now openly charge the police with undue brutality and harassment of workers, pointing to the increasingly clear class character of the system.

There are indications that policemen are becoming increasingly aware of their problematic situation and of their own class position. Most recently some policemen expressed uneasiness at interfering with a physical blockade by workers with whom they had joined hands in the public employees' strike in March 1979, and refused to act until they had contacted their union and had been prompted to go ahead. So in a speech at the National Police Association Meeting in June 1979 their chairman had to declare that there could be no doubt about the obligation of the police to enforce the law. There is hardly any clearer way to highlight the crisis of legitimacy for the police and the legitimacy of the welfare state.

NOTES

[1] See Feest, J. (1971), Feest & Blankenburg (1972).
[2] See also: PO. Johansen's and Håkon Lorenzen's articles in this volume.
[3] On one occasion, however, in 1955, angry fishermen and other inhabitants of Klaksvig in the Faroe islands, in protest against Danish government, blocked the harbour of Klaksvig for several days and harassed the emissaries from Denmark, with the result that several high officials were forced to remain in the local police station overnight. The instigators and some active participants were sentenced to prison for illegal deprivation of liberty . . .
[4] The fines were set at Dkr. 200 instead of 400 with explicit reference to the special situation of the fishermen.
[5] Actually only two of those sentenced were 'sympathizers' – the great majority were workers who had been dismissed for striking against the Terminal.

REFERENCES

The present paper is based upon an original article from 1976: Jørgen Jepsen, Arbejdskonflikter og 'den offentlige ro og orden' (Labour conflicts and 'public peace and order'), (*Retfærd,* No. 1, September, 1976), which has detailed references to Danish literature on 'physical blockades' up until that date. Another important source in Danish is the collection of material in Ph. Lauritsen (ed.), *Blokade – Frihed og Tvang i Danmark* (Informations Forlag, 1976) and its addendum *Tillæg til Blokade – Frihed og Tvang i Danmark* (Informations Forlag, 1978). In addition, a series of books, pamphlets and articles on the 'physical blockades' in Denmark have been issued since the Hope Computer-case, but none of them in languages other than Danish.

The following references in German and English have served as inspiration and background-material for the article, along with the works of the Norwegian authors Per-Ole Johansen (see his article in the present volume) and Håkon Lorentzen.

References in German:
BRUSTEN, MANFRED: Determinanten selektiver Sanktionierung durch die Polizei. pp. 31–70 in Feest J. & Lautmann R. *Die Polizei: Soziologische Studien und Forschungsberichte.* Westdeutscher Verlag, Opladen 1971.
DIETEL, A.: Ermessensschanken bei Eingriffen in das Versammlungs- und Demonstrationsrecht. p. 570 in *Deutsche Verwaltungsblatt,* Heft. 14, 1969.
FEEST, JOHANNES: Die Situation des Verdachts. In Feest, J. & Lautmann, R., *Die Polizei: Soziologische Studien und Forschungsberichte.* Westdeutscher Verlag, Opladen 1971.
FEEST, JOHANNES & E. BLANKENBURG: *Die Definitionsmacht der Polizei. Strategien der Strafvervolgung und Soziale Selektion.* Bertelsmanns Universitätsverlag, Düsseldorf, 1972.

References in English:
FORCE, ROBERT: Decriminalization of Breach of the Peace Statutes: a Nonpenal Approach to Order Maintenance. *Tulane Law Review,* Vol. XLVI, No. 3, pp. 367–493, February, 1972.

HALL, STUART, et al.: *Policing the Crisis: Mugging, the State, Law and Order.* Macmillan, London 1978, (in particular Chapter 9: The Law and Order Society: Towards the Exceptional State).

PEPINSKY, HAROLD: Police Decision-Making. (Chapter III in: Don M. Gottfredsson (ed.): *Decision-Making in the Criminal Justice System: Reviews and Essays.* Crime and Delinquency Issues. A Monograph Series. NIMH, Rockvill, Maryland, 1975).

SILVER, ALAN: The Demand for Order in Civil Society: A Review of Some Themes in the History of Urban Crime, Police and Riot. pp. 1–24 in David Bordua (ed.): *The Police. Six Sociological Essays.* John Wiley & Sons, N.Y., 1967.

The Police and Social Conflicts – The Menstad Conflict of 1931

BY *Per Ole Johansen*

On Monday, 8 June 1931, demonstrators and policemen clashed in a riot outside the Menstad warehouse and loading station in southern Norway. The riot, the climax of a serious labor dispute, was immediately known as 'the Battle of Menstad'. This dispute stands out as one of the most important struggles in the Norwegian labor movement during the period between the two World Wars.

The conflict stemmed from a special contract system which the industrial giant and saltpetre producer, Norsk Hydro, had introduced at its warehouse and loading station in Menstad in 1924, following a large strike. In that part of Norway, the Menstad harbor had a central function for Norsk Hydro's saltpetre production. Raw materials were unloaded there, and finished products shipped out. A strike at this location was bound to present a great threat to the company's interests. After the strike in 1924, the company had dismissed a large number of employees. A few weeks later, the same workers were offered jobs on condition that they accepted a so-called 'three months' contract'. This deal involved, among other things, giving three months' notice, while the other workers had a two weeks' period of notice only. The newly engaged contract workers, who did not belong to the trade union, performed the same type of work as the rest of the dock workers. The only difference was that the former had the right and duty to continue working during a strike, as long as they had not given notice three months in advance. Legally they were not strike-breakers if they continued to work while their colleagues went on strike. That was Norsk Hydro's reason for hiring this special force. The company assured itself of loyal workers in the event of a new strike.

The next strike, which led up to the 'Battle of Menstad', came in 1931. The international economic crisis was in full swing and strongly affected Norwegian industry. During the spring of 1931, employers proclaimed a nation-wide lock-out in order to press wages down. The Employers' Association considered this a necessary step if Norwegian industry were to survive against international competition. The Federation of Norwegian Trade Unions reacted by putting printers and transport workers on strike. Thereby the Menstad dock workers became involved in a huge labor dispute, in which some 80,000 workers were either locked out or on strike. However, the contract workers at Menstad continued to work, and were labelled strike-breakers by those in the labor union. This situation led to an acute labor conflict, which lasted from the middle of April 1931 until the end of the year. As time passed, what had begun as a local conflict developed into a national issue involving the state police, the military, the government, the ministries, the country's large organizations, and the entire press.

The Menstad conflict in its entirety is described elsewhere.[1] This article focuses primarily on the role of the police during the conflict, and discusses some principal criminological perspectives in connection with the police and social conflicts.

I THE POLICE, THE MILITARY, AND THE LABOR MOVEMENT

The difficult 1920s

From 1905 to 1920, the Norwegian labor movement made great progress. Membership grew, and workers gained higher wages as well as shorter working hours. In the decade that followed, prices fell while unemployment rose. Workers faced a crisis. During the concurrent tariff negotiations, the employers uncomprisingly demanded wage cuts because of the falling price index. The period from 1920 until the beginning of the 1930s was characterized by large unemployment and bitter wage disputes.

The high rate of unemployment made it easy for employers to get strike-breakers, and also easier for them to get rid of revolutionary activists at work places. Strike-breaking was a constantly recurring and controversial question in this period. With this in mind, Parliament in 1927 expanded section 222 of the penal code with a second sub-section, the so-called *tukthusloven* (an anti-labor-union law). This provision gave strike-breakers special protection, and criminalized forceful methods which for years had been paramount in the workers' combat against strike-breaking.

Ever since the 1870s–80s a rather cool relationship had prevailed between the police and the working class, partly because of the fact that the police were brought in during the more acute labor disputes. This antagonism reached a peak in the 1920s. Police officers were called in to guard industrial plants and strike-breakers, thus losing even more respect among the workers. Representatives of the labor parties voted against appropriations to the police during budget sessions in local councils and the Parliament. Labor representatives especially protested against funds to the mounted police, who were a familiar but not particularly popular element during the larger strikes. Most policemen must have disliked serving during the labor disputes. 'It is natural that in most cases, the policeman's sympathies will be on the side of the striking worker', stated the organ of the police, *Norsk Politibald*, in 1921. Among the lower ranking policemen there was sympathy for the labor movement. The police, too, felt the effects of the recession. Their wages were low and working hours inconvenient. Furthermore, many of them felt united with the working class because of their own background and circle of friends.

During the labor disputes in the 1920s, the Oslo Police Organization protested against policemen having to protect strike-breakers and in some cases even perform strike-breaking work themselves. These protests irritated the police administration, who then suspended the head of the police officers' organization. Bitter agitation followed within the police department. In 1930, *Norsk Politiblad* complained that police participation in labor disputes 'as a rule had benefited capitalist interests at the cost of labor interests'.

When the regular police could not cope, non-commissioned officers' training schools, guards' companies, and specially trained military security units were there to take over. Soldiers were on the alert and prepared to aid the police during the larger strikes. Security units guarded the military depots, since in the 1920s there was a widespread fear in the more conservative wing that strikers would help themselves to military weapons. Officers removed the bolts from the rifle actions at the warehouse depots. Military personnel organized running the trains on schedule when railroad employees were on strike. Naval vessels guarded the harbors hit by strikes, while the intelligence office of the General Staff kept watch over developments within the labor movement. Respect for the military force was at a low ebb in the 1920s. Within the labor movement, anti-militarism was customary. Labor leaders and activists were prosecuted and punished for agitation against military powers. Certain officers saw a connection between the use of soldiers in the labor disputes and the lack of respect for the military. Carl Fleischer, captain in the General Staff, wrote in 1921 that the military apparatus could not be exempted from accusations of being a class protector: 'We have enough examples of that in our own country'.

Police and military preparedness

The Norwegian government ordered an extensive mobilization of the state police, the army, and the navy during the Menstad conflict. This state of preparation had been built up by shifting conservative-liberal governments during the 1920s and was improved in 1930 and in the winter of 1931, that is, concurrently with the prelude to the nation-wide lock-out and the Menstad conflict.

In the 1920s and early 30s, the Norwegian police were financed and organized by the municipalities. The state was only responsible for the chief of police positions. However, as a counterbalance to the dominance of the municipalities, the Department of Justice had the right to recruit police from different municipalities to serve in a district experiencing demonstrations or strikes, in the event of the local police proving inadequate or refusing to go on duty. In the first place the local police were responsible for the policing of social conflicts, but it was not unusual that they were content to hand over the arena to outside policemen from distant districts. The Department of Justice had agreements with twelve municipalities, and thus a special force of 86 men was available in time of crisis. This was a large number by Norwegian standards.

The position of the central administration in relation to the local police forces was further cemented by the police code of 1927, which in certain instances gave the Department of Justice the right to send policemen from one municipality to another, even though the state had no agreement with the municipality supplying policemen. In 1930 and the spring of 1931, the central administration worked against time with a proposition to create a separate permanent state police force, to be organized as a kind of rebellion control unit under the sole command of the Department of Justice. This proposition was passed by Parliament at the very height of the Menstad conflict.

As in the case of the military, leading police quarters also started preparations in anticipation of an extensive labor dispute. The police in several of the larger towns borrowed Nagant revolvers from the Department of Justice; the Oslo police received, among other things, 300 revolvers. The police in Skiensfjorden, the area in which the Menstad conflict took place, received Browning revolvers to arm prospective police reserves. The trainees at the police school in Oslo were kept there at the end of the spring semester, so that they could serve as police reserves during the conflict. The chief of police in Oslo offered temporary jobs as policemen to individuals who had previously applied to join the corps. In Bergen, recruitment of police reserves also took place before the lock-out, and the forces were strengthened in other large towns as well.

In addition the government had at its disposition a country-wide alert system of military security forces and armed units. The military security forces had the task of guarding military depots and facilities, as well as civilian plants (such as telephone and telegraph facilities, banks, water works, gas works, prisons and official offices) in case of 'internal disturbances', as it was expressed in the military terminology of the time. The armed units of the military were to assist the police during the labor disputes. If the local police force was unable to cope, even with the help of out-of-town reinforcements, its chief of police was authorized to request military assistance.

The use of security forces and armed units was an old arrangement: nonetheless the Norwegian General Staff doubted the reliability of this usage. Would the soldiers be loyal to their military leaders during internal disturbances, or would they feel a greater sense of loyalty toward the labor union and the striking workers? In 1930 and during the winter of 1931, the generals discussed this question. In January, the General Staff sent a letter to the district commanders requesting an evaluation of the soldiers' reliability. The lack of refresher training for conscripts in the second half of the 1920s had reduced the contact between officers and soldiers. It had become more difficult to select reliable persons for security forces and armed units. The soldiers had little or no training in serving during internal disturbances.

The district commanders shared the doubts of the General Staff. The third district commander remarked that as long as officers and troops met in regular refresher courses, mutual trust had prevailed:

> Officers frequently had the opportunity to observe the individual soldier and were able to evaluate with reasonable certainty his reliability for duty in the armed units. The situation, however, has deteriorated and a reluctance to serve could be expected from a great many of the conscripts.

The report from the fifth district command was especially pessimistic. The soldiers could absolutely not be trusted: 'Social and class consciousness is too widespread among all levels of society to permit this'. The infantry regiments had had a policy of registering trustworthy recruits for future use in security forces and armed units. However, the impressions from the recruitment schools were no longer reliable:

> Those who in the year of recruit-training rightly can be described as trustworthy may a couple of years later, when the union and the political party have gained influence over them, often be among the most unreliable.

In June 1930, the Commanding General sent a report to the Department of Defense pointing out the lack of refresher training as a definite negative influence on the soldiers' morale. In spite of the strong scepticism, the Commanding General and district commanders preferred to continue to make use of conscripts during internal disturbances.

During the winter of 1931, the district commanders, following orders from the Commanding General, started to revise the organization of the security forces and armed units. Entire age groups were still to be summoned in the event of internal conflicts. However, soldiers whom the officers considered less than reliable were to be sent home immediately after reporting for duty. Radical union members should be avoided at all costs. In addition to weeding out soldiers at the reporting point, the military leaders could ensure the soldiers' loyalty by mobilizing from other and more reliable districts than the conflict area. Using young conscripts from rural areas during conflicts in industrial cities has more or less been the traditional rule.

In addition to the ordinary conscripts, the government could during internal conflicts mobilize the standing guards' companies. The guards constituted the elite unit of the national armed forces, and were particularly suited for internal police duties. They could quickly be alerted. The companies were recruited from different parts of the country, and therefore not burdened with ties of loyalty to any special district. Former guards were also included in the plans for mobilizing guards' companies in case of internal disturbances. In the 1920s and the beginning of the '30s, the head of His Majesty's Guards kept a file on former guards considered to be especially suited for extraordinary guards' service. Moreover, during the summer of 1930, the selection for regular guards' service became the object of additional scrutiny. Groundless rumors claimed that Labor Party members had infiltrated the companies.

In the spring of 1931, the navy had 12 ships available with a crew of 390 men to assist the army and the police in times of civil disturbances. In the event of delays in mustering the crews due to railroad strikes, the military authorities could requisition coastal ships for transportation. Cooperation between the army and navy became closer following a communication from the 4th district command to the Commanding General in December 1930. It noted 'the great importance of the *navy* in coastal towns and districts if some naval craft could be activated in the event of disturbances'. The respective army and navy district commanders then worked out plans for where and how these naval war-prepared vessels could contribute to maintaining 'law and order'.

In the beginning of the 1930s, the military administration, too, made some organizational changes in order to be prepared for possible civil disturbances. In the spring of 1931, the General Staff made plans for alerting officers in case of disturbances in Oslo. If an officer received information that political unrest was brewing, he was to notify his fellow officers. A pre-arranged and detailed grapevine system would see to it that the officers got the message. In case of internal disturbances, the General Staff preferred to use a civilian building as an operation and command centre. The danger prevailed that the offices of the General Staff and the most important official buildings would be occupied by revolutionaries. The officers were to meet at Norsk Hydro's office premises in Oslo, dressed in civilian clothes. Pertinent documents were kept on the premises.

A considerable escalation of the domestic state of preparation took place during the beginning of the 1930s. The fear of a revolution was still very strong among the bourgeoisie and the military. Characteristic of the atmosphere was the fact that leading officers operated with no political differentiation between the social democratic Labor Party and the Norwegian Communist Party. Apart from the general escalation, in the spring of 1931 several concrete preparatory measures were taken in the light of the country-wide labor dispute that everyone knew was brewing. Additional guards were placed at all military depots and fortifications and at the arsenal at Kongsberg. The screening of the security forces and armed units intensified. Extra weapons were sent out to several military camps and a company of guards, ready to be demobilized at the end of May, had to remain in service because of the strained situation.

The battle plan for the use of physical coercive means during social conflicts was as follows: first the local police, then, if necessary, out-of-town state police would be used. Then, if the police could not handle the situation, the infantry, the guards companies, and the navy would be sent in. This was the battle plan that was put into effect during the Menstad conflict.

II. THE CONFLICT

From negotiations to demonstrations

The majority of the workers at Menstad went on strike on 15 April 1931. At the same time, approximately 2000 other workers in the district were involved in a lock-out. The contract workers at Menstad continued to work despite the strike. That was of course the intention behind the new contract system – to have a guarantee against strike threats. From 15 April through 2 June, the Menstad conflict was a local affair. The labor union tried to negotiate with the contract workers, but to no avail. The union workers looked upon the contract workers as strike-breakers, while the company and the contract workers maintained that legally they had every right to keep the work going. The controversy about the three months' contract soon ended in a deadlock. Two conflicting political values collided. The workers' appeal for class solidarity clashed with the employers' demand for freedom of work, the notion that hiring and work conditions were a private matter between the employer and the individual worker. A basis for compromise did not exist.

The social democrats within the union were in control until the end of May, and thereafter the communists took over the initiative. The latter immediately adopted a clear-cut demonstration and confrontation policy. At that point the local police were drawn into the conflict. Norsk Hydro's harbor facility, Menstad, was situated between two smaller towns, Porsgrunn and Skien. On Saturday 30 May, the workers on strike and in lock-out marched by the hundreds from the 'People's House' in the two towns, respectively, demonstrating against the strike-breakers at Menstad.

Their patience had come to an end.

The elderly and quiet chief of police in Porsgrunn, Roll Hansen, knew about the planning of the demonstration, but had done nothing to stop the plans. Instead, he went right away to Menstad accompanied by a few members of the local force and asked the management to stop the work. This chief of police had been involved in labor disputes before, and he knew how violent a showdown between strike-breakers and pickets could become.

By the time the demonstrators had reached Menstad, the contract workers

had stopped working and most of them had departed out of the way. The few
who were caught on their way out of the factory area were made a spectacle
of and stared at as a warning to others. Their names were solemnly read out
before a large crowd, and one of the labor leaders made a speech about 'the
strike-breaker as a present day Judas':

> Judas of today is the same as at the time of Jesus. The only difference is that the modern
> Judas does not go and hang himself. Today's Judas, the strike-breakers, do not feel
> shame.

The reading aloud of the names of the contract workers continued; it was
a well-known tactic in the struggle against strike-breaking. However, such
name calling was forbidden under section 222 of the penal code. The chief
of police protested against the continuation of the reading. He also wanted
to forbid the workers to demonstrate outside the homes of the contract
workers, but gave in as soon as one of the labor leaders remarked: 'Do not
bother to stop this, but be in the lead!' And the chief of police replied kindly,
as he patted the labor leader on the shoulder: 'Well, you take the responsibility for the procession'. The demonstrators then marched past the homes
of the contract workers with union flags dipped to indicate that symbolically
the contract workers were dead for the union movement. The local police
force headed the march. The chief of police reported very neutrally to the
Department of Justice about the demonstration.

The chief of police followed a soft policy. In this manner he prevented the
police from coming into conflict with the workers. Neither the police nor the
workers looked upon the demonstration as a showdown among themselves.

After the demonstration on 30 May, the workers agreed to demonstrate
again if the strike-breakers continued at Menstad. On Monday, 1 June, work
started again and the communists announced a demonstration at Menstad on
Tuesday, 2 June. In this effort the supporters in the district far outnumbered
their own party members. The police chief had given permission for the
demonstration on condition that the demonstrators did not break into the
plant area. By the time the processions from the surrounding towns and
districts reached Menstad, between 2000 and 3000 people had gathered
outside the plant. The contract workers went into hiding, and the police had
barricaded the entrance as the demonstrators headed for the main gateway.
The police force consisted of some 16 men, the majority of whom were
middle-aged and overweight. The police had erected altogether three barricades, which were rapidly torn down by the demonstrators. The policemen
withdrew at the same time as they admonished the demonstrators and made
sure they were aware of the fact that the demonstration was unlawful. The
policeman knew quite a few of the demonstrators by name and recognized
both friends and neighbors in the crowd.

After all the barricades had been demolished, the police force gathered in front of the plant's office building, where some of the contract workers had hidden. The chief of police was convinced that the demonstrators would storm the building if the contract workers refused to come out. He could not do much more than caution and warn the demonstrators if he was to avoid provoking them. A police attack against the head of the procession of demonstrators would have been a provocation, as it proved to be later in the conflict. The chief of police thought that the most sensible thing to do was to meet the demand of the demonstrators to speak with the contract workers. A policeman went into the building and asked the contract workers to come outside; if not, they would all be beaten up.

The contract workers were led into a ring of demonstrators, and the circle persistently became smaller. The labor leaders demanded that the strike-breaking be stopped, and in order to emphasize the seriousness of the matter had the contract workers make a symbolical running of the gauntlet. The punishment consisted of curses and scornful remarks, not kicks and blows, but the experience was undoubtedly frightening enough, even though they were not physically assaulted. The police witnessed the treatment the contract workers received, but did not intervene, since 'nobody did them any harm'.

While the demonstration ended with singing 'The International', the director of the Menstad plant, engineer Trygve Nielsen, made his way to the head office in Oslo to complain about the cautiousness of the police.

Escalation

In the days that followed, the situation developed rapidly. From being a local conflict, the Menstad affair became a struggle in which the nation's central power elite took part.

Immediately after the demonstration on 2 June, Bjarne Eriksen, head of the legal section of Norsk Hydro, got in touch with the Minister of Justice, Asbjørn Lindboe, and demanded effective police protection of the contract work. The Minister of Justice was in complete sympathy.

On Wednesday, 3 June, an extraordinary conference took place at the Department of Justice. The Minister of Justice and the officials at the department were present. Mr. Nielsen and Mr. Eriksen represented Norsk Hydro. The Association of Norwegian Employers was represented by its chairman, who felt that in principle it was very important to have the work started again. Mr. Eriksen emphasized that it would be very unfortunate if the work was not resumed because of 'the malicious demonstrations'. It was of the utmost importance to society, as well as to Norsk Hydro, that willing workers were not molested. The Minister of Justice replied that the government would definitely protect those willing to work. It had already been decided to send a special force of 150 policemen to the disturbed area. Mr. Eriksen wanted soldiers sent to the district immediately, 'because it was better to get the military in a day too early rather than a day too late'. The Department of Justice was reluctant to make such a move. Mobilization would only be used as a last resort. The unions were in the process of voting over the State Mediator's proposal for wage reductions. As he was trying to achieve a compromise solution in the big labor dispute, it was important not to make a move that would hinder this solution. The presence of soldiers would be a provocation and, in addition, the police undoubtedly would manage on their own.

Later that day one of the local labor leaders, Arthur Berby, was arrested on orders from the chief of police in Porsgrunn, while on his way to a meeting which, after some pressure from the workers, the contract employees had agreed to the day before.

In the meantime the contract workers had changed their mind about participation in such a meeting. They would continue working, and demanded police protection because of their fear of being forcibly taken to the meeting. The chief of police found himself in a tight corner. He wanted to be on good terms with the unions, but at the same time the Department of Justice demanded that he should prohibit demonstrations and adopt a tougher attitude towards the workers. The workers were determined to stop the strike-breaking. What could the chief of police do? A fight between the police and the workers was the last thing he wanted. Three policemen arresting one union leader was a better bet than 20–30 policemen fighting 2000–3000 demonstrators on the fields at Menstad.

The arrest of Berby quickly aggravated the relationship between the police and the workers. From being a minor hindrance during the demonstrations, the police had turned into an enemy. Any hopes that the arrest would dampen the workers' urge to fight were put sadly to shame. The district newspaper of the Labor Party, *Telemark Arbeiderblad,* pointed out the monstrosity in having Berby arrested while on his way to a legitimate negotiation meeting: 'The police have never engaged in labor disputes without making blunders, and have not avoided them this time either'. On Thursday, 4 June, 4000 workers gathered in a demonstration and protest meeting in Porsgrunn. *Telemark Arbeiderblad* wrote:

> Workers! We find ourselves in a critical situation after what has taken place. One of us is already in jail. Nobody knows when it will suit the police to continue this mad spree (of arrests). The town is full of policemen from out-of-town. Class Law is at work.

The chief of police, Roll Hansen, had banned the demonstration in accordance with the instruction from the Minister of Justice. But he changed his mind. The chief of police in the neighboring town, Skien, had no intention of stopping the workers from marching to the meeting in Porsgrunn, and the union leaders had made it clear that there would be a demonstration, no matter what the police thought. Roll Hansen gave a dispensation from the demonstration ban, and as he explained later:

> I wanted to express my sympathy toward the workers. It is my opinion that the police should be as neutral as possible and not provoke either of the parties.

This, the Minister of Justice and Norsk Hydro had not expected. Moreover, the Minister of Justice had requested the chief of police to arrest several of the union leaders. The chief had no intention of doing that either. During the protest meeting that focused on the arrest of Arthur Berby, a delegation visited the chief of police demanding that Berby should be set free. He promised to take up the matter with his superiors and to do his best to get Berby out of jail. Talking with the Ministry of Justice, the chief explained that it was necessary for him to take a positive attitude, otherwise the meeting would have developed into riots. If one stuck to a tough policy, riots could be expected at any time. The chief of police expressed pessimism in spite of the fact that he had over 100 out-of-town policemen at his disposition, a force that he had kept waiting in the hotel during the entire afternoon and evening while the protest arrangement lasted. He had his subordinates' and his own future in the district to consider.

Later that evening Mr. Eriksen got in touch with the Minister of Justice, Asbjørn Lindboe, and once again complained that the chief of police in Porsgrunn did nothing to put a stop to the demonstrations. On top of all, the chief of police had contacted Mr. Nielsen stating that the police could no longer be responsible for the continuation of the contract work at Menstad. It would be better to stop the work until the strike was over. The Minister of Justice guaranteed that the contract work would continue regardless of the chief of police's opinion. Additional police reinforcements would be sent in. The same evening the Minister of Justice decided that the leadership of the state police force in Skiensfjorden should be turned over to a police leader on whom the Ministry could rely more. The choice fell on a younger militant chief superintendent from another district, by the name of Annar Thinn. He had previously led the state police in successful offensives against striking workers in other parts of the country. Norsk Hydro, the government, and the conservative press had great expectations regarding superintendent Thinn's efforts. At the Department of Justice patience with Roll Hansen's soft policy had come to an end. The workers' patience had also expired. At the large protest meeting in Porsgrunn, on 4 June, one of the leaders of the Communist Party in the district urged the workers to form their own means of protection:

Comrades, are we ready with the means to stop police attacks? It is doubtful. We must get red guards and choose our fighting leaders. So the situation at Menstad demands. We must be prepared. The others are more than willing to shoot down workers, women and children. We too must take precautions. There are people on the job at Menstad today. Tonight we will march together to the People's House and elect our own guards.

The open conflict

The contract workers reported at Menstad on Friday, 5 June, but work was not resumed, owing to threats of new demonstrations. The plant authority complained that the local police were doing nothing to protect the contract workers even when openly badgered by the union members. Hydro's executive, Mr. Eriksen, agreed not to resume operations on that particular day, and thereafter once more contacted Lindboe, the Minister of Justice. As opposed to Eriksen, Lindboe was optimistic.

The Minister of Justice noted that never before during civil disturbances had such a large police force been mobilized and made available to the chief of police. Besides, the Department's own man, chief superintendent Thinn, was on his way to the district to replace the local chief of police. Still, Eriksen was not satisfied. It was now necessary to call in the military forces:

I pointed out that because of the inefficiency of the police so far, the masses must have gotten the idea that they could do whatever they liked and therefore it would be the right time to send in the military.

The Minister of Justice made no comment to this suggestion.

The same day, the union leader, Arthur Berby, was released from the prison in Oslo, after pressure from the legal adviser to the Federation of Norwegian Trade Unions. Berby had been detained in Oslo because the police feared local riots. Now the Federation warned the Department of Justice that the communists would organize some 30,000 unemployed persons in the Oslo area in a demonstration and riot if Arthur Berby was not released. For the time being, the Federation had been able to keep the unemployed under control, but now the danger existed that the communists would gain control in Oslo with the aid of the huge army of unemployed. The warning was effective. As a condition for release, Berby had to agree to remain in Oslo as long as the Menstad dispute lasted. For this promise he was strongly criticized by the communist press. Undoubtedly, the police and the Department of Justice came out ahead when Berby agreed to these release conditions. The police prevented the spreading of the Menstad dispute to the capital, and simultaneously the release took the sting out of the Porsgrunn workers' protest against the arrest, without giving them their union leader back.

All was quiet at Menstad on Friday 5 June. However, a violent clash occurred between out-of-town police and strikers at Skotfoss, a smaller industrial town about 10 kilometers from Skien. Some strike-breakers had been brought in at the Skotfoss wood-processing plant, and the workers intended to do something about it. Approximately 500 of the Skien and Skotfoss workers marched out to the plant to announce their demands. The executives at the Skotfoss plant were warned and immediately contacted the police, requesting protection. The local police had, as previously, kept to the soft policy and given permission for the demonstration. However, the director at Skotfoss contacted the head of the large unit of out-of-town policemen, who for days had passed the time playing poker in the hotel. Fifty of them, under out-of-town leadership, immediately drove up to Skotfoss where they blocked off the plant area by raising some lock-bridges which the workers had to cross to get into the plant. Policemen with batons guarded the bridges. The force was ready to fight long before the demonstrators were in sight. When the crowd approached the barricades the leaders tried to address the police, partly because they wanted to send in a delegation to negotiate with the strike-breakers. The police ignored the request, and when some of the demonstrators tried to force their way past the guarded lock-bridges, the battle was soon in full swing. The policemen swung their batons and knocked out the demonstrators on the bridges, leaving them hanging over the railings. The rest of the demonstrators retorted with a hail of rocks that for the other party resulted in black eyes and knocked-out teeth. In an appeal to the workers after the skirmish, the communist leader, Godtfred Lundin, repeated that now was the time for the workers to form their own protection apparatus, so as not to be left standing helpless in the face of the police attacks. The class struggle would be intensified.

Up until the clash at Skotfoss, the local police chiefs decisively influenced the tactics. The battle on the lock-bridges warned of a change. In the days to follow these police chiefs had little to say.

At this time, the local police were under cross-fire. The labor press criticized the deployment of out-of-town units, while the conservative press was dissatisfied because the chief of police in Porsgrunn had not satisfactorily utilized the mobilized special units. The police chief had given in, and it was high time he be granted a leave of absence, demanded *Aftenposten,* the leading conservative newspaper.

To this criticism, the chief of police replied:

During all these demonstrations I have tried to act as neutrally as possible in order to curb tempers and calm those agitated. I have been strongly reproached for this conciliatory approach, and in *this* respect the conservative newspapers are not better than the workers' organs.

15. Policing Scandinavia

Following a request from the contract workers, work at Menstad also stopped on Saturday 6 June. They simply did not dare to work as long as the police protection was not more adequate:

> At this moment we feel that the situation is so critical that we would be putting our lives as well as those of our families in danger if we now went to work.

Mr. Eriksen, however, in no uncertain terms proclaimed that production would start again on Monday. Complete stoppage would mean a victory for the demonstrators and that would set an unfortunate precedent for the future. Furthermore, chief superintendent Thinn had arrived in Porsgrunn. Even Mr. Eriksen believed that thereby the police would now be in control of the situation. Superintendent Thinn had great faith in the strength of the police. His inclination toward tough policies was precisely the reason why the Department of Justice had sent him to the district. To Mr. Nielsen at Menstad, he emphasized that the contract work should unquestionably continue; 'because we must at all costs re-establish the trust in the police's ability to protect those willing to work'. But the chief superintendent entertained no doubts about being in enemy territory:

> It was easy to notice a decisive dissatisfaction in the district regarding the out-of-town police. Difficulties in billeting developed. The labor organization blocked the hotels, restaurants and shops. Taxi drivers refused to transport the police.

At the same time, the communists made preparations for a clash that everyone now felt was bound to come. An armed unit was formed, and the activists discussed what to do if they were attacked by the police:

> We had to count on being attacked when approaching the police barricades. So we decided to place a workers' guard armed with the weapons at our disposal, clubs and rocks, at the head of the procession.

The Confrontation

It was generally known in the district that there would be new demonstrations at Menstad if the work there was resumed. On Monday morning, 8 June, the contract workers were at their job and the pickets immediately started a mass mustering. Labor leaders in Porsgrunn and Skien agreed on a battle plan that entailed having the demonstrators approach Menstad from two sides as a sort of pincer action to distract the police and simultaneously detain them at the points that best suited the demonstrators. A negotiating delegation was elected, but the labor leaders thought it unlikely that the out-of-town police would let themselves get involved in any negotiations. The clash at Skotfoss indicated quite the opposite, and Superintendent Thinn had stated at a press conference on Saturday, 6 June, that if the workers dared to demonstrate again, they would be thrashed. The workers' armed unit, leading the demonstrators, had the task of storming the police barricades if necessary. For the occasion they armed themselves with clubs. At all costs the strike-breakers should be gotten rid of.

Well ahead of the time the demonstrators were expected, a police unit of about 100 men were stationed at various barricades out at Menstad. In Skien a large reserve police unit waited, and in Porsgrunn a couple of police officers with a supply of weapons and ammunition were ready to leave for Menstad on short notice. Water-hoses to be used against the demonstrators were installed at the barricades at Menstad.

Chief superintendent Thinn, the actual leader of the police force, was very optimistic. He had recently been enganged in a clash between workers and the police in the log-driving districts. He, who would have no connection with the Skiensfjorden area after the labor dispute had been settled, firmly intended to stick to the policy of tough tactics. The older and less militant police chief in Porsgrunn had his doubts. He believed that the police should be neutral and was willing to negotiate with the demonstrators. Before 'the Battle of Menstad', he was nervous and unsure. Superintendent Thinn dared to point this out, despite the difference in age and rank, when once again the chief of police warned against meeting force with force. Concurrently between 2000 and 3000 workers approached the police barricades singing 'The Internationale.'

The workers' armed unit and the demonstrators' negotiators were about 15 meters from the police's main barricade when chief superintendent Thinn went forward and raised his white-gloved hands in the air to indicate that the crowd should come to a halt. So it did, but at the same moment, some of the spectators began throwing rocks at the police. The chief superintendent gave orders to use the water-hoses against the demonstrators and spectators, while simultaneously he ordered a baton attack upon the head of the procession. In this tense situation it was almost accidental who first started the fight; things began happening very fast. Godtfred Lundin, the leader of the workers, had no difficulty in assessing what lay in store for his men. 'Go to it, damit!', he yelled, and the workers in their overalls and windbreakers rushed to meet the police with clubs and rocks in their hands. It got pretty rough. Both the police and the demonstrators were set on meeting force with force. Both groups knew that the other side was prepared to fight. The policemen put up a fight at the beginning of the hand-to-hand combat, but there was never any doubt about the outcome. The police had no chance; after about five minutes they were chased in a wild retreat leaving behind twelve more or less battered men who staggered along or lay unconscious in the dust. Several of them were really hammered by the agitated demonstrators, and the labor leaders had to step in to restore discipline in the crowd. Many of the demonstrators were also rather roughly treated before the policemen were deprived of their batons.

The police retreated to the main building at Menstad, where they equipped themselves with weapons and rounds of live ammunition. They cocked their rifles and prepared for the next wave of attacks. In the meantime the police reinforcements had arrived. But the demonstrators did not follow up their victory, since that probably would have cost them too much. The policemen were nervous, bewildered, and to some extent seriously hurt after the hand-to-hand combat. Now they stood ready with hoses and weapons; with the river on one side and the demonstrators on the other, and without much chance of escape.

The demonstrators retired and the police went back to their hotel rooms to lick their wounds. Chief superintendent Thinn was bandaged in his hotel room by the local doctor. Meanwhile Roll Hansen worriedly contemplated his future as chief of police in Porsgrunn: 'The worst of all is . . . that we have the public against us as well'.

The 130 men strong state police force had not deterred the workers from defying the ban against demonstrations. The police force was not even frightening enough to scare off the demonstrators from physical combat with the police. When it came to fighting, the policemen retreated. The Department of Justice had deployed the large police unit to Skiensfjorden in order to compensate for the local force's weakened authority. If the workers would not obey, they should be forced to. But instead of frightening the workers from defying the police ban, the police force only caused increased resistance to the law enforcement agency. 'The Battle of Menstad' meant a defeat for the police and was experienced as such.

Reinforcements

Norsk Hydro's central administration and the Department of Justice were immediately informed of the defeat of the state police force. Strangely enough, that same afternoon the Minister of Justice took part in a debate in Parliament concerning a proposition for a new state police corps. 'The Battle of Menstad' was immediately used by the conservatives as an argument for strengthening the police force, and the appropriation of funds for the proposed state police corps was doubled after a spontaneous motion made by their parliamentary leader.

The Minister of Justice no longer entertained any qualms about sending military troops to Menstad. That very afternoon during a hurriedly called conference, the situation was discussed by Norsk Hydro's Mr. Eriksen, the director of the Association of Norwegian Employers, Finn Dahl, the Defence Minister, Vidkun Quisling (better known for his role as a traitor during World

War II), the Minister of Justice, Asbjørn Lindboe, and officials from the Department of Justice. Norsk Hydro and the Employers' Association once again put forth a demand for military protection. If the state did not take care, there was a danger that the demonstrators' encroachments would become rampant.

The government summoned an extraordinary conference that same evening. Lindboe emphasized the seriousness of the situation; the government's authority was at stake. Without soldiers it would be impossible to re-establish 'law and order' and protect those willing to work. All agreed, and the Defence Minister, Vidkun Quisling, called the Commanding General and ordered mobilization.

First the guards' companies were mobilized. They were already on duty and the officers had been warned in advance that trouble was brewing. According to Captain Hermansen, the leader of the military expedition, the guards were especially suited to this assignment: 'They barely knew where Skien was situated and had no friends or sympathies there. The people were practically total strangers to them. That made the assignment much easier'. At 9 p.m. an activated guards' company stood ready with complete field equipment; field uniform, helmet, rifle and machine gun. The unit had been equipped with tear gas and special equipment for use during civil disturbances. The officers carried pistols. Before leaving the camp in Oslo, the guards received a visit by Defense Minister Quisling. He gave the necessary military orders and reminded the guards of the important task they now had to perform when revolutionaries threatened vital interests of society.

The guards' company made a discreet departure from a suburban station outside Oslo, and a specially requisitioned express train took them some 100 miles south to Skien. Early the next morning they arrived at a dismantled military camp outside Skien. The company was in a state of full emergency readiness, and around the camp a 50-meter-wide barbed wire enclosure was built to keep the soldiers isolated '. . . thereby establishing a neutral zone between the soldiers and the public to discourage fraternizing and the smuggling in of leaflets'. The soldiers were under strict orders to avoid all contact with outsiders:

> *General instructions for all sentry posts.* In addition to the usual duties according to sentry regulations, all posts are instructed to be extremely alert and suspicious of all approaching civilians. Sentries shall always pass 5 meters inside the enclosure and see to it that no one touches the barricades. When sentries stop anyone by calling out 'halt', the rifle shall at the same time be held at the ready. *It is forbidden to engage in conversation with civilians.*

All leaves were cancelled. Captain Hermansen wanted to have the entire unit in one place, but perhaps the most important reason had to do with avoiding political infiltration:

We took no chances of being tainted by the demonstrators. At that time the only way the demonstrators could do any damage to our forces was by political infiltration.

What the company needed in the way of motorized vehicles was requisitioned after it became known that no civilians dared to have anything to do with the military. For the first few days the company experienced difficulty in getting food supplies, since the local merchants refused to sell to them.

At a new government conference at 1 p.m. on Tuesday, 9 June, it was decided to send a large navy unit to Menstad, partly to protect the harbor facilities from the sea-side. The fact is that during a strike in 1924, some workers had attacked the strike-breakers from row boats and motor boats. The naval component consisted of four units; two minelayers, each with a crew of 40 and two cannons on board, and two torpedo boats, each with a crew of 22 and two cannons. The navy arrived at the troubled area on Wednesday evening, 10 June. One of the visiting journalists covering the arrival of the fleet, reported:

These two towns can not endure many more days of this tension. In itself the situation is unpleasant enough, and the nervousness which has spread and grown these past few days is blowing up this affair to unnecessary proportions among the population. A gasp went through both towns when a small German freighter came steaming up to Menstad last evening escorted by 4 warships; 2 torpedo boats anchored up in front of the freighter and 2 minelayers behind. The barrels of the cannons pointed towards the fields of Menstad and the crews were made ready for going ashore.

Immediately upon arrival, the warships put out sentries. Rifle crews received 50 fresh live rounds and 10 blanks.

Ready ammunition was placed beside the machine guns. The sailors had strict orders to remain onboard until given further instructions. The officers were not quite sure of the loyalty of the sailors, as most of them were from the working class and had gone to sea before being drafted into the navy.

In addition to the guards and the sailors, sentry posts at Menstad were augmented with a military security force, which was set up according to the pattern described earlier in this article. The politically hand-picked security force consisted for the most part of youths from the mountain areas of Telemark. In cases where the officers had any doubts about the soldier's loyalty, he was immediately sent home.

By the evening of 10 June, the military forces totaled some 400 men, while the state and local police comprised about 150 men. Later, both the army and the police force were further increased. The police reinforcement included a whole team of investigators, organizers, and combat specialists which the Department of Justice had sent to the district. The police force was reorganized on a military pattern, moved out to tents at Menstad and constantly drilled. Batons, steel helmets, and pistols made up part of the equipment.

In the evening of 10 June, the leaders of the police and the military forces gathered in a conference to discuss necessary measures for re-establishing law and order, as they called it. The police feared new disturbances, and the old dissension between the local police and the Department of Justice, represented by chief superintendent Thinn, flared up again. Like his colleague in Porsgrunn, the chief of police in Skien had asked Norsk Hydro's local manager to stop the work at Menstad, a step that would have been taken if the company's central administration in Oslo had not gone against it. The soft local policy encountered the tough central policy:

> The local and the state police had quite different opinions concerning which tactics to employ. The police chief in Porsgrunn still felt that in order to avoid riots, work stoppage at Menstad should be implemented. On the other hand, the state police pointed out that one ought to and could avoid work stoppage, and that it was necessary for the authorities to take a strong stand.

The local police chiefs got no sympathy for their attitudes. Force would be met with force, and the police were to be in the front line in order to regain their lost prestige, among other things. Chief superintendent Thinn strongly argued for having the military deployed only if the situation could not be effectively combated by the police. At the same time those taking part in the meeting decided to postpone the arrests of the union leaders. At the moment the law enforcement authority in the district was not strong enough to allow such a move.

Consolidation

The law enforcement agencies spent the time up to 19 June in consolidating. The work at Menstad was resumed, guarded by an armed state police and guards in such numbers that demonstrations were out of the question. Instead the workers concentrated their efforts on a boycott, which was quite effective for the first few days. The enforcement agencies had great difficulties in acquiring food, tobacco, hotel rooms, and taxis. The local merchants took part in the boycott, partly out of sympathy for the workers and partly because they feared losing the workers as customers. The union leaders emphasized that the local police should not be affected by the boycott. After a few days the supply problems were solved through building up stable and well-armed support lines from the army warehouse in the capital.

The police carried out surveillance of the labor leaders by telephone-wire tapping and censoring of mail. An informer was in full activity in the labor unions to pick up any information about labor leaders who had gone into hiding. The Department of Justice paid the informer.

A couple of local police officers were suspended because it was known that they sympathized with the workers. One of them had kept the labor leaders informed of the state police's plans.

The chief of police in Porsgrunn much disliked the fact that Norsk Hydro had started production again:

> I find it very stupid of Hydro to aggravate the situation at this time. Principles are fine, but unfortunately they can be dangerous, too.

The state police and the soldiers were on call at all times in case it became necessary to intervene during one of the workers' meetings. Police and military units contacted each other via topnotch technical equipment.

Even before the 'Battle of Menstad', police chief Roll Hansen had been relieved of his command over the state police dispositions. At a meeting of police leaders on Sunday, 14 June, it became clear that he had also lost control over the investigation work. The chief of the state police division in Østfold county, Sig. Jensen, had on orders from the Department of Justice gone to Porsgrunn to lead investigations. The police had consolidated their position, and work was in full swing again at Menstad. But police executives still feared that the arrest of labor leaders could stir up new riots. Therefore Sig. Jensen suggested that they should wait before arresting the most popular leaders. It would be better to start arresting some of the less known demonstrators, and preferably those with a criminal record. It should not be difficult to find some of that category; after all, nearly 4000 people were present at the 'Battle of Menstad'. By accusing the first arrestees of violence against the police, Sig. Jensen hoped to win the sympathy of the people. At the same time he wanted to avoid giving the arrests a political character, which certainly would happen if he first arrested the labor leaders. The presence of criminals would compromise the demonstrations and concurrently legitimize the police arrest of the labor leaders the second time around:

> The general situation was discussed and I formed . . . a plan for the investigation work. I suggested that for the time being the aim should be to arrest some of the persons who were suspected of attacks on the police on 8 June at Menstad, and preferably those who were known as doubtful characters. In this manner I hoped to win over the people who were still quite agitated because the authorities had started prosecution. This plan was accepted. For tactical reasons I have presently not arrested those who organized or glorified the riots, but the police have been told to weed out and arrest those who have committed crimes of violence in connection with the riots, meanwhile seeking to collect evidence against the leaders to have available when we detain them later. I feel it is opportune to choose this policy in the light of the situation we now are in . . . At the moment things are quiet here, and public opinion is beginning to turn against the riots that have taken place. It seems as if the responsible fraction of the workers is against more uprising and feels that things have already gone too far. If we let the investigations take on, shall I

call it, a political character, and go in for apprehending those who have organized the riots or demonstrations, that might lead to new unrest and in any case the labor press would have an excuse for exciting the masses. For the time being, by marking out the violent criminals and arresting them, I expect to get the public accustomed to arrests in connection with the riots, and at the same time the newspapers can not decently reproach the police for this type of arrest. When the state of affairs has become more clarified, and especially if there is any sign of an amicable settlement of the conflict, I will take action against the leaders based on the material I expect to have gathered. As far as I can see, they are for the most part communists, and with a labour settlement in sight, I do not believe that the Labor Party will find it in its interest to become deeply involved in defending these persons.

The arrests followed this plan and started immediately after the meeting. Altogether 19 persons were arrested in the following days, and 16 of them were kept in prison until the country-wide lock-out ended. The first arrest took place on Sunday afternoon, 14 June. 'The man has previously been convicted several times, is unmarried and a fly-by-night type of person', stated the police's description of the arrestee. *Telemark Arbeiderblad* gave the arrest a rather cool coverage: 'He is previously an old aquaintance of the police who is remanded for taking part in the demonstrations. He has no real connection with the labour movement'. To the newspapers, the police consistently referred to the first people arrested as violent criminals who were accused only of acts of violence. Subsequently came the arrest of the labor leaders. But the concurrent investigations progressed slowly because the local population hesitated in speaking out to the police. The local police assisted the state police with the investigations; at least some of them did. Those who sympathized with the workers could not seem to remember a thing from the 'Battle of Menstad'. Without local assistance it would have been difficult for the police to pick out the different labor leaders and investigate their roles in the conflict.

The settlement

For the time being, the government and state powers of authority had full control over the situation. A general strike proposal by the communists was voted down in the union organizations. The moderate social democratic leaders had regained control. In Skiensfjorden, machine guns and cannons had confronted the workers' clubs and rocks. The physical supremacy of the state law enforcement agencies was indisputable. But the control over the workers was brief, it might be added. As the dispute began to drag out, both Hydro and the government started looking around for a way out that would give peace with honor. Although they had the upper hand, they uneasily felt that in the long run they would lose by using force against force.

The danger of new clashes was there if the workers gathered their strength again. Even worse, the fact was that the use of the state police and soldiers threatened to poison the political climate for years to come. Everyone was aware that a high price had to be paid for the use of physical coercive measures in a social conflict.

The contract workers started work again at Menstad, and the strike-breakers were allowed to work undisturbed. All the same, Norsk Hydro's leaders decided to give them a vacation after only one week's work. Officially the reason had to do with the shipping season being nearly over. Of course, the contract workers were used to getting a summer vacation, but not all of them at the same time as was now being planned, and not for as long as the 6 weeks granted this time. By letting them work for one week before the 'vacation', the state had proved its ability to protect those willing to work and the company had not been embarrassed. By sending them on vacation, Norsk Hydro managed to end a labor dispute that had developed into a real headache for the company. This tactic was clearly expressed by Mr. Eriksen:

> Provided that the authorities succeed in maintaining law and order while the loading is going on of the ships waiting for cargo, then as far as I can see, the state has shown its ability and willingness to protect those willing to work. When the loading is completed, it can not be counted as any 'defeat' either for the state or Norsk Hydro that the workers get a vacation. To then continue the work, which for practical reasons would have no other purpose than just to prove that work *can* continue would, I believe, be an unnecessary provocation vis-à-vis public opinion.

The Menstad conflict occurred simultaneously with a nation-wide lock-out, which the workers' and the employers' organizations tried to bring to a swift close through a compromise. Norsk Hydro's leaders read the writing on the wall. The Federation of Norwegian Trade Unions would not go along with any compromise if the strike-breakers at Menstad continued working, and the Employers' Association was unenthusiastic about allowing a nation-wide lock-out to drag on because of some contracts at Menstad:

> We can not . . . count on members of the Association to approve of the present dispute continuing indefinitely just to protect the 26 monthly salaried workers at Menstad.

On 19 June, the contract work stopped and a 6 weeks' shutdown of the plant began. When the contract workers returned after the vacation, the entire contract system had been abolished. The contract workers were placed in other types of jobs at the plant that did not oppose the union's views. In the course of an hour one morning toward the end of August, the contract system that had caused so much strife was thrown overboard. The tariff negotiations that followed the lock-out pointed toward a compromise that both parties saw as beneficial. But the Federation of Norwegian Trade Unions demanded that the contract system at Menstad be permanently abolished. If Norsk Hydro persisted with this system, the collective interests of industry would be threatened. The company's principles thus had to yield in the face of tough economic realities. The State Mediator made it clear that it was high time that all responsible powers showed moderation and got the country out of the crisis.

In spite of the resolute use of state police and soldiers, even the government began to suspect that the employment of coercive means in a labor dispute is a complicated matter. In the long run it would be costly to rely on the large coercive apparatus to deter the workers from demonstrating unlawfully. Prime Minister Peder Kolstad gave his support to the resumption of the contract work on 13 June, but he had his doubts. He asked his colleagues if it was 'justifiable to start up work that could trigger new and more serious fights than the previous ones?' In several smaller disputes taking place at the time of the Menstad conflict in other parts of the country, the Minister of Justice refused to use soldiers. He had acknowledged the warning from the State Mediator, and through talks with representatives from the Federation of Norwegian Trade Unions he learned that the central union leaders also wanted to avoid new confrontations:

As things progressed, I got the definite feeling that the Federation tried to apply a moderating influence, wanted to get the dispute settled, and by and large retained the leadership vis-à-vis most of the workers.

The relative moderation on the part of the Department of Justice was not due to acute moral scruples, however. At the time of the central tariff negotiations and the lock-out, the government and the Minister of Justice secretly effectuated a huge apparatus for a nation-wide mobilization of reliable military forces in the event of a continuation of the lock-out and the outbreak of new labor disturbances. However, events did not follow that course. The state police and the military units were gradually withdrawn from Skiensfjorden after 19 June. The plans for a nation-wide mobilization were shelved after the Federation of Norwegian Trade Unions and the Association of Employers agreed to a compromise in the wage question. Once again 'peace and quiet' prevailed. Labor leaders were released from the out-of-town prisons; the police had intentionally avoided imprisoning them in politically radical districts. The leaders of the state police and the military units had time to evaluate their experiences. Most of the reports concluded with suggestions as to how the police and the soldiers could be deployed more effectively in the event of social conflicts. The head of the investigation work, Sig. Jensen, urged the Department of Justice to study the experiences from Menstad:

Investigations reveal that the riots which have taken place are of a peculiarly nasty and fairly dangerous character, and I would like to recommend that the central authorities thoroughly study the investigation material as an aid in tactical planning for future disturbances of that type. It appears that the police armament was not adequate to cope with a situation of this nature, and it is further shown that a special police unit should be established and trained to meet similar situations.

The senior police officials' journal, *Politiembedsmennenes Blad,* seconded the demand for police rearmament. Moreover, the time had come for taking away the central administration of Norway's police from inexperienced departmental lawyers and turning it over to the police agency's own people: 'The Norwegian police must as soon as possible be granted real policemen as their leaders.'

The state police corps, which was just getting organized, was expanded, and during later disturbances it made use of the experiences gained at Menstad. The corps' leaders were granted requisition rights, which meant that rooms, food and motor vehicles, etc. could be requisitioned in the event of the local population refusing to let or sell what the police needed. The police were thus prepared for possible boycott actions. A law was passed that automatically put the leader of the state police in a superior position to the local chief of police in any district where the state police operated. Thereby one had an effective means of preventing a repetition of the discordant exercising of authority which was evident during the Menstad conflict.

The leader of the naval forces that were sent to Menstad, Captain Diesen, inquired about a change in regulations giving military chiefs the right to intervene in labor disputes according to their own judgement. The chief of the guards' company, Captain Hermansen, emphasized the importance of keeping the soldiers isolated from the local population. The Minister of Defense, Vidkun Quisling, asked that the military alert system be reformed in order to assure an even swifter and more reliable mobilization during future labor disputes:

> The present regulations for military deployment to maintain law and order seem no longer to be in accordance with the demands of our time. The Commanding General is therefore requested to advance proposals for: 1. New regulations concerning cooperation with the civilian authorities. 2. New regulations concerning emergency situations. Taking into account the experience gained from the recent deployment of security forces and armed units, it is assumed that the Commanding General will take care of the necessary changes in the existing plans and preparations. Among other things, the existing plans do not seem adequate for a swift and reliable mobilization.

The plans for emergency preparedness were improved. But the Norwegian political situation in the 1930s developed differently from what the clamor for weapons in the beginning of the decade would indicate. Four years later the Labor Party gained control of the government, and the relations between the Employers' Association and the Unions' Federation were marked by a policy of cooperation.

III. CRIMINOLOGICAL PERSPECTIVES

Law or morale

The opposing views during the labor conflicts in the period between the two World Wars were not only concerned with strike-breaking; the opposition was also rooted in the very definition of strike-breaking. The labor union placed far more meaning in the term than the employers and the legislators did.

The legislators became involved in the dispute about strike-breaking by passing a law in 1927 which set strict limits to the means workers could use to stop strike-breakers. Publication of names, attempts to influence strike-breakers to stop by demonstrating against them, shadowing them, keeping them under surveillance and so forth became illegal. This law, section 222, subsection (2) of the penal code, known in labor circles as an anti-labor law and called *tukthusloven,* is an extreme example of a law being introduced contrarily to the sense of justice in large segments of the population. The law was interpreted as being so basically immoral that neither the law itself nor its enforcement had any possibility of creating a law-abiding attitude. Laws generating from a sense of justice among the majority of the population will have a great chance of being followed and respected. Even laws that do not stem from basic values can become more than dormant laws if by and large that which is forbidden does not mean very much to us. The gain from crime is then not proportionate to the possible discomfort of breaking the law. It can even be imagined that over a long period of time such laws can influence the formation of new moral concepts. The situation is completely different, however, when a law criminalizes behavior and actions which are significant for a group's or a class's struggle to secure their interests. *Tukthusloven* was such a law. It contributed least of all to creating new morals. Quite the contrary, contempt of strike-breaking increased along with the convictions. Instead of becoming a new defense for strike-breaking, it aroused indignation and contempt as never before. The convicted were honored and not disgraced by their own people. Enforcement of the law was not frightening enough to enable the strike-breakers to work undisturbed; too much was at stake for the labor union.

A large part of the labor movement felt that *tukthusloven* verified that the law favored the employers and that this was the intention. Biased laws have been known to discredit the entire body of laws. When laws are considered to be tools for class interests of privileged groups, there is a great danger that the body of laws will lose its legitimacy.

In the years between the World Wars, the Norwegian working class was just as divided as other groups when it came to questions of politics or legislation. Many of the workers voted for the Labor Party, but quite a few gave their vote to the conservatives, and a minority voted communist. Some did not vote at all. The labor movement was not particularly interested in criminal policy. The majority of the working class voters hardly had more radical viewpoints than other groups when it came to how traditional law-breakers should be treated. It was quite a different story, however, when it came to strike-breaking and the hostile legislation. Regarding this matter, the workers were by and large united, independently of their political differences or degree of political engagement. The great majority of labor voters took a fundamentally different attitude toward strike-breaking from that taken by employers and legislators. In Norwegian society no common sense of justice prevailed in that area; no real or imagined societal interests surpassed the social class distinction.

In 1935, *tukthusloven* had become ripe for abolishment. For some time, and far beyond the circle of workers, strike-breaking had been looked upon as immoral and dishonorable. It was no secret that members of the state police declined to have anything to do with strike-breakers. Some employers, too, scorned the strike-breakers much in the same manner as officers have looked down upon foreign deserters, in spite of their valuable services. Among the liberal lawyers in the country, there was a general feeling that *tukthusloven* produced the reverse of its desired effect. It was, in other words, the much disputed *tukthusloven* that the understaffed police in Skiensfjorden had the job of demanding respect for during the Menstad conflict. Right from the start it made the local police's position very difficult.

Social control and social closeness

The local police were short-handed. For example, during the demonstration on 30 May 1931, 6 policemen were on duty. During the demonstration on 2 June, the force was not more than doubled. Short staffing, however, was not the police's main problem. As a rule the policemen worked singly or in pairs. In his daily work, on the other hand, the policeman experienced quite a different situation to the one prevailing during the Menstad conflict. The population on the whole respected what he did and said. He had authority. The laws being enforced by the policeman were in accordance with the majority's sense of justice. Some, of course, took an indifferent attitude toward some of the laws and occasionally broke them, but only a minority of the people held a directly hostile attitude towards the police. The local policeman did not daily confront large groups of people who rejected and actively opposed what he stood for.

During the Menstad conflict, the local police force, among other things, acted against the workers in accordance with *tukthusloven,* although in a very diplomatic manner, to be sure. However, the law and the police intervention went against the workers' sense of justice, and the police chief lost authority. The workers no longer listened to his words. And, the district did not have enough policemen to compensate for the lost authority with sheer physical strength. Even if the local police force had been considerably larger, nonetheless it would have created a major problem for the police if they had started a physical conflict instead of letting the demonstrators pass.

The somewhat elderly policemen in Skiensfjorden lived in the small-town society. They took part in the social life, were active in clubs and organizations, and like many others did not mind stopping by a neighbor's house for a beer. The policemen had friends and neighbors among the demonstrators and were familiar with the background of the conflict. They knew enough both to understand and to sympathize. It would have become very unpleasant if any of them had been anything else than reasonable and friendly in such a situation. Most of the policemen had tried other jobs before they joined the force and were closer to the workers than to the middle and upper classes. Their only police training consisted of what they had learned on the job. They might react against methods used by some of the workers, but still many of them felt sympathy for the actual cause. The benefits for which the labor movement had been fighting for decades, such as higher wages and shorter working hours, were something the lowly policeman sorely missed in his own working day. The leaders of the labor movement, both in Skiensfjorden and elsewhere in the country, had recognized that the police agency was not so unambiguously politically reactionary as its role during the labor disputes might indicate. In time the union movement was able to build up a good relationship with the policemen who were sympathetic toward the workers' struggle.

The closeness to the local society which usually was an asset to the police became a problem during the Menstad conflict. It would not have been very pleasant to use batons against friends and neighbors. The chief of police and his men had a life to live in the district after the Menstad conflict. The workers knew the policemen. Tough actions could give the police trouble with ordinary police functions which otherwise were performed fairly smoothly. The police depended upon the goodwill of the public. Economically, the police were completely dependent upon the local society. After all, the municipalities in Porsgrunn and Skien appropriated funds for salaries and equipment.

The conservatives strongly criticized the local police, but in relation to the labor movement that was no problem. The local policeman experienced neither boycott nor nuisances. The labor leaders emphasized that the boycott only applied to out-of-town police. There was no need to take action against the local police, and like the policemen, the workers had reservations against fighting with people they knew well from everyday life. The relationship between the local police and the local labor movement remained positive even after the Menstad conflict. Arthur Berby's arrest was soon forgotten.

The local police's vulnerable position during the Menstad conflict sheds light on a central problem in connection with social control, what we may call *the dilemma of social closeness*. Quite a bit of control in social and political contexts is based on sheer physical force, but often the control will be more effective if grounded in natural authority resulting from close contact and familiarity with the persons and surroundings being controlled. Through his knowledge of local conditions, the controller will more easily be able to estimate the impact of his moves. And, if he is accepted in the environment, that circumstance alone will give greater authority. The close relationship to the environment being controlled may, on the other hand, create problems in executing the intended control. A similar viewpoint is put forth in an interesting article by the Norwegian criminologist Anne Marie Støkken:

> Where the one who controls and the one who is controlled are closely linked to one another, the formal control will probably be somewhat reduced. Frequent interaction leads to the controller also being controlled by the other party.[2]

It often happens that persons with authority keep at a distance from the persons who are to be controlled. We see this in the relations between police and the criminal, officer and soldier, captain and crew, teacher and pupil, doctor and patient, guard and prisoner, social worker and client. For many, the distance makes the job easier. This approach to the problem is well-known in sociology, nevertheless, the principle of distance has too often been looked upon as a law of nature. The distance can have quite a different cause than just making it easier to control fellow beings. In many cases the controller has to deal with so many people that he has no time to get to know each one individually.

To combine closeness with control might not necessarily be a problem for a control apparatus such as the police. Closeness will often give valuable insight. The groups that the police traditionally have the most contact with will in any case not possess much to set up against the control encroachments, partly because convicted individuals can not count on much social or political support outside their own circles. The combination of closeness and control does not ever need to be a problem in relation to the larger groups in society, that is, as long as the population accepts the laws that the police enforce. A heavy fine might hurt, but few people will favor unrestricted speed limits in densely built-up areas.

The population must have an overview of what the police are doing if the police's closeness to the environment is to present a problem for the controller. The police's enforcement of rules of order is generally quite visible, especially in smaller places. It was in connection with maintaining these rules at Menstad that the police showed moderation. But the public often knows little or nothing of other aspects of the activities of the police or the controller. The union did not know that certain persons from the local police force participated in the investigations during the Menstad conflict, a form of assistance that the state police could hardly have managed without. The investigation work greatly benefited from a thorough knowledge of local conditions, and at the same time the status of the local police was not threatened. The relationship between the local and the state police bore more evidence of conflict than cooperation, but the experience from the work of investigating reveals that a tough centralized police strategy and a local velvet-gloved police policy are not necessarily in opposition to one another. In other situations the central police authorities have on purpose used both tough and soft control measures by letting different police sections be responsible for the diplomatic and iron-fist aspects, respectively.

The closeness to the local environment first becomes a problem when the controller openly acts in such a way that large groups of the population react negatively. The situation becomes even more difficult if the controller himself does not have faith in the laws which are to be enforced, as was the case at Menstad. It can be argued that the soft policy of the local police was due to the personality of the chief of police in Porsgrunn. Roll Hansen was, in his way, something of an original, who preferred a bicycle and sports clothes to a car and a uniform when performing official assignments. He was no militant chief of police according to the old military prototypes. He got into an unaccustomed and unpleasant situation during the Menstad conflict which made him labile, nervous, and unsure of himself. The chief's personality traits were important enough, but the vulnerable social position of the local police was the main reason for the caution that they demonstrated during the social conflicts. This pattern is repeated both in Norwegian and European police history. A chief of police can of course introduce a tough policy even if the feelings in the district and the corps indicate otherwise, but in such instances it is certainly advantageous to turn over the command to other police leaders.

Social control and social distance

The Department of Justice chose the tough policy. In order to carry it out, considerable police reinforcements were necessary to make up for the local force's lack of authority, and it was necessary that the 'tough' reinforcements were not inhibited by local ties of loyalty.

16. Policing Scandinavia

The police's need for social distance to the public in connection with unpopular control functions raises a new control dilemma, *the dilemma of social distance*. Distance makes it easier for the controller to perform an unpleasant control function, but at the same time it is easier for him to misjudge the situation, because he is so far removed from the people who are to be controlled.

The state police at Menstad came from out of town. Few of them had any knowledge of the local conditions. As opposed to the local police, they had no personal contacts in the population. A great many of those called in for duty were uninterested in politics. The chiefs preferred police cadets who were politically neutral rather than conservative young men. The men were not supposed to sympathize with any party in a social conflict. The chief of police in one of the largest towns was known for hiring only 'political idiots', as he himself called them. Policemen should not have sympathies or antipathies that would show up in law enforcement situations. The chiefs were particularly fond of athletes, understandably enough at a time when the physical strength of a policeman played a relatively important role. But the fact that competitions and training usually preoccupy athletes' time might also have influenced the recruitment. The recruits had had neither time for nor an interest in politics.

Undoubtedly, there were men in the state police who sympathized with the workers even if they did not know them personally. But these policemen depended on their job in the force. The 'Battle of Menstad' took place in a time of great unemployment. Generally, applications for employment in the police increase during economic depressions and diminish when conditions improve. It could scarcely be said that those who applied for police jobs were especially authoritarian persons. Like everyone else, the police applicants just sought work where work could be found. Part of the workers showed the same preference when the fear of losing their jobs made them vote against the communists' proposal for a general strike. Some of the policemen held conservative attitudes. They were skeptical of the labor movement and loudly proclaimed that it was about time the communists learned that they had to deal with the police. All the out-of-town policemen had in common their distance to the conflict district. They were anonymous, and there was not much danger of future reprisals. Nothing tied them to the district once the conflict ended. Distance and anonymity cure qualms about using harsh tactics. The use of specially chosen officers for distinctly unpleasant assignments is an old policy strategy. Norwegians have been used as policemen in Stockholm, and Swedes in Norway's capital. Rural youth have always been welcome to urban police forces.

The state police formed the back-up in case the local force failed, coupled with the army and navy, in their turn, if even the state police did not manage to re-establish 'law and order'. The soldiers were under a stricter disipline than the policemen, and the legal consequences of not obeying orders could entail long prison sentences. In that respect, the military leaders had better control over their front-line personnel than the police had over their men. Nonetheless, the military leaders made sure that the soldiers were protected by the same social distance as the state corps when mobilized during civilian disturbances. Soldiers were mustered from remote districts, preferably rural areas, and at the same time the soldiers' political reliability was checked. But the danger with having a large social distance between the controller and the controlled is that the controller misjudges the situation and makes moves unfortunate for all parties concerned. The leaders of the state police misjudged the situation during the Menstad conflict, made provocative statements in official contexts, and used force without even trying to negotiate with the workers first. The distance to those controlled can reduce the controller's inhibitions and thereby leave too few remaining restraints. The controller makes misjudgements and ends up aggravating the situation. The choice of police tactics partly defines how 'hot' the war between the police and the demonstrators will be. In fact, in this context we can talk about a definitional effect and a self-fulfilling prophecy. The use of a well-equipped riot squad, mounted police, water hoses, and so forth, decisively has an impact in defining a situation as 'dangerous' and critical, and often does so in comparison to what the riots or demonstrations were like before calling in the police. Extraordinary police forces signal that an unusual occurrence is emerging. Furthermore, in connection with demonstrations and social conflicts the use of such harsh police tactics commonly has the effect of provoking rather than subduing; the situation becomes more critical. Certain police leaders never seem to learn this elementary fact. In the period between the two World Wars, as well as in more recent times, we have frequently seen examples of the well-known 'snowball effect' that such offensive and militant police initiatives cause. When called in during a demonstration or riot, the police, in addition to their provocation, attract to the scene large crowds of spectators, who in turn mix with the persons involved from the beginning. Subsequently, the police feel their position being threatened and call for reinforcements with better equipment, often mounted police and motorcycle squads. By that time the crowds really begin to gather. Screaming sirens from dozens of police cars and motorcycles make it known all over that something is about to happen in the central areas of the city. This can continue for hours, and in most cases the police efforts are to no avail. The crowd can be herded from one section of the city to another, but experience has shown that only when the police have started withdrawing their forces do tempers cool and people go back home.

A developed plan for emergency preparedness might increase the chances of the controller using harsh means. The physical resources are available, and the controller has been trained to use them. Participants in the police's emergency units are experts on physical violence. They have learned to use batons and tear gas, not friendliness and diplomacy. Besides, as a group they will easily develop a professional pride that, among other things, entails a desire to justify their existence through demonstrating their proficiency. The distance to those who are to be controlled and the general isolation from the population which often characterize both the regular police force and the special units in the larger towns, give rise to a 'corps spirit' and a separate police culture. This circumstance will in turn support the offensive and hard police strategies. The Norwegian criminologist Nils Christie has in several books discussed how the probability of resorting to violence and ill-treatment increases when a person feels that the one to be controlled is foreign and unpleasant. The probability that the controller will look upon people in such a negative manner increases with the personal and social distance to the opposite party.[3]

When social and political crises develop, it can also be tempting to use resources designed for other purposes. In Norway in 1920, for example, the state entered into an agreement with several municipalities to supply a special (alcohol) intoxicant squad who were to keep an eye on smuggling and illicit distilling. Unlawful production and trade was widespread in the mid-20s owing to prohibition, which was in effect in Norway as well as in several other countries. But after prohibition was abolished, the intoxicant squad continued to exist, and this unit was later used during the major labor disputes.

The dilemma of deterrence

Johs. Andenaes, professor in criminal law at the University of Oslo, states that it may be true that some individuals do not let themselves be deterred, but that the threat of punishment does have an effect upon the majority. Professor Andenaes uses the sentencing of the Norwegian labor leader, Marcus Thrane, in the middle of the nineteenth century as an example:

> Marcus Thrane's sentence . . . completely destroyed the movement he had started. The labor movement's later progress had no connection with this pioneer movement. In present day dictatorships we see how an adequately effective and hardhanded criminal prosecution can clear out all organized political opposition against the ruling powers.[4]

Professor Andenaes has an interesting viewpoint concerning the effects of general preventive measures. Physical coercion can be effective if the oppression is extensive and brutal. Control based on physical coercion has been the rule as far as a great many regimes are concerned. Mobilization of the army and navy deterred the workers from new demonstrations and fights with the police during the Menstad conflict in 1931. A protest march heading towards cocked rifles and machine guns could have ended in a blood bath, as happened in Sweden in a similar situation a few weeks earlier. However, no general rule states that the use of physical coercion and threats of hard punishment deter a political opposition. In some cases when the state power re-establishes the status quo, this happens through rendering the opposition harmless rather than through deterrence. In connection with the Norwegian authorities' struggle against the Marcus Thrane movement in the 1850s, a strong element of the latter tactic was evident. The central leaders landed in prison for several years, with no possibility of carrying on political activities. During the Menstad conflict the entire local labor leadership was put behind bars and kept there until the reason for the conflict had been removed. Threats about convictions and imprisonment will have considerably less deterrent value with regard to well-organized and politically conscious groups than vis-à-vis groups that are both organizationally and politically weak. The Norwegian working class was in quite a different position in the period between the two World Wars than during Marcus Thrane's era. By then society at large was different and considerably more industrialized. The working class as a whole had grown a great deal larger and commanded a more dominant position in society. The labor movement could boast of considerable organizational strength, and the political level had altogether changed and become more conscious. *Tukthusloven* and the related sentences provoked and almost stimulated the political opposition.

Threats of physical coercion can deter opponents from demonstrating unlawfully and from using their own physical means of coercion, as we observed during the Menstad conflict. But the political opposition will easily find new paths as long as the coercion does not wipe out every trace of resistance. During the Menstad conflict, the workers stopped their unlawful demonstrations and did not again attempt hand-to-hand combat with the police, but their struggle continued in the form of boycott actions, protest meetings, press campaigns, leaflets, and psychological warfare.

In a discussion of the possible deterrent effects of law enforcement and punishments on political opposition groups, it is integral to ask what price a political system must pay when using physical coercion. To begin with, the use of coercion, seen in a purely economic sense, is an expensive way of governing. To have the state police, the navy and the army at Menstad cost the Norwegian government enormous sums of money. The investigation work and the extensive trials in the months following the conflict were also very expensive. If a political regime loses legitimacy and then bases its existence on threats of punishment and police control, it will require such a multitude of resources that in the long run the strain will be enormous on a society accustomed to the moderate budgets that are typical for a more traditional and civilian police force. Prime Minister Peder Kolstad once remarked when

Defense Minister Vidkun Quisling spoke out against the communists: 'It presents certain practical problems to put an entire political party in prison'.

An even higher price to pay is the loss of legitimacy encountered when a system of government must resort to physical coercion against large groups of people who are accustomed to better treatment. The extreme threats of imposing martial law had a certain effect during the Menstad conflict, but the government, as well as Norsk Hydro and the Employers' Association, realized that if the control over workers during lock-outs and strikes had to be founded on pure coercion, serious political problems would emerge. The use of police and soldiers in political conflicts would not be easily forgotten. Such dramatic events as the Menstad conflict take on their own significance and become an integral part of the labor movement's political inheritance. Characteristically enough as regards long-range effects of the use of coercion, the labor disputes of the 1920s and the 30s are today used as arguments against police rearmament. The Norwegian defense forces are finding that they have a political skeleton in their cupboard, now that researchers and journalists are delving into previously closed files. The Menstad conflict has survived as a political example; in fiction, theater, ballades and debates.

Power, legitimacy and stigmatization

During the Menstad conflict, the police hesitated to start making arrests. The presence of the out-of-town police was most unpopular, and contributed to reducing the prestige of the police. The police leaders were afraid that police prestige would be further weakened through making arrests, while, on the other hand, the arrests paradoxically enough were looked upon as necessary, since the local police with the aid of their natural authority did not manage to maintain 'law and order'. By first arresting those with criminal records, the police hoped to compromise the demonstrators and at the same time legitimize their own presence and also the arrests of the labor leaders.

Usually it was not necessary for the police to legitimize the apprehension and incarceration of law-breakers, whether for crimes of sex, theft or violence. In such instances, most people were either positive or slightly indifferent to police arrests.

True, police actions against liquor smuggling and illicit distillers were not especially popular but, nevertheless, the local police's position was extreme and vulnerable during the Menstad conflict. It was most unusual that such large groups of the population rejected the police's right to intervene in a conflict situation. The police intervention was looked upon as immoral, unreasonable, and unnecessary. In other words, what the police did was not legitimate.

During the Menstad conflict, both the local and state police leaders experienced prestige and authority crises at first hand. It was the police who had to find a solution to the coercion dilemma. How were they to follow up the politicians' demands for a tough strategy without the enforcement agency losing legitimacy?

The police could have claimed that the workers broke the law when they demonstrated unlawfully and fought with the policemen. However, in relation to the working population, such claims were not enough to legitimize the hard police tactics. The Menstad demonstrators' protest was too deeply rooted in the majority's sense of justice. Legislators had criminalized the workers' traditional means for struggle against strike-breaking with the help of *tukthus-loven*. But most people did not thereby regard the struggle against the strike-breakers as criminal. To utilize political accusations would have produced the reverse of the desired effect. Stronger medicine was needed to legitimize the arrests and the tough police tactics. By picking out demonstrators with a criminal record and charging them with acts of violence, the police took advantage of the stigmatization and contempt that follow the traditional criminal – the old prejudice against the criminal as a more or less 'contaminated' and 'dishonest' person. The criminal's bad reputation threatened to rub off on all who had anything to do with him or her. The superstitions about criminals' 'contamination' subsided as time went on, but the contempt for the individual criminal continued to exist.

Much would have been gained if the police had succeeded in presenting the demonstrators as criminals. The demonstrators would have emerged as an isolated deviant group on the fringe of what was acceptable; a group from whom the authorities could freely demand respect and submission. The criminal label would have legitimized the hard police policy.

The sociologist Hovard Becker has written about the great changes that can take place in a person's life when he or she is labelled deviant.[5] In people's minds the actual or alleged deviance becomes the most important thing about that person. The deviance is the main feature. The person's other characteristics, such as profession, political views, and personality traits, are of secondary interest. The deviant person is treated accordingly. He or she is no longer entitled to express opinions in good company. His or her acquaintances are prejudiced. The deviant label brings and legitimizes a harsher treatment of that person than of others. Becker's views can lead on to an analysis of the situation political opposition groups can get into, especially in a system with a political or economic crisis. The road to arrest, incarceration, and physical suppression is short if those in power manage to label the opponents as different, crazy, dangerous or criminal. Stigmatization can be the beginning of the final clearing of the opposition. It is considered legitimate to fight against individuals who break the laws of the country and threaten the interest of the state. A movement with criminals and other deviants in its midst has no right to be taken seriously. It has placed itself beyond the pale. The criminal label can legitimize actions which the rulers otherwise would not have taken and in addition it is diversionary. The background of the conflict and the central questions are displaced. The rulers claim that the opposition consists of 'outsiders'. The scapegoat is named. It has been convenient for regimes in political and economic crises to be able to blame so-called inside and outside enemies. Ethnic minorities, foreigners, those in political opposition, and convicted persons have, one after another, served in the role as scapegoat.

Emil Durkheim is known for his theory on the functions of crime and punishment.[6] Punishment, according to Durkheim, has the effect of creating solidarity. By punishing the criminal, the other members of society are brought closer to one another. In their condemnation of the crime, they unite in a perceived fellowship of interests. The criminal thus serves to strengthen the unity among well-adjusted citizens. The solidarity function is an unintended effect of the punishment. The motives and arguments for punishment are something quite different. The Menstad conflict differed from Durkheim's model. The police intentionally planned to use convicted persons as scapegoats. They would legitimize the arrest of labor leaders. The expected uproar around the criminals and the acts of violence should create unity among the people against the demonstrators. Things did not work out in that way. The attempt at stigmatization had no effect on the workers; hardly any others than the police leaders themselves reflected over the order of the arrests.

The arrests of some local 'criminals' did not confer legitimacy, because in itself the use of the state police and the military was felt to be an outrageous enchroachment on the part of the authorities.

State power and neutrality

It is a basic fact that the use of physical coercion has played a part in Norway's political development, though to a much lesser degree than we have witnessed in other countries. The enforcement agency's chances of remaining neutral during a social conflict are usually lessened when political and social contrasts in a society become acute. Control through the state's resources of physical power is sharpened during times of crisis, especially in politically labile societies. In the period between the two World Wars, the Norwegian police had a great deal of independence under normal service conditions. This independence came to an abrupt halt during the large labor disputes. The Department of Justice strengthened its control over police authorities, employers demanded police protection, and the bourgeois journalists kept a close watch on police activities.

The criminologist Jørgen Jepsen has, in a study of Danish labor disputes, discussed how the media's detailed coverage of the conflicts served to curtail the local police's freedom of movement. Until the labor disputes were covered by the media, the police kept out of the troubled districts as much as possible. It became more difficult for the police to stick to this soft strategy after the journalists had done their reporting from the scene where the police were conspicuously absent. The conservative public reacted to the passiveness of the police and demanded that they should intervene against the striking workers and factory occupants.[7]

Police and military leaders have in some instances warned against bringing in policemen and soldiers in social conflicts because, among other reasons, such an intervention damages the prestige of the ruling power. In other instances, especially in the inter-war period, some of the police and military chiefs argued for a rearmament to meet an alleged revolutionary threat. This war-like attitude partly expressed an honest fear of a revolution, but often the 'hawks' in the police and military used this threat to suit their own needs and insure their own interests. The Norwegian defense apparatus had to accept several drastic budget cuts in the period between the two World Wars, as did large parts of the municipal and state administration. It was not uncommon for officers to meet proposals on budget cutbacks with arguments that the defense forces would be less able to counteract revolutionary uprisings. However, independently of the attitudes of police leaders and officers, this power structure has also been subject to political control, and politicians have in some situations called on the police and the military for assistance. The police and the military have, in fact, been given a concrete role in critical situations. Accordingly, detailed emergency plans were worked out during the inter-war years. These plans were utilized on several occasions and, interestingly enough, the use of policemen and soldiers led the 'hawks' to demand further escalation and training of the power apparatus for usage during civil disturbances.

How important a role this power structure plays, will vary from the peripheral to the central and depend on, among other things, the stability and the legitimacy of the governing system. As previously pointed out, the use or threat of physical coercion will most likely sharpen political antagonism, even though for a while the demonstration of power can deter an inferior opposition. Most political systems, especially those with democratic traditions to preserve, will thus as long as possible refrain from using methods of physical coercion against large groups of the population. The police and the military represent extreme resources which preferably are only employed when other control and mediation methods have failed.

NOTES

[1] Per Ole Johansen, *Menstadkonflikten 1931*. Tiden Norsk Forlag, Oslo 1978. 380 pages, illustrated.

The quotes in this article are from *Menstadkonflikten 1931*, which has utilized several primary sources, such as files from the local police, the state police, the Department of Justice, the Department of Defense, the military departments, Norsk Hydro, the Skienfjord municipal administration, local labor unions, the Association of Employers and the Federation of Norwegian Trade Unions. All of the country's newspapers that came out during the conflict have been examined. The author has interviewed some 50 persons who were active during the Menstad conflict.

[2] ANNE MARIE STØKKEN, *Politiet i det norske samfunnet* (The Police in Norwegian Society) Oslo 1974.

[3] NILS CHRISTIE, *Hvor tett et samfunn* (How close a Society?) Oslo 1975.

[4] JOHS. ANDENAES, *Straff og lovlydighet* (Punishment and Law Abidance), Oslo 1974.

[5] HOVARD BECKER, *The Outsiders*, New York 1972.

[6] EMIL DURKHEIM, *The Division of Labour In Society*, New York 1969.

[7] JØRGEN JEPSEN, 'Arbeidskonflikter og Den offentlige ro og orden' in *Retfaerd*, 1976, No. 1.

THE AUTHORS

ANDERS BRATHOLM, born 1920, cand. jur. 1948, dr. jur. 1958. Professor of Law at the University of Oslo, Norway, since 1960. He is editor of the Norwegian legal journal *Lov og Rett*, and has published a number of books and articles on penal law and procedures, as well as on civil law and criminology.
Author's address: *Institute of Criminology and Criminal Law, University of Oslo, Karl Johansgt. 47, Oslo 1, Norway.*

JAN FORSLIN, born 1939, Ph.D. in psychology 1978. Research fellow at The Swedish Council for Personnel Administration. Has carried out studies on work adjustment of various occupational groups and on social impact of technological change in industry. Has published books and articles on these topics.
Author's address: *Swedish Council for Personnel Administration, Box 5157, S-10244 Stockholm, Sweden.*

MARTTI GRÖNFORS, born 1942. He studied sociology and anthropology in New Zealand and criminology at Cambridge before taking his Ph.D. at the London School of Economics. He has taught criminology, social anthropology and methodology at Helsinki and Tampere universities, and has published two monographs based on his fieldwork among Finnish gypsies: *Blood Feuding Among Finnish Gypsies* (1977), and *Ethnic Minorities and Deviance: the Relationship Between Finnish Gypsies and the Police (1979).*
Author's address: *Institute of Sociology, Franzeninkatu 13, 00500 Helsinki 50, Finland.*

RAGNAR HAUGE, born 1933, cand. jur. 1959, Director of the National Institute for Alcohol Research in Norway. He was attached to the Institute of Criminology and Criminal Law, University of Oslo, 1960–1975, from 1967 as a research fellow. During 1961–62 he studied criminology at the University of Cambridge. He has published a number of books and articles on criminology and alcohol research.
Author's address: *National Institute for Alcohol Research, Dannevigsveien 10, Oslo 4, Norway.*

JØRGEN JEPSEN, born 1930, cand. jur. 1956, Lecturer in criminology, Institute of Criminal Science, University of Århus. Formerly secretary to the Scandinavian Research Council for Criminology, and research associate at the Institute of Criminal

Science, University of Copenhagen. Has written on 'Equality before the Law', treatment of deviants, drug addiction, pollution and on labour conflicts, and – with Lone Pal – on forecasting of crime. At presently working on economic crime, in particular relation to labour safety violations.
Author's address: *Institute for Legal Procedure and Criminal Science. Århus University, 8000 Århus C. Denmark.*

PER OLE JOHANSEN, born 1945, MA in sociology 1970. He was attached to the Institute of Sociology 1971–1972 – and became a lecturer in criminology in 1972 at the University of Oslo. He has published books and articles on the sociology of deviance and criminology.
Author's address: *Institute of Criminology and Criminal Law. University of Oslo, Karl Johansgt. 47, Oslo 1, Norway.*

HENNING KOCH, born 1949, cand. jur. 1974. Since then he has been attached to the Institute of Criminology – since 1976 as research fellow, and 1979 as senior research fellow. He has published articles on criminology, criminal procedure, and police history. His major research activity concerns the work and efficiency of the uniformed police.
Author's address: *Institute of Criminology, University of Copenhagen, Sct. Peders Straede 19, 1453 Copenhagen K, Denmark.*

LEIF LENKE, born 1941, cand. jur. 1969. He is teaching Criminology at the Department of Sociology at the University of Stockholm, Sweden. He has done research and published articles in the fields of drug problems, crimes of violence and criminal policy.
Author's address: *Department of Sociology and Criminology, University of Stockholm, 106 91 Stockholm, Sweden.*

HÅKON LORENTZEN, born 1946, MA in sociology 1977. Attached to the Institute for Sociology of Law, University of Oslo. Engaged in a research project on industrialization, network and social control.
Author's address: *Institute of Sociology of Law. University of Oslo, Sporveisgaten 35, Oslo 3, Norway.*

TUIJA MÄKINEN, born 1946, MA in sociology 1969. Research officer at the Research Institute of Legal Policy from 1973. Her publications include studies on crime damages, closed institutions, and illegal sale of alcohol.
Author's address: *Research Institute of Legal Policy, Siltasaarenkatu 12 A, 00530 Helsinki 53, Finland.*

SVEN SPERLINGS, born 1942, cand. phil. 1969. Project leader of the Demographic Database, Stockholm. He was attached to the Institute of Criminology, University of

Stockholm, 1973–77 as research assistant. His research concerns the history of crime in Stockholm.
Author's address: *Demografisk databas, Sturegatan 10, S-114, Stockholm, Sweden.*

HANNU TAKALA, born 1946, jur. lic. Research officer at the Research Institute of Legal Policy in Helsinki from 1972. He has been counsellor of legislation 1974–75 and 1979. He was secretary for the Penal Law Committee 1972–74, and has from time to time taught criminal justice, criminology and sociology of law at the Law Faculty, University of Helsinki. He has written a number of articles on criminology and criminal policy.
Author's address: *Ministry of Justice, Law Drafting Department, PL 1, 00131 Helsinki 13, Finland.*